IN THE NAME OF THE CHILD

STUDIES IN THE SOCIAL HISTORY OF MEDICINE

In recent years, the social history of medicine has become recognized as a major field of historical enquiry. Aspects of health, disease, and medical care now attract the attention not only of social historians but also of researchers in a broad spectrum of historical and social science disciplines. The Society for the Social History of Medicine, founded in 1969, is an interdisciplinary body, based in Great Britain but international in membership. It exists to forward a wide-ranging view of the history of medicine, concerned equally with biological aspects of normal life, experience of and attitudes to illness, medical thought and treatment, and systems of medical care. Although frequently bearing on current issues, this interpretation of the subject makes primary reference to historical context and contemporary priorities. The intention is not to promote a sub-specialism but to conduct research according to the standards and intelligibility required of history in general. The Society publishes a journal, *Social History of Medicine*, and holds at least three conferences a year. Its series, Studies in the Social History of Medicine, does not represent publication of its proceedings, but comprises volumes on selected themes, often arising out of conferences but subsequently developed by the editors.

Margaret Pelling, Series Editor

Volumes in the series include

Life, Death and The Elderly
Edited by Margaret Pelling and Richard M. Smith

Medicine and Charity Before the Welfare State
Edited by Jonathan Barry and Colin Jones

IN THE NAME OF THE CHILD

Health and welfare, 1880–1940

Edited by Roger Cooter

London and New York

First published 1992
by Routledge
11 New Fetter Lane, London EC4P 4EE
Simultaneously published in the USA and Canada
by Routledge
a division of Routledge, Chapman and Hall, Inc.
29 West 35th Street, New York, NY 10001

Typeset in Linotype Stempel Garamond by
Falcon Typographic Art Ltd., Edinburgh & London
Printed in Great Britain by
Biddles Ltd., Guildford, Surrey

British Library Cataloguing in Publication Data
In the name of the child: health and welfare,
1880–1940. – (Studies in the social history of medicine)
I. Cooter, Roger II. Series
362.7950942

Library of Congress Cataloging in Publication Data
In the name of the child: health and welfare,
1880–1940/edited by Roger Cooter.
p. cm. – (Studies in the social history of medicine)
Originated in a conference held at the Institute of Historical Research
in Oct. 1987, sponsored by the Society for the Social History of
Medicine and the British Paediatric Association.
Includes bibliographical references and index.
1. Children–Health and hygiene–History. 2. Child welfare–History.
I. Cooter, Roger. II. Society for the Social History of Medicine.
III. British Paediatric Association. IV. Series.
RJ101.I5 1992
362.1'9892'009–dc20   91–20287   CIP
ISBN 0–415–05743–4

6003629593

CONTENTS

CONTENTS

vi

ILLUSTRATIONS

CONTRIBUTORS

Jennifer Beinart is a research fellow at the London School of Hygiene and Tropical Medicine working on the history of hepatitis B with the AIDS Social History Programme, and a research associate at the Wellcome Unit for the History of Medicine, Oxford. She is the author of *A History of the Nuffield Department of Anaesthetics, Oxford, 1937–1987* (1987), and papers on the history of tropical medicine and child health in Africa.

Linda Bryder is a lecturer in the Department of History at the University of Auckland and the overseas editor of *Social History of Medicine*. She is the author of *Below the Magic Mountain: A Social History of Tuberculosis in Twentieth-Century Britain* (1988), co-editor with Joan Austoker of *Historical Perspectives on the Role of the Medical Research Council* (1989), and editor of *A Healthy Country: Essays on the Social History of Medicine in New Zealand* (1991).

Roger Cooter is Senior Research Officer at the Wellcome Unit for the History of Medicine, University of Manchester, and one of the editors of *Social History of Medicine*. The author of *The Cultural Meaning of Popular Science* (1984), and *Phrenology in the British Isles* (1989), he has also edited *Studies in the History of Alternative Medicine* (1988). His *Surgery and Society in Peace and War, 1880–1948* is soon to be published.

Harry Ferguson is a lecturer in the Department of Social Studies at Trinity College, Dublin. He contributed to and collaborated in editing the Violence Against Children Study Group's, *Taking Child Abuse Seriously: Contemporary Issues in Child Protection Theory and Practice* (1990), and is currently completing a Cambridge doctoral thesis on the history of welfare practices and the abused child.

Harry Hendrick is Senior Lecturer in British social history at Oxford Polytechnic. He is the author of *Images of Youth: Age, Class and the Male Youth Problem, 1880–1920* (1990) and is currently preparing for Routledge a textbook history of children and social policy in twentieth-century England.

Susan E. Lederer is Assistant Professor of History in the Department of Humanities at the Pennsylvania State University College of Medicine at Hershey, Pennsylvania. She has published on the history of anti-vivisection in *Isis* and elsewhere, and is currently working on a history of human and animal experimentation in twentieth-century America.

John Macnicol is Reader in Social Policy at Royal Holloway and Bedford New College, University of London. The author of *The Movement for Family Allowances, 1918–45* (1980), he is also co-editor of *Aspects of Ageing* (1990). He is currently completing studies of the history of old age and retirement, and of the reconstructions of the idea of an 'underclass' in Britain and America over the past hundred years.

Elaine Sharland is a research fellow at the Department of Psychiatry, Park Hospital, Oxford, where she is conducting a study into the policies, practice and effectiveness of health and welfare interventions in child sexual abuse. She previously worked with Cathy Urwin at Cambridge on a study of the psychotherapist Margaret Lowenfield and on popular childcare orthodoxies.

Carolyn Steedman is Senior Lecturer in Arts Education at the University of Warwick and a member of the *History Workshop* collective. Her previous publications include *The Tidy House* (1982), *Policing the Victorian Community* (1984), *Landscape for a Good Woman* (1986), *The Radical Soldier's Tale* (1988), and *Childhood, Culture and Class in Britain: Margaret McMillan, 1860–1931* (1990).

Deborah Thom teaches history at Robinson College, and in the Social and Political Sciences Faculty at the University of Cambridge. She is currently completing a study of educational psychology, and conducting research on both child guidance in Britain and women's employment. She has published on intelligence testing, education and, with Antonia Ineson, on TNT poisoning and women workers in the First World War.

Cathy Urwin was formerly the Margaret Lowenfeld Research Fellow based in the Child Care and Development Group, University of Cambridge. She is now working in London. She is co-author of *Changing the Subject: Psychology, Social Regulation and Subjectivity* (1984) and a co-editor, with Carolyn Steedman and Valerie Walkerdine, of *Language, Gender and Childhood* (1985), and with John Hood-Williams of *Child Psychotherapy, War and the Normal Child: Selected Papers of Margaret Lowenfeld* (1989).

Paul Weindling is Senior Research Officer at the Wellcome Unit for the History of Medicine, University of Oxford. He is the author of *Health, Race and German Politics Between National Unification and Nazism, 1870–1945* (1989), and has edited *The Social History of Occupational Health* (1985) for the Society for the Social History of Medicine.

PREFACE AND ACKNOWLEDGEMENTS

This volume originated in a conference on 'Child Health, Healing & Mortality' held at the Institute of Historical Research in October 1987 under the aegis of the Society for the Social History of Medicine in collaboration with the British Paediatric Association. Although only two of the papers presented at the conference appear in this volume (those by Carolyn Steedman and Paul Weindling), the editor remains indebted to all the participants for their many insights and encouragements. Summaries of all the conference papers appeared in the Society for the Social History of Medicine's journal, *Social History of Medicine*, volume 1, April 1988. Special thanks are owing to Mary Fissell, Bill Luckin, Margaret Pelling and Helen Cooter for their generous support and counsel in the preparation of this volume.

INTRODUCTION

Roger Cooter

Few fields of study have grown so vigorously as the history of childhood. Before the publication in 1960 of Philippe Ariès *Centuries of Childhood: A Social History of Family Life*, the subject barely obtained the status of a footnote. Three decades later, the yield of articles, dissertations and monographs is such that printed bibliographies have had to give way to sophisticated data banks.[1]

Such interest and industry cannot be attributed simply to the work of Ariès, fruitful though that may have been in stimulating debate.[2] Underlying all, if not directly animating it, has been the apparent transformation of attitudes towards children in the modern family. As with histories of the body, sexuality, and gender produced in recent years, the study of childhood has been, first and foremost, a means of illuminating and explicating the present at the remove of the past. Moreover, since everyone experiences childhood, it has proven itself remarkably open to a wide range of reflections. Historians of art and antiquity, no less than those of labour and leisure, have been moved to comment, and to join forces with anthropologists, psychologists, sociologists and literary scholars in fuelling academic debate. *Annaliste*, Marxist, Freudian and Foucaultian perspectives abound, some overlaid with feminist theory, others deeply ensconced in discourse analysis. Indeed, so many perspectives and thematic foci now compete that the history of childhood has come to be described as 'a mass of tangled strands'.[3] But the resulting complexities have also been recognized as integral to the richness of the field.

'Intellectually rich' and abundant is hardly the best way to describe the current state of the history of child health and welfare, however. Although much attention has recently been directed to the history of the medicalization of birth and infant

1

nurturing,[4] there have been few such undertakings in the area of the health and welfare of *children* (meaning primarily the school-aged, between 4 and 14 years).[5] Despite the psychological impact and near-universality of the experience of childhood illness, and the sociological recognition of how sickness and deprivation transform experience,[6] the child as patient or 'welfare object' has hardly obtained a toe-hold in historical studies. It has been acknowledged that towards the end of the nineteenth century the concept of childhood became far more socially homogeneous by virtue of its reconstruction in predominantly psycho-medical terms.[7] But a literature detailing the how, where and why of this process has yet to emerge.[8] There are surprisingly few references to the subject even within those writings that seek to reveal 'medicalization' as a blunt form of social control exercised by the medical profession.[9] Likewise slim is the literature dealing with the history, conceptualization and politics of agencies and institutions for the care and custody of children. George Behlmer's pioneering study of the development of concern over child abuse in late-Victorian Britain, and Linda Gordon's more recent American work in this area are among the notable exceptions.[10]

Mostly, the knowledge, practices and policies articulated in the name of child health and welfare are encountered only in passing in histories of education, psychology, child employment, child protection legislation, and in the literature treating the late-Victorian 'discovery of poverty', the rise of public health, the history of social policy, and the origins of the 'welfare state'.[11] Supplementing these are hagiographic accounts of paediatrics,[12] and celebratory histories of individual children's hospitals.[13] Above all, for the period that concerns us in this volume, child health and welfare has been subsumed within the history of infant mortality, and has thus come to be dominated by historical demography. While some of the best of the demographically oriented work heeds developments in medical knowledge, practice, and professionalization,[14] most is excessively causal, quantitative, and scientistic. It is preoccupied with isolating the factors that affected infant mortality in different urban environments and between social classes, and with measuring and comparing the impact of different social, medical and political strategies upon that mortality. Only rarely do such studies venture into the morbidity of the school-aged child. When they do, as in one recent study which devotes a chapter to the neglected subject of the school health service, it is principally to highlight what is regarded as the more historically problematic, more 'complicated' *infant* welfare movement.[15] The latter, moreover, is usually coupled with the study of 'maternal welfare'.[16]

'Stuck in infancy' also characterizes one of the few general social histories of medicine to contain a chapter on 'Childhood and Youth', F. B. Smith's *The People's Health, 1830–1910* (1979). Opening with the observation that 'the years between four and fourteen constituted the least hazardous stage of life', Smith's chapter is in every sense a sequel to his preceding one on 'Infancy', which attends to the relative impact of different factors on the decline of infant mortality as viewed from the present.[17] Although he omits to note that towards the end of the nineteenth century nearly one-third of the population of England and Wales was under 14 years of age,[18] Smith is here wholly on the terrain of historical demographers. Like them, he perceives the decline in the ravages to children from measles, diphtheria and scarlet fever, for example, as sufficiently arresting facts in themselves about 'the world we have lost' as to require little further comment.[19] If they do require anything, it is only by way of supplement with still more statistics, such as on accidents, which by the early twentienth century were becoming an overwhelmingly important cause of death and disability among children.[20]

Left unquestioned, however, is why contemporaries chose to dwell more on the epidemiology of infectious diseases than on 'non-infectious' causes of death, or why, within epidemiological discourse, they appear to have been less concerned with, say, measles (a major killer) than with smallpox (the near least). Nor, more generally, do we obtain any insight into the political creation and uses of such facts and figures. Rather, we learn only that the great interest in, and 'really effective' measures for the improvement of child health and welfare in the early twentieth century emerged simply in response to the 'shocking' revelations on the state of Britain's national health. Typically, the classic exposés by Charles Booth, the scandal caused by military recruitment during the Boer War, the *Royal Commission on Physical Training in Scotland* (1903) and the *Report of the Inter-departmental Committee on Physical Deterioration* (1904) are regarded as sufficient in themselves to account for the introduction of such measures as the medical inspection and feeding of schoolchildren, clinics for infants and mothers, health visitors, state maternity benefits and so on.[21] Of course, no self-respecting social historian would regard such measures as straightforwardly 'progressive', or as unallied to political and ideological interests. But the absence of attention to the latter in relation to the history of medical and welfare provision for children has left its study curiously detached from the social, intellectual and cultural history of childhood.

This book has been conceived to bridge this gap. Its chapters are concerned mainly with detailing specific ventures in child health and welfare during the decades before and after the first World War, and with drawing attention to some of the social and political interests behind those ventures. These essays thus depart from the 'causalities' of historical demography as much as from the estimates of 'progress' that preoccupy so much of the history of medicine and social policy. Directly and indirectly they reveal how initiatives in this field were intimately a part of wider socio-economic and cultural change, of which, indeed, the revaluation of childhood at the end of the century was itself a part.

To the extent that each chapter is written from such an understanding, the work of one scholar in particular, the sociologist Viviana Zelizer, might be regarded as providing a backdrop to the volume as a whole. In her *Pricing the Priceless Child* (1985), Zelizer makes clear how the introduction of child labour laws and compulsory education in America towards the end of the nineteenth century transformed the wage-earning 'non-child' of the labouring poor into the category of the economically worthless child-scholar. Thereby, for the first time, the *majority of children* came to be appropriated into a neo-romantic middle-class ideal of childhood in which the child became emotionally 'priceless'.[22] The defining characteristics of 'the child' today, such as parental dependence, economic and sexual inactivity, and absence of legal and political rights – criteria that did not necessarily apply in past societies[23] – were largely born out of this end-of-the-century transformation which was common to the whole of the industrialized Western world.[24]

The essays in this volume discuss aspects of the intellectual, social, medical, commercial, political and professional interests in child health and welfare which in different ways were constitutive of this transformation of childhood. Carolyn Steedman addresses the issue directly, using evidence from the writings of the child welfare reformer Margaret McMillan to explicate how working-class childhood was remade within the organicist social vision of the Independent Labour Party. Harry Hendrick approaches the issue from the perspective of the debate over part-time child workers – ambiguously both 'scholars' and 'labourers' – and considers how medical intervention helped to shape this debate. While concentrating on how this issue assisted medical officers of health and school medical officers in their own professional struggles, he also raises themes taken up in other chapters. One of these themes, the medicalization of school life, is central to Linda Bryder's chapter on the open-air schools, which were catering for over 16,000 children in Britain by the late 1930s. In Bryder's schools, as in Hendrick's debates over child labour, medicine can be seen as conferring a 'special nature' upon children. More visible in the schools, however, is the promotion of the idea of children being brought into communion with an idealized 'nature'. Bryder suggests that in the cold and damp reality of Britain's hungry thirties, such ideas were increasingly felt to be out-of-date, and the scientific rationales for exercising preventive medicine through fresh air – as opposed to better diet – were permitted to slip quietly away. Eroded, too, was the spectre of the tuberculous and 'pre-tuberculous' hordes of children upon which the movement for the establishment of these schools had been based. But what could not be discarded was the medical identity of children; once the schoolroom was transformed into a laboratory for physical and mental measuring and monitoring, those identities were affirmed.

What transpired in schools might be regarded as but the thin end of the medical wedge when viewed from Susan Lederer's discussion on the exploitation of children for experimentation in American orphanages and foundling homes. Pressure from the anti-vivisectionist lobby and vivisectionist reformers compelled some physicians to confront the ethics of such experimentation. Ironically, the 'progress' of social welfare meant the dehumanization of children in this context of commercial gain and professional prowess through scientific research. But as Lederer contends, it is too easy simply to moralize in retrospect on the experiments conducted on orphans to test new diagnostic techniques such as those for syphilis and tuberculosis. Since such measures were carried out against opposition and in the name of better paediatric care, Lederer provides a more sophisticated explanation acknowledging competing professional obligations and commitments.

Paul Weindling, too, is concerned with professional and scientifically based strategies (some of them deriving from child experimentation) and with the public and state responses to them. By a comparison of the reception of serum therapy for diphtheria in Berlin, Paris and London, Weindling identifies a crucial historical stage. Not only did the politics of such therapy bring together both state and medical researchers, and voluntary and state financial and administrative resources, they also turned public health priorities away from water supply, sewers and conditions of poverty. Instead, new priorities in hospitals and dispensaries established child health as a hospital-based medical specialism.

Weindling's concern with the shift from the 'isolation' of infected children to 'active therapy', or to ever greater medical intervention and custodial surveillance by new professional groups, is complemented by Harry Ferguson's chapter on the construction of 'child abuse' in the English county of Cleveland and the implementation of modern child protection practices there over the 1880–1914 period. 'Active therapy' in this case consisted of intervention by middle-class 'child protectors' into working-class domestic spheres for purposes of regulating child–parent relations. As might be expected during the implementation of such a radically new national welfare policy, local ambivalences and tensions did much to shape the form and content of local practice. By 1914, 'child abuse' and child protection practice had been established in Cleveland, but the emphasis was still on the duties and responsibilities of parents rather than on the state or the institutionalization of the child.

Whether abused or diseased, children's bodies have never been the sole object of the advocates of child health and welfare. Children's minds and emotions have been equally important. Addressing this subject, the chapter by Cathy Urwin and Elaine Sharland on childcare advice literature, and that by Deborah Thom on the child guidance movement in England also move us forward into the inter-war period. Both chapters are concerned, to varying degrees, with the introduction of dynamic psychology and psychoanalysis, and – extending the insights in this area of Nikolas Rose[25] – both challenge current historiography. But whereas Urwin and Sharland aim at broad correlations between the prescriptions within the advice literature and national and international preoccupations and anxieties, Thom concentrates on grass-roots developments and reveals a plurality of forces and historical contingencies behind child guidance clinics. Both routes lead us further into the complex of social, political, economic and professional worlds that structured the 'advisors' and the 'advised'.

While Urwin, Sharland and Thom sketch the framework for the modern interiorizing of self through the psychologizing of the child, Jennifer Beinart turns to a context – Africa – in which, well on into this century, the child remained largely 'undiscovered' except as a unit of labour, and where, paradoxically, adult men remained 'boys' in the eyes of their colonial masters. Drawing on collections of photographs, Beinart outlines a history in which children in health and illness could only be perceived – literally brought into the picture – after having adopted the cultural and ideological trappings of colonial domination. Beinart's 'African child' functions in many respects as an inversion of those whose social construction is plotted elsewhere in this volume. As such it holds up a mirror to the European experience.

In the final chapter, John Macnicol extends the comparative dimension through a transnational study of the complex forces operating for and against the introduction of family allowances. Macnicol's chapter does more than merely remind us of one of the recurring themes in this volume, that of the increasing invasion of the state into the organization of family life in general, and child health and welfare in particular. The theme of child benefit recalls us once more to the 'priceless' child no longer capable of contributing to the family income. Moreover, Macnicol's demonstration of the political and economic interests which completely overshadowed the poverty of children in debates over child benefit serves forcefully to remind us of the seen-but-not-heard presence in whose name everything and anything might be negotiated.

As changes in the contemporary family have set the agenda for the history of childhood in general, so recent events in the health and welfare of children have had an important bearing on this volume. Crucial, in particular, has been the controversy surrounding child sexual abuse, one of the effects of which has been to illuminate the webs of power that have come to surround and sustain the modern construction of the child. As Ferguson reminds us in the introduction to his contribution, for all its human tragedy, the Cleveland child abuse affair in Britain has played a vital role in exposing the all-too-often unquestioned nature of professional authority in child welfare discourse. Not only did events in Cleveland in 1987 render the veracity of social workers, psychologists, psychiatrists and paediatricians open to contestation by parents, politicians and the media, they also made hitherto value-neutral appearing technologies for the detection of child sexual abuse deeply problematic. No longer could it be believed that children's bodies were simply objects for disinterested clinical gaze: 'childhood' itself, together with 'best practice' in children's welfare, became transparently a part of moral, political, class, and gendered discourse.[26] Nor can it be overlooked that the context of the 'Cleveland affair' was one in which government was not only intent on destabilizing the economic and intellectual bases of the medical, legal, academic and teaching professions, but also was concerned to reconstruct a 'Victorian' ideology of 'the family' in which the rights of women and children would be marginal at best. Here, in fact, lies the ideological and historiographical starting point for this volume – a plea to observe the oft-concealed role of interests in the construction of the medicine and welfare imposed on children, and to indicate the relation of those constructions to wider social contexts.

To pursue these objectives is to pursue the social history of medicine as it has matured over the past few decades. It should come as no surprise, therefore, that in their general approach these essays have much in common with Jane Lewis's study of the politics of motherhood in the infant and maternal welfare movement in early twentieth-century England.[27] None of the contributors adopts Lewis's self-consciously feminist stance, or writes from precisely the same social history of medicine perspective that she adopted in defiance of histories of social policy written 'from above'. They do, however, parallel Lewis's effort to explicate the mutually constitutive social and medical contexts in which the ideology of motherhood was generated and politically deployed. Indeed, the subjects are cut from the same cloth inasmuch as the celebration of the child proceeded hand-in-hand with the celebration of the domestic role of woman.[28] For both women and children this was accompanied by increasingly institutionalized medical care in the hands of professionals.

As yet, however, far more is known about the turn-of-the-century idealization of the child, on the one hand, and the medicalization of women, on the other, than about the social and intellectual connections between these two processes. Ornella Moscucci, for instance, has pointed to the ways in which the construction of the man/woman dichotomy, fundamental to the rise of gynaecology in the nineteenth century, parallels that of the adult/child dichotomy drawn at the base of paediatric practice.[29] Moscucci has also indicated how the invention of the 'science of woman' was crucial to the representation of female pathology as akin to, and classifiable with, that of the child. By the end of the century, medicine was legitimizing an understanding of both women and children as

8

'incomplete' or 'undeveloped' – hence socially dependent and in need of protection. Such a depiction was not unlike that which was applied to the 'primitive' peoples who were coming under colonial rule at this time. But while Western women and children were linked in their social dependency, issues of gender divided discourse on mothers from that on children. As women came to be characterized as inferior as a result of their sexual biology,[30] so children, as a part of what Zelizer terms their 'sacralization', were de-sexed, cast into a gender-free zone of attributed innocence – at least until Freud.[31] At the same time, the hitherto unified teaching of the 'diseases of women and children' was divided up.[32] This separation was accompanied by the gradual disappearance towards the end of the nineteenth century of hospitals for both women *and* children, and the subsequent rise of special institutions for each.[33] As hospitals for women embodied distinctive ideologies of 'femininity',[34] so those for children implicitly embodied social and moral notions of childhood.

These shifts in the conceptions of, and relations between, women and children constitute only a handful of the themes which await systematic inquiry by social historians of child health and welfare. Among others, which are not formally addressed in this volume but which deserve mention as areas for future research, are those implicated in the politics of medical professionalization. As yet we know little about how and why it came to be believed that children differed from adults with respect 'particularly to etiology, pathology, symptomatology, diagnosis, and treatment' (as an American 'pediatrist' put it in 1907),[35] or how children came to be seen as exhibiting their own distinct repertoire of behavioural problems and physical disorders.[36] Such attributions do not appear to have stemmed from the practice of anatomy – the absence of post-mortem dissections of children being perhaps of significance. It seems that neurology, psychology, pathology and, above all, physiology, were more central. However, like medicine as a whole, these disciplines were never outside culture and politics in defining the body and potentials of children. As Steedman's chapter amply demonstrates, to point to the physiology of growth in the 'discovery' of childhood is to beg much larger questions about the meaning of physiology and growth.

More basic, though not separable from questions about medical knowledge and professionalization, are those about the place, nature and meaning of the practice of children's medicine. Here too, even at the relatively 'visible' level of institutions, our knowledge is skimpy. No one has yet produced a history of children's hospitals, despite the evident growth of these institutions in late nineteenth-century Britain.[37] Only half a century earlier, when the 'pioneer' institutions were opening as outpatient dispensaries – in Liverpool in 1851 and in London a year later – it was being lamented that there was as yet no hospital exclusively for children in the entire British Empire.[38] Indeed, it was complained that there was little space for children in general hospitals at this time (mainly, it seems, from the fear of their spreading infection). An enumeration in the general hospitals in London in January 1843 found only 136 children under 10 years of age, '41 [of whom] had been admitted in consequence of accidental injury, 69 for the surgical treatment of some local ailment, and only 26 [all between the ages of 3 and 10], or less than one per cent, for the cure of internal disease'.[39]

It was commonly the case in the nineteenth century that special hospitals were promoted by those who were outside the medical establishment. Setting up such a charity institution (usually no more than a house with a few rooms) and practising within it, was a means of earning a reputation. Even if not a means of entry into the medical élite, such specialist foundations were often pathways to lucrative private practice, the primary objective of much medical activity. But children's hospitals are historically significant precisely because of their anomalies in these respects. There was, after all, little money to be made through the practice of this medicine, since the overwhelming bulk of child ill health was among the poor. Those patients belonging to parents with incomes were zealously guarded by general practitioners; women and children being the monetary mainstay of middle-class general practice.

A further interesting feature of at least some of the children's hospitals is the fact that their founders were not only emigrés, but were also political radicals. This is evident in the case of mid-Victorian Manchester, where east Europeans who had been involved in the revolutions of 1848 established children's dispensaries and clinics.[40] Abraham Jacobi, the so-called father of American paediatrics, was among those who made his way to Manchester after escaping from prison in Berlin in 1853 (though he was soon compelled to move to the USA for want of local custom).[41] Yet it remains unclear how many of these men were involved in children's medicine before they left the Continent, and what the connections may have been between their visionary politics, their religious beliefs, and their professional field. It cannot be regarded as merely coincidental that many of the 'pioneers', like many of those who would later be involved in psychoanalysis, were Jewish. Their faith may well have possessed a significance beyond its compounding of an already highly marginalized cultural status. Perhaps Jewish faith was analogous to gender; perhaps it was the constraints in both cases that functioned to promote philanthropic and medical endeavours for children.[42] Like the implications of the economic and intra-professional constraints on the development of paediatrics, the answers to these questions remain wide open.[43]

Institutionalized paediatrics scarcely constitutes the sum of the history of child health and welfare, however, as the essays in this volume confirm. Paediatrics may in fact become insignificant to historical accounts once research develops on, say, the role of the medical missions and children's dispensaries that were established in most urban slums towards the end of the nineteenth century, or on the role of poor law medicine and poor law infirmaries.[44] The growth of children's surgery, much of it conducted from outpatient departments and concerned with the removal of adenoids, tonsils and foreskins, presents yet another focus. Nearly two-thirds of inpatients in children's hospitals by the end of the century were 'surgical', and for aspiring consultants an honorary appointment to such a hospital could be an important career-step, providing a training-ground for entry into general surgical consultancy among fee-paying adults. Not all surgery was invasive, though. The majority of surgical cases that came to fill children's hospitals were sufferers from tuberculosis of the bone and joints for which 'conservative surgical', long-term open-air remedies were advocated by an increasingly powerful orthopaedic lobby.[45] The proliferation of orthopaedic clinics for crippled children during the first few decades of this century was matched by the growth of Local Education Authority health clinics, infectious diseases hospitals, 'colonies' for epileptic children, provision for the mentally handicapped, and so much more.

In the twenty pages of close-typed print under the entry 'Children' in the 1881 series of the *Index-Catalogue of the Library of the Surgeon-General's Office* there were some seven sub-categories. But by the 1922 series the entry ran to over thirty pages of new publications, even though topics such as 'child-labor', 'school-children', 'child welfare', and 'cripples' were now catalogued under separate headings. Included among the thirty-one headings under 'Children' were 'anthropology of', 'illegitimate', 'delicate and weak', 'delinquent', 'precocious and exceptional', 'growth and development', 'nutrition', 'hygiene', 'protection', 'education and training', 'hospitals and asylums', and 'diseases, periodicals on'. This offers a clear indication not only of the intensification of interest in children over these years, but also of how medicine had come to perceive itself as central to all aspects of their physical and mental surveillance, classification, treatment, and institutionalization. Historians who use the term 'child health and welfare' reflect this process of consolidation. In 1880 child health and welfare was not yet medicalized; instead it was a set of interests converging on the idealization of the child. But by the 1920s child health and welfare was not only medicalized, it was serving as a powerful argument for extending the role of the state in health and welfare generally.

No single volume can cover all aspects of this history, nor fully explicate the medicalization of the child. In deploying the term 'medicalization', Foucault was identifying a complex process, 'involving not only the extension and improvement of medical services and health institutions, but also the spread of a "somatic culture", shaped and controlled by an increasingly powerful medical profession'.[46] This volume offers only a sample of some of the national, institutional, scientific, intellectual, political and economic contexts in which this process occurred. If it goes some way towards historicizing the social and other interests which lie behind the development of 'child health and welfare', it will have fulfilled its primary aim. It will have done even more if it illustrates how the history of enterprises conducted in the name of the child cannot be other than part of the social history of medicine and childhood proper.

ACKNOWLEDGEMENTS

It is a pleasure to thank Harry Ferguson, Mary Fissell, Harry Hendrick, Susan Lederer, Jane Lewis, Bill Luckin and the anonymous referees of this volume for their helpful comments. Responsibility for the views expressed is my own.

NOTES

1 For example, Neil Sutherland, Jean Barman, Veronica Strong-Boag, *Bibliography of Canadian Childhood*, University of British Columbia,

12

Vancouver; cf Harry Hendrick, *The History of Childhood and Youth: a guide to the literature*, Oxford Polytechnic, Faculty of Modern Studies, Occasional Papers, 1, 1981.

2 See Adrian Wilson, 'The infancy of the history of childhood: an appraisal of Philippe Ariès', *History and Theory*, 1980, 19: 132–53; see also the papers on the history of childhood studies in France and in Germany by Marie-France Morel and Brigitte Niestroj, respectively, in the special issue of *Continuity and Change*, 1989, 4: 323–57. For other appraisals within a lucid assessment of the state of the art, see Ludmilla Jordanova, 'Children in history: concepts of nature and society', in Geoffrey Scarre (ed.) *Children, Parents and Politics*, Cambridge: Cambridge University Press, 1989: 3–24.

3 Diana Gittins, 'Disentangling the history of childhood', *Gender & History*, 1989, 1: 342–9.

4 There is now an extensive literature on these subjects, albeit mostly American; for recent work with useful bibliographies, see Judith Leavitt, *Brought to Bed: childbearing in America, 1750–1950*, New York: Oxford University Press, 1986; Ann Oakley, *Women Confined: towards a sociology of childbirth*, Oxford: Martin Robertson, 1980; Sylvia Hoffert, *Private Matters: American attitudes toward childbearing and infant nurture in the urban north, 1800–1860*, Illinois: University of Illinois Press, 1989; Rima Apple, *Mothers and Medicine: a social history of infant feeding, 1890–1950*, Madison: University of Wisconsin Press, 1987; Valerie Fildes, *Breasts, Bottles and Babies: a history of infant feeding*, Edinburgh: Edinburgh University Press, 1986; Sally G. McMillen, *Motherhood in the Old South: pregnancy, childbirth, and infant rearing*, Baton Rouge: Louisiana State University Press, 1990; and Deborah Dwork, *War is Good for Babies and Other Young Children: a history of the infant and child welfare movement in England, 1898–1918*, London: Tavistock, 1987. For references to American scholarship in the history of child-rearing, see Peter N. Stearns and Timothy Haggerty, 'The role of fear: transitions in American emotional standards for children, 1850–1950', *American Historical Review*, 1991, 96: 63–94; for some of the British literature, see Urwin and Sharland's chapter in this volume and Hendrick, *Guide to the Literature*, 21–5.

5 Nearest to any kind of systematic survey are John Cule and Terry Turner (eds) *Child Care Through the Centuries*, Cardiff: British Society for the History of Medicine, 1984; and 'Child health', in Robert Bremner (ed.) *Children and Youth in America: a documentary history*, Cambridge, Mass: Harvard University Press, 1971, 2: parts 1–6. For a pioneering social historical study of child health in the early modern period, see Margaret Pelling, 'Child health as a social value in early modern England', *Social History of Medicine*, 1988, 1: 135–64.

6 See Howard Brody, 'How sickness alters experience', in his *Stories of Sickness*, New Haven: Yale University Press, 1987.

7 Harry Hendrick, 'Constructions and reconstructions of British childhood: an interpretative survey, c. 1800 to the present', in A. James

13

and A. Prout (eds) *Constructing and Reconstructing Childhood*, Basingstoke: Falmer Press, 1990.

8 However, see Peter W. G. Wright, 'Babyhood: the social construction of infant care as a medical problem in England in the years around 1900', in M. Lock and D. R. Gordon (eds) *Biomedicine Examined*, Dordrecht: Kluwer Academic, 1988: 299–329; and David Armstrong, *Political Anatomy of the Body: medical knowledge in Britain in the twentieth century*, Cambridge: Cambridge University Press, 1983: esp. ch. 6, 'Child life and health'.

9 Ivan Illich, for example, only mentions in passing the medical interventions into childrens' lives in his *Limits to Medicine. Medical nemesis: the expropriation of health*, Harmondsworth, Middlesex: Penguin Books, 1977: 93. Compare this understanding of 'medicalization' with that provided by Foucault, quoted at the end of this Introduction.

10 George K. Behlmer, *Child Abuse and Moral Reform in England, 1870–1908*, Stanford: Stanford University Press, 1982; Linda Gordon, *Heroes of Their Own Lives: the politics and history of family violence, Boston 1880–1960*, London: Virago, 1989. For other sources on this subject, see Harry Ferguson's chapter in this volume.

11 This is true of narrative accounts, such as that by Ivy Pinchbeck and M. Hewitt, *Children in English Society*, London: Routledge, 1969, 1973, 2 vols, as well as more sophisticated recent studies, such as Colin Heywood, *Childhood in Nineteenth-Century France*, Cambridge: Cambridge University Press, 1988; Lee Shai Weissbach, *Child Labour Reform in Nineteenth Century France*, Baton Rouge: Louisiana University Press, 1989; and Clark Nardinelli, *Child Labor and the Industrial Revolution*, Bloomington: Indiana University Press, 1990. An exception, from the point of view of its singular focus, is Marjorie Cruickshank, *Children in Industry: child health and welfare in north-west towns during the nineteenth century*, Manchester: Manchester University Press, 1981.

12 For a list of such works (within a sharply contrasting sophisticated sociological study), see Sydney A. Halpern, *American Pediatrics: the social dynamics of professionalism, 1880–1980*, Berkeley: University of California Press, 1988: 161–2.

13 See, for example, Derrick Mercer, *Children First and Always: a portrait of Great Ormond Street*, London: Macdonald, 1986; Douglas Guthrie (ed.) *The Royal Edinburgh Hospital for Sick Children, 1860–1960*, Edinburgh: Livingstone, 1960; Edna Robertson, *The Yorkhill Story: the history of the Royal Hospital for Sick Children, Glasgow*, Glasgow: Board of Management for Yorkhill, 1972; Clement A. Smith, *The Children's Hospital of Boston*, Boston: Little, Brown, 1983; Rachel E. Waterhouse, *Children in Hospital: a hundred years of child care in Birmingham*, London: Hutchinson, 1962.

14 See, for example, Richard A. Meckel, *Save the Babies: American public health reform and the prevention of infant mortality, 1850–1929*, Baltimore: Johns Hopkins University Press, 1990; Simon Szreter, 'The importance of social intervention in Britain's mortality decline, c. 1850–1914: a re-interpretation of the role of public health', *Social*

History of Medicine, 1988, 1: 1–37; and Dwork, *War is Good for Babies*.

15 Dwork, *War is Good for Babies*. Cf Bernard J. Harris, 'Medical inspection and the nutrition of schoolchildren in Britain, 1900–1950', Ph.D. thesis, University of London, 1988; and J. David Hirst, 'The growth of treatment through the School Medical Service, 1908–18', *Medical History*, 1989, 33: 318–42. For other sources on the School Medical Service in Britain, see Hendrick's chapter in this volume.

16 For example, Valerie Fildes, Lara Marks and Hilary Marland (eds), *Women and Children First: international maternal and infant welfare, 1800–1950*, London: Routledge, 1992.

17 F. B. Smith, *The People's Health, 1830–1910*, London: Croom Helm, 1989. Smith opts for the introduction of mothercraft and health visiting as the best means to explain the decline in infant mortality over the period 1903–8: 113ff.

18 See B. R. Mitchell and Phyllis Deane, *Abstracts of British Historical Statistics*, Cambridge: Cambridge University Press, 1971: 12. For the more variable European situation, see Richard Lawton and Robert Lee (eds) *Urban Population Development in Western Europe from the Late-eighteenth to Early-twentieth Century*, Liverpool: University of Liverpool Press, 1989.

19 Peter Laslett, 'After the transformation: English society in the early twentieth century', in his *The World We Have Lost*, London: Methuen, 1965: 200–26. Mortality from measles in England and Wales between 1898 and 1948 fell from 13,000 to 300, and for diphtheria, from 7,500 to 150, while scarlet fever fell one-hundredfold (ibid: 221). Cf the social policy/politics of health care perspective on diphtheria in Jane Lewis, 'The prevention of diphtheria in Canada and Britain, 1914–1945', *Journal of Social History*, 1986, 20: 163–76.

20 See George Wolff, *Death From Accidents Among Children and Adolescents*, Washington, DC, US Department of Labor, Children's Bureau, 1944, and other sources cited in Viviana Zelizer, *Pricing the Priceless Child: the changing social value of children*, New York: Basic Books, 1985: 233 n. 25 and *passim*; and Smith, *People's Health*: 173–4.

21 For an extreme version of direct causal thinking in this connection, see Michael S. Teitelbaum and Jay M. Winter, *The Fear of Population Decline*, San Diego: Academic Press, 1985: esp. 31, 34. For similar, see Ann Oakley, 'Children of the Nation: the beginnings of antenatal care 1900–18' in her *The Captured Womb: a history of the medical care of pregnant women*, Oxford: Blackwell, 1984: 34–61 at 35. Dwork (*War is Good for Babies*) offers a fuller treatment and seeks to place both the Boer War and the First World War in perspective by locating concern about race deterioration in scientific and intellectual discourse from the mid-nineteenth century.

22 Zelizer, *Pricing the Priceless Child*: 6. Of course neither the neo-romantic idealization of childhood nor the appropriation of working-class children into it were peculiar to the late nineteenth century. See Hendrick, 'Constructions and reconstructions'.

23 Jordanova, 'Children in history': 10.

24 For statistics on school attendance in Britain after the Education Act of 1870, see Anthony Wohl, *Endangered Lives: Public Health in Victorian Britain*, London: Dent, 1983: 137.

25 Nikolas Rose, *The Psychological Complex: psychology, politics and society in England, 1869–1939*, London: Routledge, 1985.

26 See also Carol-Ann Hooper, 'Rethinking the politics of child abuse', *Social History of Medicine*, 1989, 2: 356–64.

27 Jane Lewis, *The Politics of Motherhood: child and maternal welfare in England, 1900–1939*, London: Croom Helm, 1980. The difference between Lewis's orientation and Dwork's is captured in Dwork's criticism of Lewis's book as 'perceiv[ing] the remedy of maternalism as a restrictive social control solution [to infant mortality]': Dwork, *War is Good for Babies*: 227. Also included in this criticism is the work of Anna Davin and Carol Dyhouse, which similarly focuses on the ideology of maternalism (though rather more causally than Lewis): Davin, 'Imperialism and motherhood', *History Workshop Journal*, 1978, 5: 9–65; Dyhouse, 'Working-class mothers and infant mortality in England, 1895–1914', *Journal of Social History*, 1978, 12: 248–67.

28 See Carl Degler, *At Odds: women and the family in America from the revolution to the present*, New York: Oxford University Press, 1980: 73–4, and Barbara Ehrenreich and D. English, *For Her Own Good: 150 years of the experts' advice to women*, London: Pluto, 1979: ch. 6, 'The century of the child'.

29 Ornella Moscucci, *The Science of Woman: gynaecology and gender in England, 1800–1929*, Cambridge: Cambridge University Press, 1990: 4.

30 See, for example, Cynthia Russett, *Sexual Science: the Victorian construction of womanhood*, Cambridge, Mass: Harvard University Press, 1989.

31 See Dean Rapp, 'The early discovery of Freud by the British general educated public, 1912–1919', *Social History of Medicine*, 1990, 3: 217–43.

32 R. Barnes, 'The teaching of midwifery and Mr Syme's committee on medical education', *Lancet*, 1868, cited in Moscucci, *Science of Woman*: 68. Partly, this was for reasons connected to professionalization in obstetrics.

33 See Gordon, *Heroes of their Own Lives*: 57ff. For comparisons with earlier periods, see Pelling, 'Child health': 137, and Brian Abel-Smith, *The Hospitals, 1800–1948*, London: Heinemann, 1964: 13–14, 24–5.

34 Moscucci, *Science of Woman*: 75.

35 Le Grand Kerr, *Diagnostics of the Diseases of Children*, Philadelphia: W. B. Saunders, 1907: 17.

36 However, see Peter C. English, '"Not miniature men and women": Abraham Jacobi's vision of a new medical specialty a century ago', in Loretta M. Kopelman and John C. Moskop (eds) *Children and Health Care: moral and social issues*, Dordrecht: Kluwer Academic, 1989: 247–73. According to Armstrong (*Political Anatomy*: 61), in Britain it was not until the early years of the National Health Service (post-1948)

that the view was adopted of the child body being fundamentally different from that of the adult.

37 Malcolm Newby, *Sick Children's Hospital Nursing in Nineteenth-Century Britain*, Bath: History Inc., 1989.

38 Robert Ellis, *Disease in Childhood, its Common Causes, and Directions for its Practical Management*, London: G. Cox, 1852: 8.

39 Report of a Committee of the Statistical Society, cited in ibid.: 8. See also Eduard Seidler, 'An historical survey of children's hospitals', in Lindsay Granshaw and Roy Porter (eds) *The Hospital in History*, London: Routledge, 1989: 181–97.

40 John V. Pickstone, *Medicine and Industrial Society: a history of hospital development in Manchester and its region, 1752–1946*, Manchester: Manchester University Press, 1985: 116–19. On Louis Bauer (1814–98), the Pomeranian radical and specialist in children's orthopaedics who settled in Manchester before eventually making a name for himself in St Louis, see Alfred Shands jun., *The Early Orthopaedic Surgeons of America*, St Louis: Mosby, 1970, and Bruno Valentin, *Geschichte der Orthopädie*, Stuttgart: Thieme, 1961: 183.

41 See the entry on Jacobi in the *Dictionary of American Biography*.

42 On the latter theme, see Frank Prochaska, *Women and Philanthropy in Nineteenth-Century England*, Oxford: Clarendon Press, 1980; and Pickstone, *Medicine in Manchester*: 114, 120, who argues that in the Manchester region at least, the late-Victorian renaissance in voluntary hospitals 'began in the special charities of the city which devoted themselves to the diseases of women and children'. This was philanthropy mobilized by doctors, but directed by middle-class women. Pickstone admits, however, that the changing interactions between lay and medical interests are complex and 'require further investigation'. On Jewry, women and philanthropy in a rather different connection, see Lara Marks, '"Dear Old Mother Levy's": the Jewish maternity home and sick room helps society 1895–1939', *Social History of Medicine*, 1990, 3: 61–88.

43 Little has been written on the development of paediatrics in Britain or the rest of Europe to compare with Halpern's study of American paediatrics (note 12). In Britain this was not a continuous story; the Society for the Study of Diseases in Children (est. 1900) floundered long before the British Paediatric Society was established. The composition of these two groups was also radically different. On Germany, see Georg Liliethal, 'Paediatrics and nationalism in imperial Germany', *Bulletin of the Society for the Social History of Medicine*, 1986, 39: 64–70.

44 But see K. J. Heasman, 'The medical mission and the care of the sick poor in nineteenth-century England', *Historical Journal*, 1964, 7: 230–45; Ruth Hodgkinson, *The Origins of the National Health Service: medical services and the new poor law, 1834–1871*, London: Wellcome Institute, 1967; G. M. Ayers, *England's First State Hospitals and the Metropolitan Asylums Board, 1867–1930*, London: Wellcome Institute, 1971; and M. A. Crowther, *The Workhouse System, 1834–1929*, London: Batsford Academic, 1981: ch. 7.

45 See Roger Cooter, *Surgery and Society in Peace and War: orthopaedics and the organisation of modern medicine, 1880–1948*, London: Macmillan, forthcoming.
46 Foucault, 'La politique de la santé au XVIIIe siècle' (1976) as quoted in Ute Frevert, 'Professional medicine and the working classes in imperial Germany', *Journal of Contemporary History*, 1985, 20: 637.

1

BODIES, FIGURES AND PHYSIOLOGY

Margaret McMillan and the late nineteenth-century remaking of working-class childhood

Carolyn Steedman

As for the history of the physiology of growth, it is soon written. We still know lamentably little about the mechanisms by which human growth is so precisely controlled. We do not know why the velocity of growth gets steadily less from birth to puberty. We do not know what causes a fast tempo, what a slow one.

(J. M. Tanner, *A History of the Study of Human Growth*, 1981)

Upon what depends this tendency to multiplication of anatomical elements, and this tendency to increase in size of individual anatomical elements of organs, until a certain approximate limit has been attained, is absolutely unknown. We know to a certain extent that the process of *growth* depends upon and is influenced by certain circumstances . . . but yet the knowledge is wanting that would tell us why, when a certain limit has been attained . . . growth ceases.

(Arthur Gamgee, 'Growth, Decay and Death',
Encyclopaedia Britannica, 9th edn, 1885)

INTRODUCTION

In this chapter ideas about child health and growth in childhood, current at the end of the last century and at the beginning of this, will be considered from the perspective of working-class childhood. The philanthropic and political attention focused on sickly, adenoidal, and ill-nourished schoolchildren in the first decades of this century is, of course, well known. It has been recorded within the kind of administrative history that seeks the 'origins' of the welfare state, within the annals of educational history, and also, within newer accounts, of state attention paid to women and children in this period.[1] Recent accounts of the 'discovery' of childhood poverty and ill health have shifted historical focus from the aftermath of the Second Boer War and its attendant revelations of working-class deterioration, to the First World War, and the reorganization of child welfare that it entailed.[2] However, none of these general historical narratives of revelation of social evil and response to it, have endeavoured to place this series of widely attended 'discoveries' of working-class childhood in its contemporary theoretical context. It is this theoretical context that this chapter is intended to outline.

By 'theoretical' is meant not only the way in which childhood came to be understood and described within various disciplines and bodies of thought (developmental linguistics, paediatrics, medicine, education, social welfare work, and so on), but also the way in which childhood, in a much more general sense, was reformulated to mean something new – something abstract yet explanatory, something 'true' – for a large number of people seeking explanations of human subjectivity, and the meaning of life.

Whilst it is argued here that physiological paradigms and their popularization structured many imaginative uses of the idea of childhood in this period, evidence for this altered imagination is taken from two fairly restricted sources. In the second part of this chapter, the evidence of literary history is considered, in order to explore a specifically late nineteenth-century transmutation of 'the Romantic child', the literary figure that since the late eighteenth century had married innocence to death. In the period under discussion here, this literary figure became an explanatory device for the mysteries of growth and decay that (as the epigrams to this chapter indicate) contemporary physiology put so perplexingly on the cultural agenda of the late nineteenth century.

This transmutation can be read across many forms of social and political writing, but the first half of this chapter concentrates on just one of them, on the idea of childhood in the construction of a political programme by the Independent Labour Party (ILP) in the years leading up to the First World War. Late nineteenth-century British socialism (particularly the ILP version) with its organicist social vision – its search for a means of analysis that put aside the idea of economic individualism for the image of the totality of social relations – made particularly interesting use of contemporary ideas about growth and decay. Though the ILP was formed as a national party in January 1893 with a political programme directed along the parliamentary road, it actually rose to political importance within specific localities, and through municipal contests. Between 1893 and 1897 the national conferences of the party ratified a programme that was based on socialist objectives: on the nationalization of land, the collectivization of the means of production and exchange, and the redistribution of income through taxation. Within this broad socialist framework, specific struggles for reform were outlined, including a 48-hour week, the abolition of overtime, piecework and child-labour, and social provision for the sick, the disabled, the old, and for widows and orphans. Over the first five years of the new party's existence, this basic programme was elaborated by a more detailed attention to education, to the whole question of child-labour, and to the school-leaving age, which was the focus of the politics that emerged from the distinction between the schooled child and the working child. This turning of the working-class child from a component of the labour force into a subject of education was a question that exercised many more political constituencies than the ILP, and can be seen as one of the major political and social shifts of all Western societies in the late nineteenth century.[3] In the case of the ILP, the working-out of a set of practical policies on the half-time system was the ground where two views of childhood were contested. The part-time labour of children, particularly in the textile trades of Lancashire and Yorkshire, brought the politics of rescue and child welfare into sharp conflict with trade union principles and the pattern of working-class life, at both a national and local level.[4] These arguments and conflicts, exercised at ILP, Social Democratic and Trades Union Congress conferences, and, after 1906, in the Labour Party, influenced the Liberal government's evolution of a statutory system of national child welfare and rescue. By the 1920s, with establishment of a system of state care for the nation's youngest children, the conflict between the labouring child and the schooled child was brought to rest, and a new conceptualization of childhood can be said to have come into being.[5]

Margaret McMillan (1860–1931), one of the party's most charismatic propagandists, spent a political lifetime conjuring working-class childhood before her audiences, in political speeches and pamphlets, in educational manuals, and in the heart-wrenching romantic socio-fictions of slum childhood that she produced for the

21

Labour press. Her technique was to symbolize scientific knowledge about growth and development in childhood, by personifying it in fictional working-class children. This was done for the purposes of propaganda, in order to sway opinion and change hearts and minds, and so the processes at work are particularly easy to discern, and open to historical analysis.

Margaret McMillan emerged as the party's theorist of working-class childhood and physiology through her experiments in welfare and education in Bradford and Deptford, between 1894 and 1930.[6] To say that in these years McMillan *rewrote* working-class childhood is not to employ some metaphor, vaguely invoking discourses of the social subject (in this case, that of 'the working-class child'); it is rather to consider seriously the huge output of her writing, the lectures she gave, and the books she published on this topic.[7] The figures of working-class children that McMillan presented to the readership of the *Clarion* and the *Labour Leader*, and in the romantic fiction that she produced for these and other journals in the 1890s, alert us to the need, when reading literary *and* scientific accounts of childhood, for a form of analysis that can deal with their subjects as both invented and real: as literary figures, and as representatives of actual children living in particular social circumstances. For what helped shape ILP and later, Labour Party, policy on childhood, was not just sets of statistics concerning child ill health and hunger, not just the sociological shape of deformed and defrauded childhood; but also, and at the same time, the moving, sentimentalized, and 'sacralized' child-figures who dwelt in McMillan's prose and platform oratory.

The term 'sacralization' is used by Viviana Zelizer in *Pricing the Priceless Child*, in her account of the way in which 'a profound transformation in the economic and sentimental value of children' took place between 1870 and 1930, in the United States. Through a consideration of child labour, public reactions to the death of children (particularly in street accidents), changing patterns of childcare, baby-farming, abandonment and adoption, and changing patterns in the practice of insuring children's lives, Zelizer shows that in the USA in this period, economically useless children (useless because of their recent transformation from workers into scholars) became emotionally priceless, to their parents in particular, but also to wider communities than the family.[8]

The argument for these particular late nineteenth-century processes taking place in Europe (as opposed to the USA) has not

22

yet been made, although it can be claimed that Ariès, in *Centuries of Childhood*, demonstrated a form of 'sacralization' of children taking place in early modern times. Nevertheless, the particularity of Zelizer's argument (though she does not herself make this point) must concern the rapid establishment of national *compulsory* school systems in the Western world, from the mid-century onwards, and the large-scale affective changes that the turning of working-class children from labourers into scholars wrought in the adult society. It is therefore possible to suggest that living through these times, McMillan and the ILP were both influenced by this shift in perspective, and also played an important role in what may have been a specifically British transformation of the meaning of childhood, for McMillan's work and writing, and its political use, allows an exploration of what may be a general development in terms of class, and the particular ambiguities that attached to the 'sacralization of child life' when it was the children of the unskilled labouring poor who were under consideration. The difficulties involved in the reification of this particular category of children had much to do with their social and class status, and the position of their parents within ILP thought.

It was developments within physiological thought that largely framed ILP policy on childhood. In the reconstruction of the meaning and purpose of working-class childhood may be found an 'origin' of the welfare state, in a child written about, wept over, rescued, in the columns of the *Labour Leader*, at ILP and Labour Party national conferences: in a child-*figure*, in this historically illuminating conjunction of symbol and sociology, within a popular use of scientific thought.

BODIES

In 1900, McMillan published *Early Childhood*. During the previous year, Keir Hardie had given three columns a month to it in the *Labour Leader*, where it appeared as a series on primary education. Both the series and the book were addressed to the wife of that symbolic addressee of much late nineteenth-century socialist argument, 'John Smith of Oldham'. It was, Hardie thought, 'written more for the mother than the Dominie'.[9]

Early Childhood drew together and made explicit the theories of child development that McMillan had been working with throughout her Bradford years. It shows a continuing use of the technique she had practised there, in the columns of the *Bradford Labour Echo*, of simplifying and conveying an array of technical information to a non-professional audience. Eight years later, in a review of her three books on childhood in the *Highway* (the journal of the Workers' Educational Association) it was claimed that McMillan's achievement had been to make 'the discovery of the child' and its educational implications accessible to a general public: 'It is only within late years that the necessity of a knowledge of childhood as a condition antecedent to the arrangement of any education programme' had become 'that prescribed by the child's own nature and stages of development'.[10]

The body of a child, as described by McMillan in 1900, was a physiological entity in that its varying functions – movement, speech, thought – were presented as the sum of many different interactions within the body. However, it was the neurological system that mapped out this physiological organization. McMillan told her readers that, in babies, the nervous system was undifferentiated, and that early impressions were received by the child through 'the sympathetic system, with its wide channels, its central ganglions'.[11] Not pausing to explain what a ganglion was, she went on to describe how the arterial system that conveyed blood around the organism was large in proportion to the baby's body, and she located the place where mind developed within this system, describing how

> the living cells, whilst building up the pabulum or food-stuffs into their own substance, ever respond to the influences that play on them like breezes on a lake, but they respond in a peculiarly effective way during the earlier months ... Occasionally we are reminded of the permanent character of these records by dim recollection, and emotions awakened in us we know not how or why. The perfume of a flower, the tone of a voice, the sight of a face or of a scene which we cannot remember to have visited fills us with vague delight or tenderness. The origin of these mysterious emotions lies deep-rooted in the subconscious life – the life we lived when as feeble recipients we accepted the impressions which flowed in on us from every side and left their traces in us for ever.[12]

McMillan described the baby and the small child gaining control of the finer muscles through movement, and then presented the order of limbs in which this control was achieved. Each fine movement awakened intelligence, and McMillan explained how 'movements are registered in the brain, and involve the awakening of brain cells'.[13]

The notion of a brain centre was introduced by McMillan, and *Early Childhood* laid out clearly what McMillan called the 'topography' of the brain:

> in a kind of arch many motor centres are ranged. And these are believed by many neurologists to be not merely centres of movements, but centres too, for the reception and record of innumerable sensations ... the cerebrum is the organ of innumerable functions and activities ... each part lives because it is stimulated through vibrations arising from without. It is the *nervous* current which is the mother of energy.[14]

This energy then, in McMillan's account, was both cerebral and muscular: a tired child might receive 'a rain of stimulating vibrations', which, if they were dispatched to the brain, would generate energy – 'the muscles ... now limp, regained their tenacity; nutrition became more active'.[15]

Physiological organization also produced language, in McMillan's account. In *Early Childhood*, child language was described as a matter of production, as the actual result of a material formation, that is, 'the form of the mouth and the larynx'. Given this formation, any interference, from poor breathing for example, would prevent the production of speech.[16] Thought itself was described as the ultimate operation of organs – particularly that of the 'Royal Organ', the heart – as muscle and blood moved within the system: 'the most casual thought, the vaguest emotion sends a red tide flowing to the brain'. As specific intellectual endeavour took place, in studying for example, 'the muscles are involved ... the activity of the blood setting in a swift river towards the cerebral centres where the great movements are taking place to which we give the name of *thought*'.[17]

This system of understanding was structured around the idea of growth and development, it allowed for comparisons to be made between children, and, most important of all as a basis for a social policy on childhood, it rooted mental life in the material body and the material conditions of life. In this way, working-class children could be seen as having been robbed of natural development, their potential for health and growth lying dormant in their half-starved bodies. Indeed, McMillan's political point was to draw attention to the way in which a vast number of children were deprived of organic development. But what was also organized in her writing was a way of seeing. She turned to the child of her symbolic addressee, and said

> Here is a boy called John Smith attending the elementary school. His age is eleven. He is short by two and a half inches of the normal stature of a boy of the upper-middle class. His chest is too narrow by six or seven inches. He breathes from the upper part of his chest. The nostrils are light, and the upper lip is probably stiff and motionless. Ask him to take a deep breath . . . [He] cannot . . . has not taken one for years.[18]

John Smith, Jun. represents a significant shift in perception of working-class children that can be located in McMillan's development as a writer and thinker, and can be speculated about in more general historical terms. In *The Political Anatomy of the Body*, David Armstrong reflects on large-scale shifts in understanding of the human subject, seen through the filter of medical knowledge.[19] He suggests that 'the gaze commenced with the child', by which he means that 'psychologists played an important part in the discovery of the normal child, in revealing the detailed stages of child development, in classifying behaviour problems and in developing techniques of educational surveillance and child-rearing'.[20] We can be more specific than this if we consider McMillan's conclusion to eight years of reading in medical and neurological literature and her acquaintance with children in Bradford's elementary schools. At the beginning of the new century, McMillan looked inwards, saw little John Smith as a branching system of nerves, his brain centres imperfectly fed by his shallow breathing, his skin a barrier to sensation rather than its transmitter. It was this understanding of a child as a physiological interiority – a body containing depth and space within it – that she worked to convey in political terms, to the ILP and a wider audience.

Early Childhood had in fact, a clear political purpose, which was to show what a restorative educational programme might look like, and to demonstrate that 'all true education is, primarily, physiological. It is concerned not with books, but with nervous tissue'.[21] Here, McMillan was making direct reference to the most consistent source for her work, the writing of Édouard Seguin (1812–80), the French physiologist and psychologist, whose work with abnormal children entered the mainstream of British educational thought after Maria Montessori publicized it in 1911.[22]

Seguin trained as a medical doctor under François Itard when Itard was involved in the care of the Wild Boy of Aveyron. He went on to found a school for mentally retarded children in Paris in 1837, and published observations on his method in *Traitement moral, hygiène et éducation des idiots* in 1846. As well as dealing with mentally deficient children, he worked with deaf mutes, and in the teaching of the deaf, placed himself within the educative tradition of Pereire and Rousseau.[23]

Until 1850, when he left France to settle permanently in the USA, he was a well-known and esteemed medical physiologist whose writing was educational in import. He was also a Saint-Simonian, who consistently understood his own endeavours in the light of Saint-Simon's *Nouveau Christianisme* of 1824, situating his work in the political context of a 'striving for a social application of the principles of the gospel; for the most rapid elevation of the lowest and poorest by all means and institutions; mainly by free education'.[24] It was for this reason that Seguin aligned himself with Itard and his work, even though Itard 'never so much hinted at the possibility of systematising his views for the treatment of idiots at large, nor organising schools for the same purpose', but because 'he was the first to educate an idiot with a philosophical object'.[25] This vision, of a form of physical and material education undertaken to show that the common lot of the common people could be dramatically improved, was the central political understanding of McMillan's life, and was almost certainly formulated around a reading of Seguin's work.

Seguin's *Idiocy and Its Treatment by the Physiological Method* was written in English and available in Britain after 1866. McMillan travelled from Bradford to read this and his *Report on Education* of 1875 in the British Museum.[26] Seguin's *Rapport et mémoire sur l'éducation des enfants normaux et anormaux* was also available in 1895. Never translated into English, it was certainly read by McMillan along with his other works. It contained Seguin's thorough-going speculation about the possibility of using his educational methods with ordinary children.[27] It was in fact, Maria Montessori who made the most famous experiments in this direction in her slum nursery school in Rome, using Seguin's work as a guide – a history of the transmission of ideas that always irritated McMillan.[28] It remains the case however, that Seguin's theories entered British educational thinking via Montessori's work, rather than McMillan's.

When Seguin called his method of teaching retarded children 'physiological', what he meant was that his understanding was based on a view of a structure of bodily organs inseparably connected with their function. To change, improve or modify a function, the appropriate organ – the wasted hand, the unseeing eye, the gaping mouth – had to be acted upon. The educator could do this, as the organs of sensation were external.[29] Seguin's method began with the training of the muscular system and the senses, through a variety of exercises and activities. Then, he led children from the education of the senses to general notions, or understandings, and from general notions to abstract thought. Physiological education of the senses had to precede the development of mind.[30] It was on this point that Seguin distinguished his approach from that of his teacher Itard. Itard had repeated visual and auditory sensations endlessly with Victor, the Wild Boy, but had not led the child towards abstraction. It was at this point too, that Seguin took issue with Friedrich Froebel, the founder of the kindergarten movement, whose activities with children, he claimed, remained at the sensory level. Seguin was insistent that his methods led from what was imitative in the child to what was creative in human thought.[31] It was to this set of arguments that McMillan referred when in 1913, discussing 'Backward Children', she described a boy at her Camp School in Deptford swinging from a tree, being told to get down, but an hour later being asked by the remedial gymnast to perform exactly the same set of movements. Nature, she argued, and 'the woods, do not offer the advantages of the higher order of school. The wild boy of Aveyron, educated in the woods alone, was an animal, not a human'.[32]

'Physiology' then, described an interactive and interconnected system, contained within the body of a child, and a 'physiological education' was a means of acting upon that system. 'Physiology' in this sense also described the child in a social setting. Seguin paid attention to the future work that children were likely to do, and tried to promote a respect for manual labour.[33] McMillan's emphasis on hands, the role of hands in labour and in the development of intelligence, and her interest in technical education has its origins here (though Peter Kropotkin's work on manual labour was also an important influence).[34] Other central features of her educational programme that can be directly traced back to Seguin were the importance of the physical setting of the school, detailed attention to the children's clothing and the food they ate, the role of water in the awakening of the senses, and the particular role of women as the natural caretakers of young children.[35] To say that she learned the educational vocabulary of love, nurture and physical activity from Seguin is another way of describing his influence, but it is also to point to him as a literary influence, as well as a physiological and educational one. For instance, he highlighted the human hand in his account of normal and abnormal development in his exegesis of 1866, in a way that still leaps from the page:

> If any part of us challenges definition, it is the hand, its excellencies being so many that a single definition cannot comprehend them all ... When we say prehension, we mean the complex action of taking, keeping, losing hold; otherwise to seize, hold and to let go; these three terms are the beginning, the object and the end of the act of prehension. This act, so simple for us in its trilogy, is either impossible to, or incidentally performed [sic] by the idiot.[36]

This is a description of the human and social subject as much as it is a biological account. For McMillan what was described were the little Bradford millhands whose brain centres were atrophied through the simple repetition of monotonous movements. An industrial system stood condemned by what it had done to the hands of the people, where 'the whole burden of [the worker's] task falls on the forefinger and thumb of one hand'.[37] Indeed, it was the hand that her audience were asked to concentrate on in *Early Childhood*:

> Look at the hand of the defective child. The fingers are probably stunted and ill-formed – cold and blue – the nails broken, the palm stiff. Indeed, the whole hand often hangs stiff and motionless, moved like a dead thing from the wrist. Suppose a teacher wants to train his hand: how does she begin. By maxims? By lessons in reading and writing? No. By movement – by exercise.[38]

In the same way, McMillan's presentation of education – waking a variety of learners from sleep – can be traced to Seguin and his description of backward children waking from unconsciousness through physiological education.

Although McMillan wrote and worked in an era when segregation and control of defectives had replaced an earlier optimistic and humanist belief in their educability (a humanism exemplified in fact, by Édouard Seguin), she continued to draw that democratic impulse from the earlier body of work, and structured her own theory of childhood around the belief that the life of children condemned to physiological and neurological sleep by a social system, could actually be enlarged. Seguin's work allowed her to perceive and understand two central points: first, that there existed a developmental order and an optimum functioning of the human body; and second, that even for children deprived of this, amelioration was possible.[39] Her consistent assertion was that poor children were the same kind of children as more favoured ones, that their inabilities were not innate and fixed – even though 'some manage to believe still that the masses are born dull'.[40] The working-class girl, she said in 1909, 'is not a distinct species. It is not in her nature and its general law of development, that she differs from the so-called upper class girl, but only in her prospects and circumstances'.[41] Although deprived, of growth, of nutritition, of stimulation, these things could be put right – with political will, human effort and a little money. It was this broad optimism that she had reinforced by Seguin's work, not a perception of working-class children as deficient or defective. We should remember as well, that in the period when McMillan was writing, the term 'idiot' was in transition from being a clinical description to a degrading insult. Whilst perhaps exonerating McMillan from an eliding of idiocy with the conditions of working-class life, there is no denying the deleterious effects of this connection, that was made out of her work and that of her contemporaries, in the construction of much twentieth-century educational theory concerned with the schooling of working-class children.

Late nineteenth-century physiology has been described as a paradigmatic science, marking a fundamental change of under-standing of systems that spread to most other areas of biological and social thought.[42] In particular, the practice of physiology, which was highly and explicitly experimental, moved first from an assumption of idealism (in which matter was seen as secondary to its conceptualization or abstract apprehension) to that of materialism, in which matter was understood to exist independently of any perception, account, or conceptualization of it. Within this under-standing, a system or an entity was studied through its parts, and the sum of those parts was taken to be a description of the whole. Later in the century, physiological accounts converged towards a more dialectical materialism, in which the actual *interaction* between the different parts of a body, or other biological entity, were understood to constitute the description of the whole.[43]

McMillan used this interactive paradigm, despite the constraints of her source in the popular physiology of Édouard Seguin – which she indeed popularized still further.[44] Indeed, in Seguin's work (and in all the books that praised him) we can see the powerful grip of natural theology that Geison has described holding British physiological thought in the mid-nineteenth century, and which, adhering to the belief of design in nature, dictated the impossibility of understanding function as separated from structure.[45] What allowed McMillan to break away from the functionalism of her source, was partly to do with the body of the subject she dealt with, that is, a *child's* body, which is not a fixed and permanent thing, but is rather, in a dramatic state of change through the process of growth. The child's body was a way of representing – of thinking through and symbolizing – those interior and generally hidden processes that the new and popularly written physiology of the late century was making plain – that uncharted darkness through growth to decline into death, that Arthur Gamgee, writing in the the ninth edition of the *Encyclopaedia Britannica* (and providing one of the epigraphs to this chapter) described as 'absolutely unknown'. That the child's body was able to provide a symbol for this process was of course to do with its rapid physiological development, and the many disciplines that had focused on aspects of its growth, in the last quarter of the nineteenth century. But it also had much to do with the way in which children had been represented – pre-figured – in the preceding century.

FIGURES

We need at this point to start dealing in literary terms, for it was in those terms that working-class childhood was reformulated and assigned new social and political meaning in the period under discussion. We are familiar, from Peter Coveney's pioneering work, with the establishment of the romantic, post-Wordsworthian child in literature, from the 1830s onwards, and with Coveney's argument that the particular legacy of romanticism for British social thought, was the idea of the child – at least, the represented child, the literary figure of the child – as a conjunction of innocence and death. Coveney's argument, in *The Image of Childhood*, is sometimes appropriated to a more general history of childhood, in which the late eighteenth and nineteenth centuries 'discover the child', and

Wordsworth, and Rousseau before him, are seen as key figures in the process of discovery.[46]

If we follow the historians who have looked at the debates surrounding child welfare in the nineteenth century, we will see that working-class children present particular problems within the romantic construction of childhood. Both Hugh Cunningham, in his work on child labour, and Deborah Gorham, in her account of the scandal surrounding the publication of W. T. Stead's *Maiden Tribute* in 1885, and the age-of-consent debate, suggest that the children of the labouring poor could be seen as both children and as 'not-children' in order to resolve the contradiction between a prescribed innocence, and the necessity of child labour.[47]

Following the argument about child labour, child welfare, innocence and corruption through parliamentary commissions of inquiry, parliamentary debates, sociological and journalistic enquiry, we see it proceeding by the same set of figurative devices as the novel. At the same time, despite the powerful restraints of class, we can witness an appropriation of the children of the labouring poor to the romantic ideal of childhood, from the middle years of the nineteenth century onwards.[48] Were an account of this appropriation to be written, then McMillan would have a significant place within it, for her high output of fiction concerning working-class children served to show them as the romantic reclaimers of social life.

Within this broad figurative sweep we should add the impact of the kindergarten movement in this country, the publicity machine of the Froebel Society, and its propagation of the idea of childhood as a garden, and the propriety of returning all children to their proper setting, which is also a Garden.[49] McMillan called Froebel 'the first great practical Restorer of the child to nature and a natural environment',[50] and it is in the camp school at Deptford that we can see the symbolic enactment of these currents of nineteenth-century thought, or apotheosis of various theories of childhood.

The Deptford Camp School developed in a fairly *ad hoc* way between 1910 and 1914, when McMillan made up beds in the garden for children who had received treatment in her clinic. From the start, the Camp School was simply an open space in which children who lived in the surrounding neighbourhood could spend the night, whether they had been ill or not. It was a garden in a slum, a space between the huddled houses and the open sky. Official visitors found the arrangements ramshackle; but almost all of them commented on the prettiness of the children sleeping and waking in the garden: it was almost impossible for journalists and other commentators to avoid horticultural imagery when describing the place.[51] Parents were meant to be able to see what was going on: not only were there parents' evenings and entertainments, but looking out of their back windows they witnessed a constant object lesson in child health and child nurture. 'It is an open-air residential school', wrote McMillan in 1914, 'that does not separate the child from his home'.[52] She hoped in the future for covered passage ways between groups of fifty or so houses, and a camp school in the middle of them. Watching the children grow healthy and strong, the parents would recognize the children as beautiful, would understand their former deprivation of their own children's health and beauty, would feel themselves to be 'the Wronged', and would then vote for the new party.[53] The working-class parents of Deptford were, in this way, to be introduced to a nineteenth-century development of thought and feeling that showed childhood as both a stage of growth and development common to all of us, abandoned and left behind, but at the same time, a core of the individual's psychic life, always immanent, waiting there to be drawn on in various ways: a means for the adult to speculate on the meaning of his or her own life.

Not only had childhood been represented in this new way from the mid-century onwards, but histories were written of it. McMillan herself wrote fragments of this kind of history, using the markers of literature and painting to measure out a nineteenth-century 'invention' of childhood.[54] John Ruskin's art-history of working-class childhood was published in 1884, and it seems likely that McMillan's account was derived from his. In 'Fairyland', Ruskin noted the beauty with which children were depicted in the work of Rubens, Rembrandt and Van Dyck, and then went on to describe how 'the merciless manufacturing fury, which today grinds children to dust between millstones and tears them to pieces on engine wheels' had compelled British painters to represent working children in 'wickedness and misery'. Using the same literary landmarks as McMillan was to employ, he suggested that 'in literature we may take the "Cottar's Saturday Night" and the "toddlin' wee things" as the real beginning of child benediction'.[55] Some fifteen years before he wrote this piece, John Ruskin had walked through St Giles on the way from his house to the British Museum, looked at the faces of the children playing in the streets, and considered 'the marvel [of] . . . how the race resists, at least in its childhood, influences of ill-regulated birth, poisoned food, poisoned air, and soul neglect'.[56]

Other men had walked thus, some with cameras, others with notebooks, seeing as Ruskin did those faces, which 'through all their pale and corrupt misery' reminded him of 'the old "Non Angii", and recall it not by their beauty but by their sweetness of expression, even though signed already with trace and cloud of the coming life'.[57] McMillan's depiction of working-class childhood, the precise evocation of beauty in sordid surroundings, the *meaning* of the child thus depicted as an already-thwarted possibility, lay within this tradition of literary, aesthetic and cultural criticism. In a striking, though probably not conscious evocation of Ruskin's vision, Katharine Bruce Glasier recalled, after McMillan's death, an incident of 1896 when, after lecturing in Oldham one October night, they both watched 'the undersized workers pour out from a factory . . . and asked ourselves in bitterness of spirit: "How much would slaves of this kind have fetched in an old Athenian slave market?"'[58] This child, noticed by many 'in pale and corrupt misery', was the means by which the city might be held up for condemnation. Ruskin noted in 1884 a number of artists who had 'protested, with consistent feeling, against the misery entailed on the poor children of our great cities – by painting the real inheritance of childhood in meadows and fresh air'.[59] McMillan's Camp School in Deptford was an intensely practical manifestation of this romantic critique of capitalism: children's adenoids were operated on, remedial gym straightened backs, and children put on weight rapidly. But *written* about, within this aesthetic and cultural tradition, the children who were healed and schooled there became figures that represented the multi-layered meanings of 'natural' childhood. 'The love of spring may have been chilled for the moment by the cold wind of our industrial system', wrote McMillan in 1906, evoking the possibility of lowering national rates of infant mortality. 'But it is bound to revive. And it is love that will save the myriads who embark on the rough seas of life from going down so soon into the dark waters.'[60] The child as potential rescuer, or reclaimer of corrupt adulthood, was and is a feature of the post-Wordsworthian depiction of childhood, and as a literary territory, the nineteenth-century component of this understanding has been very well mapped out.[61] One of McMillan's literary achievements may come to be seen in the way she wedded this particular legacy of romanticism within British culture to socialist thought, in a new and politicized version of an established literary figure, 'the child'.[62] For not only were the children of Deptford (and of the unskilled labouring poor in general) to be rescued, but once saved, would reform their parents as well.

Both the fictional children and the real Deptford children that McMillan described in her journalism had been thwarted in development. More fortunate children, operating through play, gathered material 'for the higher mental life which is to follow, just as in the sub-conscious life of infancy, they once gathered materials for the conscious life today'. The way in which she depicted working-class child life operated then as a warning to her readers, that 'the mental life flows from the sympathetic and sub-conscious, and from these alone it is nourished. Woe then to those whose life-river is troubled near its source'.[63]

I have suggested a way in which a particular theory of physiological development, the theory embodied in the work of Édouard Seguin encouraged McMillan to believe that working-class children could be rescued from deprived circumstances, made whole, well and strong, and educated to become agents of a new social future. But Seguin's work apart, there was another set of ideas, popular in the 1890s, that allowed working-class children to be seen as possible agents of the new life. In McMillan's writing and propaganda work a telling phrase echoes: 'little children have brought us all up from barbarism'.[64] The source of this phrase is to be found in a now-forgotten but contemporaneously immensely influential book, Henry Drummond's publication of the Lowell Lectures in *The Ascent of Man*, in 1894. Drummond's book was an exegesis on what the author called 'the evolution of love'. Darwinism, he argued, had been misunderstood, in that the struggle for existence had been confused with evolution itself. In fact, in his account, there are two struggles to be seen taking place in the history of the human race, one being for life, and the second for the love of others: 'from selfdom to otherdom', said Drummond, 'is the supreme transition of history'. *The Ascent of Man* set out to reveal 'the stupendous superstructure of Altruism'.[65]

Drummond argued that, in human history, it was 'in the care and nurture of the young, in the provision everywhere throughout nature for the seed and the egg, in the infinite self-sacrifices of Maternity' that altruism had found its main expression.[66] Within this revision of evolutionary biology, human children had a particular significance, because the human mother was able to recognize her children as *being like herself*, and thereby able to move evolution on from a mere 'solicitude for the egg', to a full-blown maternity:

35

if a butterfly could live until its egg was hatched . . . it would see no butterfly come out of its egg, no airy likeness of itself, but an earth bound caterpillar. If it recognised the creature as its child, it could never play mother to it.[67]

But with the creation of human children, 'Altruism found an area for its own expression as had never before existed in the world.'[68] Drummond's work, and her use of it, allowed McMillan to establish working-class childhood as both an arena for political action *and* as a figurative device.

Between 1911 and 1912, McMillan gave typical literary shape to her politics of working-class childhood, in a series of pieces she wrote for the *Highway*. With the overall title of 'In Our Garden', the third and most reprinted piece was an account of the night when the first Deptford child slept out in the garden of the Clinic.[69] In describing the progress of Marigold's arrival, disrobing, washing, and settling down to sleep under the stars, McMillan made great literary claims for this Deptford seven-year-old, a costermonger's child, calling her, in her title to the piece, 'the English Mignon', and using as an epigraph the opening line from the infinitely sad song of yearning that Mignon, the child heroine of Goethe's *Wilhelm Meister* sings, and that was later set to music by Schubert: 'Kennst du das Land . . .'[70]

In evoking this particular child-figure, McMillan attached a weight of meaning to her own Marigold. The import of Mignon lay in the eighteenth-century fictional child's strangeness, deformity, retarded growth, and in her potential as reclaimer of sensibility in the adults around her[71] and it is likely that McMillan did intend the reader to make all these connections between Mignon and Marigold, and to bestow on the working-class seven-year-old of 1911 the same depth of interiority, dignity and meaning that Goethe gave to his child-figure. (Mignon was in fact, much in the news at this time, for an earlier version of *Wilhelm Meister*, entitled *Wilhelm Meister's Theatrical Mission*, written by Goethe in the 1770s and 1780s, had recently been discovered in Germany, and reported on in the British press.[72] However, the only direct reference that McMillan made to *Wilhelm Meister* was when she presented the child's facial beauty. 'She wears', wrote McMillan,

> the poor raiment of the slum child – a thin, soiled pinafore, long skirts and clumsy shoes; but on her head, over a triangle

of short, thick golden hair, is a blue knitted cap, which blot of vivid colour draws the eyes away from the poor raiment. Then one notes the beauty of the face, the broad, low brow, the exquisite lines of lip and chin, the nose, which like Goethe's Mignon, is extremely lovely, and above all the ethereal blue eyes, set rather far apart under wide, dark eyebrows . . .

In *Wilhelm Meister*, Mignon marks the hero's particular failure of sensibility, and when she dies, he understands, too late, the aetiology of that failure. Mignon herself, and McMillan's reworking of her, are both examples of the way in which, from the late eighteenth century onwards, children themselves became the central repository for the sense of loss and yearning that the words 'too late' embody. Robert Pattison, in *The Child Figure in English Literature*, has noted that in post-Wordsworthian sensibility, childhood is understood as 'a condition which for the vast majority of men is irretrievably lost as soon as completed'. He further describes it as 'a lost realm, somewhere in the past of our lives and the past of our culture'.[73] This idea can be approached, as I have suggested earlier in this chapter, in a different though complementary way, by pointing to the massive development in understanding of human growth witnessed by the century we are discussing. The building up of scientific evidence about physical growth in childhood described an actual progress in individual lives, which increased in symbolic importance during the nineteenth century, whereby that which is traversed is, in the end, left behind and abandoned, as the child grows up and goes away. In this way, childhood as it has been culturally described is always about that which is temporary and impermanent, always describes a loss in adult life, a state that is recognized too late. Children are quite precisely a physiological chronology, a *history*, as they make their way through the stages of growth. The solution of the writer trying to use the social fact of childhood in a symbolic way, and as representative of an adult state of mind, is usually to kill the child-figure. In *Wilhelm Meister* for example, Mignon dies at the realistic level because she has suffered too much, but at the symbolic level she expires because Meister has achieved adulthood, maturity and an inner integrity, and Mignon is no longer useful as representative of his former disharmony.[74]

We must suppose that by so deliberately operating this set of references, by making Marigold a version of Mignon, McMillan was both making a political statement, telling her readers at a practical level, that help needed to be given to inner-city children at the optimum time for human development, and also, at the same time, manipulating much that was unspoken. Marigold was not doomed, as Mignon is, and she does not die; but whilst McMillan's child expresses hope, she also means: *it is too late*, a fact of which her author was quite aware. McMillan wrote tenderly of her, asleep in the garden; and then asked

> Will she go back to the dark ugly house? Yes. As the nights grow long and chill, she must go back. She will sleep again in a foetid room, and for this poor resting place the coster must pay such a heavy rent that there is little left over to spend in food and other things for Marigold.[75]

Marigold, it seems, could only achieve the beautiful land of Mignon's song for a very short time; she was a moment of possibility, before she had to leave the garden.

POSSIBILITIES

When Goethe was writing his first version of *Wilhelm Meister* and of the character Mignon in the 1780s, he was also engaged in collecting botanical and geological specimens for his studies in morphology, 'exploring the natural world on every side in the attempt to understand its laws',[76] and it was his visits to Padua in September 1786 and to Palermo in April 1787 (particularly to the botanical gardens in Palermo) that promoted his understanding of botanical growth not as replication, not as one form repeating and taking the place of a similar one, but of growth as an unfolding, from a central and essential form: 'the point that we call leaf, that is the real Proteus, that could hide or reveal itself in all plant formations. Forwards or backwards, the plant is always only leaf.'[77]

So too Ruskin, some ninety years later, working on *Fors Clavigera*, and taking tea with a lady acquaintance who had just attended a lecture on botany, heard from her that she had learned at the lecture that there was '"no such thing as a flower"'. He went back to Goethe by way of explaining to the lady what her lecturer could have meant, and in order to insist upon the symbolic flower (if not the botanical one), writing that

> the poet Goethe discovered that all the parts of plants had a kind of common nature, and would change into each other.

38

Now this was a true discovery and a notable one; and you will find that, in fact all plants are composed of essentially two parts – the leaf and root – one loving the light, the other darkness . . . But the pure one which loves the light has, above all things, the purpose of being married to another leaf, and having child-leaves, and children's children of leaves, to make the earth fair forever. And when the leaves marry, they put on wedding robes . . . and they have feasts of honey, and we call them 'Flowers'.[78]

Ruskin's understanding of growth, which he traced back so precisely to Goethe's morphology, was as a kind of prewritten form, and the popularization of nineteenth-century physiological investigation made this understanding a diffuse social metaphor. A result of this was that the form itself, when considered in imaginary terms, became curiously timeless, both the essence of a living entity as it unfolded itself (there in the past), and that for which it strove (there in the future). 'We may well ask ourselves', wrote Alfred Mumford in some puzzlement at the beginning of his most serious and unmetaphorical account of physiological development in schoolboys of 1927, 'whether there is not some perfect form or build with which all boys may be compared, and which – given appropriate feeding, training and methods of upbringing – all should imitate or approach'.[79]

This was an understanding that could most economically and easily be represented by the idea of a child (even if, as in Ruskin's conversation with the lady, the child is a leaf rather than a human child). In their turn, these questions of form, of growth and development, and the cessation of growth and development, allowed Ruskin to see the sadness of the doomed and thwarted children, playing in the streets of St Giles, just as McMillan turned to Goethe's Mignon (who as a child-figure had her very real roots in late eighteenth-century physiological thinking) to present her own account of working-class childhood at the beginning of the twentieth century.

J. M. Tanner, at the end of his extraordinary study of the ways in which, throughout history, people have attempted to understand the phenomenon of growth, suggests that such investigations may have been in part responsible

for the change in how the adult world regarded children, that took place between the end of the seventeenth and the end of the nineteenth century. While children were regarded as small adults it was natural for them to be worked not reared ... But when children's growth began to be studied, that forced a different view on the organism, the view of a developing organism.[80]

Tanner may use a teleological and now largely discredited history of childhood, in which modern times are seen as the only true begetters of childhood. But that is not the point of this insight, which suggests an oscillation between physiological knowledge and social perception: 'the process', he claims, 'was circular, growth studies being both caused by, and stimulating, the new view'. Growth studies remind us too, perhaps, that the new child thus delineated was also quite precisely an expression of the adult's problem, written in the name of the child across many discourses and from many political perspectives. It was the problem that late nineteenth-century physiology showed so sharply: that growth stops; that the child grows up and goes away. And not just away. The end of a period of growth that defined the end of childhood also marked the beginning of the decline of the physiological body. We ought to consider how far a popularized physiology suggested that the name of the child was also death.

NOTES

1 B. B. Gilbert, *The Evolution of National Insurance in Britain*, London: Michael Joseph, 1966; J. Hurt, *Elementary Schooling and the Working Classes, 1860–1918*, London: Routledge & Kegan Paul, 1979; J. Lewis, *The Politics of Motherhood*, London: Croom Helm, 1980.

2 Deborah Dwork, *War Is Good for Babies and Other Young Children: a history of the infant and child welfare movement in England, 1898–1918*, London: Tavistock, 1987.

3 This shift has been generally neglected by historians, but Eric Hobsbawm reflects on it in *The Age of Empire, 1895–1914*, London: Weidenfeld & Nicolson, 1987: 149–50.

4 David Howell, *British Workers and the Independent Labour Party, 1888–1906*, Manchester: Manchester University Press, 1983: 343–85.

5 C. Steedman, *Childhood, Culture and Class in Britain: Margaret McMillan, 1860–1931*, London: Virago, 1990.

6 Steedman, *Childhood, Culture and Class*; E. Bradburn, *Margaret McMillan, Portrait of a Pioneer*, London: Routledge, 1989.

7 The bibliography to *Childhood, Culture and Class* contains references to 400 pieces of journalism (certainly an underestimate), as well as to her major books: *Early Childhood* (1900), *Education Through the Imagination* (1904, 1923), *Labour and Childhood* (1907), *The Child*

and the State (1911), *The Camp School* (1917), *The Nursery School* (1918, 1930), *Life of Rachel McMillan* (1927).

8 V. A. Zelizer, *Pricing the Priceless Child: the changing social value of children*, New York: Basic Books, 1985: 3–21, 208–28.

9 London School of Economics, Francis Johnson Collection, 1899/16, John Keir Hardie to David Lane, 6 April 1899. 'John Smith' was Robert Blatchford's creation, the audience for his *Merry England* (1894). M. McMillan, *Early Childhood*, London: Swann Sonnenchein, 1900.

10 J. W. Slaughter, 'Labour and childhood: the books of Margaret McMillan', *Highway*, December 1908, January 1909. McMillan, *Education Through the Imagination*; *Labour and Childhood*.

11 McMillan, *Early Childhood*: 11.

12 McMillan, *Early Childhood*: 11–12.

13 McMillan, *Early Childhood*: 31–2.

14 She made unacknowledged reference to what is probably Paul Broca's (1824–80) work on p. 39 and pp. 157–8 of *Early Childhood*. She made explicit reference to his work on accumulation in M. McMillan, 'Forecast of civilisation', *Ethical World*, 21, 28 October 1899.

15 McMillan, *Early Childhood*: 156.

16 McMillan, *Early Childhood*: 55–6.

17 McMillan, *Early Childhood*: 169–70.

18 McMillan, *Early Childhood*: 49.

19 D. Armstrong, *The Political Anatomy of the Body*, Cambridge: Cambridge University Press, 1983: 8–10.

20 Ibid.: 114.

21 McMillan, *Early Childhood*: 35.

22 For Seguin, see M. E. Talbot, *Édouard Seguin*, New York: Teacher's College Press, 1964, and the important account in H. Lane, *The Wild Boy of Aveyron*, St Albans: Paladin, 1979: 261–78. There is some account of the Itard/Seguin/Montessori route in S. Phillips, 'Maria Montessori and contemporary cognitive psychology', *British Journal of Teacher Education*, 1977, 3: 55–68.

23 For Itard's and Seguin's work with the deaf, see Lane, *Wild Boy*: 185–254; and É. Seguin, *Traitement moral, hygiène et éducation des idiots*, Paris: Ballière, 1846. For Jacob Pereire, see also H. Lane, *When the Mind Hears: a history of the deaf*, Harmondsworth: Penguin, 1988: 67–71.

24 For Saint-Simonianism, see G. Ionescu, *The Political Thought of Saint-Simon*, Oxford: Oxford University Press, 1976: 1–13, 29–57, 204–18; G. G. Iggers, *The Doctrine of Saint-Simon*, New York: Schocken, 1972: ix–xlvii; G. D. H. Cole, *Socialist Thought: the forerunners, 1789–1850*, London: Macmillan, 1953: 37–61; K. Taylor, *The Political Ideas of the Utopian Socialists*, London: Frank Cass, 1982: 132–59; É. Seguin, *Idiocy and Its Treatment by the Physiological Method* (originally published 1866), New York: Augustus M. Kelly, 1971: 29; and McMillan, 'Backward children: a new method of teaching', *Christian Commonwealth*, 29 January 1913.

25 Seguin, *Idiocy*: 28.

26 É. Seguin, *Report on Education* (originally published, 1875, New York: Augustus M. Kelly, 1976).

27 É. Seguin, *Rapport et mémoire sur l'éducation des enfants normaux et anormaux*, Paris: Bibliothèque d'Education Spéciale II, 1895.

28 In 1923 McMillan wrote that 'Seguin's work, carried on for many years after his death was the text book and Bible which began to be taken as a guide in the 90s and which I strove to popularise at the time; but it was to receive a more dramatic recognition through the writings of Montessori in later years'. Ten years before this, she had defensively told the readers of the *Highway* that 'the new education is not new ... it was developed in Bradford fifteen years ago'. She described here the experiments at Belle Vue infants school made by the Infants' Mistress Florence Kirk, and observed tartly that 'I do feel that charming as the little Romans may be, they are not more charming, trustful or artistic than the Bradford babies of Belle Vue'. Margaret McMillan, 'The "new" education', *Highway*, June 1913. See Phillips, 'Maria Montessori', and Lane, *Wild Boy*: 281–6 for the use by Montessori of Seguin's ideas. See also Margaret McMillan, 'The Montessori system', *Christian Commonwealth*, 26 June 1912; and 'Backward children'.

29 Seguin, *Idiocy*: 104–18.

30 Seguin, *Idiocy*: 137ff.

31 Talbot, *Seguin*: 44.

32 McMillan, 'Backward children'.

33 Seguin, *Idiocy*: 116–18.

34 McMillan, *Early Childhood*: 34–46. See also McMillan, *Labour and Childhood* for her promotion of Kropotkin's work.

35 Seguin, *Report*: 10, 14, 26.

36 Seguin, *Idiocy*: 110–11. For a similar description, see Sir Charles Bell, *The Hand: its mechanism and vital endowments*, London: John Murray, 1854.

37 McMillan, 'Forecast of civilisation'. See also M. McMillan, 'One of the trespassers', *Clarion*, 5 November 1895; 'Economic aspects of child labour and education', *Transactions of the National Liberal Club, Political and Economic Circle*, 18 December 1905, 5, no. 9.

38 McMillan, *Early Childhood*: 34.

39 M. McMillan, 'The claims of the "practical" in education', *Highway*, January 1910.

40 McMillan, 'Backward children'.

41 McMillan, 'Claims of the "practical"'.

42 G. E. Allen, *Life Sciences in the Twentieth Century*, Cambridge: Cambridge University Press, 1978: xi–xxiii, 18–19.

43 Ibid.: xxi–xxii.

44 Much other educational writing brought Seguin to the attention of the new century. See particularly, E. Holmes, *What Is and What Might Be*, London: Constable, 1911, and H. Holman, *Seguin and His Method of Physiological Education*, London: Pitman, 1914.

45 G. L. Geison, *Michael Foster and the Cambridge School of Psysiology*, Princeton: Princeton University Press, 1978: 21.

46 Peter Coveney, *The Image of Childhood*, Harmondsworth: Penguin, 1968.

47 H. Cunningham, 'Slaves or savages? Some attitudes to labouring children, 1750–1870', unpublished paper, 1987; D. Gorham, 'The "Maiden Tribute of Modern Babylon" re-examined: child prostitution and the idea of childhood in late Victorian England', *Victorian Studies*, 1978, 21: 353–79.

48 For a brief account of the figuring of children in mid-nineteenth-century sociological inquiry, see C. Steedman, *The Tidy House*, London: Virago, 1982: 110–31.

49 For the Froebelian movement, see E. Lawrence, *Freidrich Froebel and English Education*, London: Routledge & Kegan Paul, 1952; and for childhood and gardens, Steedman, *Childhood, Culture and Class*, ch. 4.

50 McMillan Collection, Rachel McMillan College Library, A2/13, lecture notes, n.d.

51 'Our ailing schoolchildren: and then?', *Wheatsheaf*, January 1912.

52 Margaret McMillan, 'The camp school', *Transactions of the National Liberal Club, Political and Economic Circle*, London, 1914, part 89a.

53 The clearest expression of this process is to be found in Margaret McMillan, 'How I became a socialist', *Labour Leader*, 11 July 1912; the need for working-class people to recognize their own exploitation, to see themselves as 'the Wronged', was an argument of her earliest journalism; see Margaret McMillan, 'Help', *Christian Socialist*, April 1891.

54 Margaret McMillan, 'The half time system', *Clarion*, 12 September 1896.

55 J. Ruskin, 'Fairyland', from 'The art of England' (1884), *The Library Edition of the Works of John Ruskin*, 33, London: Allen & Unwin, 1908: 338–42, 327–49. See also 'Design in the German school', from 'Ariadne Florentia' (1874), *The Library Edition of the Works of John Ruskin*, 22, London: Allen & Unwin, 1906: 390–421.

56 John Ruskin, 'Humility', from 'Time and tide' (1867), *The Library Edition of the Works of John Ruskin*, 17, London: Allen & Unwin, 1906: 405–9.

57 Ruskin, 'Humility': 406.

58 K. Bruce Glasier, *Margaret McMillan and Her Life Work*, Manchester: Northern Workers' Publishing Co., n.d.

59 Ruskin, 'Fairyland': 341.

60 Margaret McMillan, *Infant Mortality*, London: Independent Labour Party, 1906.

61 Particularly by Coveney, *Image of Childhood*.

62 R. Pattison, *The Child Figure in English Literature*, Athens: University of Georgia Press, 1978: 47–75.

63 M. McMillan, 'Education in the Primary School', *Labour Leader*, 27 April 1899.

64 Rachel McMillan College Library, McMillan Collection, Letters, A1/1, Margaret McMillan to Sally Blatchford, 22 February 1895.

65 H. Drummond, *Lowell Lectures on the Ascent of Man*, London: Hodder & Stoughton, 1894: 282.

66 Ibid.: 288.
67 Ibid.: 346–7.
68 Ibid.: 338.
69 Margaret McMillan, 'In a garden', *Highway*, June 1911; 'In our garden', *Highway*, July 1911; 'In our garden: Marigold, an English Mignon', *Highway*, September 1911; 'In our garden, I–V', *Highway*, April–September 1912. See a reprint of 'Marigold, an English Mignon', *Christian Commonwealth*, 3 January 1912.
70 J. W. von Goethe, *Wilhelm Meister's Years of Apprenticeship* (trans. H. M. Wardson), 6 vols, London: Cape, 1977. For the song, 1, Book III: 167–8. For the musical arrangement, 'Mignons Gesang', *Schubert-Lieder*, vol. III, Frankfurt, C. F. Peters, n.d.: 221–4.
71 W. Gilby, 'The structural significance of Mignon in *Wilhelm Meisters Lehrjahre*', *Seminar*, 26 (1980): 136–50.
72 See *The Times*, 22, 28 February and 22 April 1910, and the *Times Literary Supplement*, 14 April 1910. For transcriptions of this earlier manuscript, see *Wilhelm Meisters Theatralische Sendung*, Zurich: Rascher, 1910, and *Wilhelm Meister's Theatrical Mission* (trans. Gregory A. Page), London: Heinemann, 1913.
73 Pattison, *Child Figure*: 58.
74 Gilby, 'Mignon': 149.
75 There was another writing of this moment by McMillan, in her *Camp School*, London: Allen & Unwin, 1917: 82–3: ' "Was she saved by the Camp?" some gentle voice may ask. No, she was not. Some were saved … [but] Marigold was not among them. She tasted the joy of one new summer. Then her father, the hawker, was killed. Her mother "moved". We saw her long after. Her lovely face had coarsened so as be almost unrecognisable … Why dwell on one tragedy among so many thousands?' See also McMillan, *The Nursery School*, London: Dent, 1919: 182.
76 W. H. Bruford, *Culture and Society in Classical Weimar, 1775–1806*, Cambridge: Cambridge University Press, 1962: 236–62 for Goethe's botanical journey to Italy.
77 Quoted in ibid.: 244.
78 J. Ruskin, 'Fors Clavigera' (1871), *Library Edition of the Works of John Ruskin*, 27, London: Allen & Unwin, 1907: 83–4. Ruskin got Goethe's history of metamorphosis severely wrong in this account.
79 A. A. Mumford, *Healthy Growth*, London: Humphrey Milford for the Oxford University Press, 1927: 4.
80 J. M. Tanner, *A History of the Study of Human Growth*, Cambridge: Cambridge University Press, 1981: 402.

2

CHILD LABOUR, MEDICAL CAPITAL, AND THE SCHOOL MEDICAL SERVICE, c.1890–1918

Harry Hendrick

We are familiar with the view that during the period *circa* 1880–1920, social, political and economic upheavals compelled governments and ruling classes to reconsider their positions. We know also that consequently, despite differences of opinion, they revised their analyses and amended their strategies as they searched for a more comprehensive order, sufficiently inclusive to incorporate new and competing interests. In the festival of reform that characterized those decades, the education, health and welfare of children, especially those from urban areas, were major concerns for a number of reformers, politicians, organizations and professions.

As Carolyn Steedman has indicated in her contribution to this volume, the tranformation of working-class children from labourers to pupils was central to the reconstruction of childhood at the end of the nineteenth century.[1] However, besides children from poor families who evaded the school attendance officer to continue to be full-time wage earners or mothers' helps, and in addition to those who worked as 'half-timers', principally in the northern textile mills, many thousands of others were employed before and after school hours. All these part-timers occupied an ambiguous territory: on the one hand, in their own right they never constituted a major social problem relative to other well known contemporary anxieties; and yet, in so far as they continued to represent the child as worker, rather than as scholar, they were obviously relevant to the conceptual difficulties involved in the reconstruction process.

This chapter is less concerned with the inherently conceptual

45

problems surrounding part-time child labour, than with medical perceptions of, and interests in, the topic, and with how medical interventions helped to shape the debate. In particular the focus is on 'child labour' as it assisted medical officers of health (MOHs) and school medical officers (SMOs) in their search for responsibility and authority within the newly established School Medical Service (1907).[2] This is not to suggest a simple correlation between reformers' unease about working children and the status of school doctors, who were often young and low paid, and combining the jobs of SMO and MOH. The intention is to show why and how, 'in the name of the child', a professional group, within the context of a national reform programme (and this fact should not be overlooked), sought to use the issue to assist in substantiating its claim to control the health and welfare of the classroom.

To understand the medical commentary, and the role of the Service, we need to see the debate itself as a factor in two larger and related concerns, whose immediate origins lay in 'the rediscovery of the Condition of England Question' in the 1880s. One, involving a variety of reform interests, emphasized the general welfare of children, and considered virtually every aspect of their lives including education, nutrition, recreation, protection from parental neglect and cruelty, and 'manners and morals'. The other concern was much more the province of doctors, psychiatrists and medical-psychologists, who concentrated on child health in terms of individual physical and mental development, though they were by no means ignorant of, nor uninterested in, broader environmental influences.[3]

Thus when the specific debate on part-time child labour opened in the late 1890s, it was an item added to an already-crowded agenda which had been under discussion for a decade or more. A prominent and innovative feature of this addition, however, was the part played by what can be described as developing medical perceptions. It is true that doctors had expressed medical opinions for and against the employment of children during the nineteenth century; but the circumstances were different around 1900. By this time not only had compulsory schooling successfully altered public attitudes towards child labour, but also the increasing number of MOHs and SMOs, who through their annual reports provided diffuse information on specific groups of school-age workers, were beginning to lay claim to an expertise and, therefore, a jurisdiction in this area of child health.

I

Medical intervention in the general welfare of schoolchildren (other than their employment) emerged during the 1880s in the course of 'a sustained public discussion of the[ir] health and capacities . . . of quite a new kind'.[4] Doctors were interested in anthropometric studies, mental and physical defectiveness, and in the social and physical condition of children as revealed by the 'rediscovery of poverty'.[5] According to the historian of the 'people's health', 'The sheer amount of bodily infirmity in the common schools alarmed medical contemporaries, and drove them to make even larger, ever more gloomy – and self-fulfilling – investigations'.[6] One development above all turned children into attractive research subjects, namely, the opportunities offered to inquirers by compulsory mass attendance. The medical profession, in common with sociologists and philanthropic workers, soon recognized that the school could be used as a laboratory in which it hoped to produce 'scientific' (always an important adjective) surveys of the pupils.[7]

The inauguration of the 'public discussion' began in 1884 with the publication of a report by the prestigious Dr, later Sir James, Crichton-Browne, on 'over-pressure' (mental strain) in elementary schools.[8] Four years later, after hearing Dr Francis Warner, Physician to the London Hospital, address its psychology section on 'Examining Children in Schools as to their Development and Brain Condition', the British Medical Association (BMA) established an investigative committee which was led by Warner and supported by the Charity Organization Society and the British Association for the Advancement of Science. Over the next few years other committees were formed to pursue similar inquiries in the classroom, some of which were also directed by Warner. In 1896, one of these committees, on the Mental and Physical Condition of Children, whose council of forty included nineteen with medical qualifications, reconstituted itself, choosing as its first title the Society for the Promotion of Hygiene in School Life. This was soon changed to the Childhood Society, with a new thirteen-member council, including five medical figures, among whom were Drs John Langdon Down, G. E. Shuttleworth, and Warner, and a general membership which was mainly specialist, with doctors having the largest representation.[9]

The Society was not alone in advocating the scientific inspection of children. By the 1890s, the interest of medical practitioners in the classroom was to a certain extent contested by that of psychologists, who were looking to education to assist them in their quest for a recognized professional role. In 1894, inspired by the American child psychologist, G. S. Hall, a couple of teachers at the Ladies' College, Cheltenham, with the support of Langdon Down, formed a London Child Study group. Several provincial branches were soon established, and in 1898 these were federated into the British Child Study Association, with the noted psychiatrist, Sir Thomas Clouston as its president. Vice-presidents included Shuttleworth and Professor James Sully, founder of the first laboratory for experimental psychology. The Association's journal, the *Paidologist* stated its objectives and identified its audience: it would help parents 'with observations of the periods and aspects of child life'; it would interest teachers by offering them 'guiding principles'; and it would prove of interest to those involved in 'education, psychology, biology and medicine'.

The Child Study Association differed from the Childhood Society in having a more mixed membership, and an emphasis on 'the natural development of individual children', rather than the condition of the child population as a whole. In 1907, however, the Society amalgamated with the London branch of the Association to form the Child Study Society (London). It seems that the Association dominated the proceedings, and was supported by most of the leading contemporary psychologists and educationalists. Doctors appear to have been fewer in number, perhaps reflecting the 'complex and ambivalent relationship of psychology with medicine'.[10] The significance of the Child Study movement is that through its literature and lecture programmes, and the practice of its influential members, it served as an important arena for exchanges between psycho-medical professionals, teachers and parents.

However uneasy the relationship between psychology and medicine, as Nikolas Rose has argued, the influence of the doctors went unabated, for example, as witnessed at the international conferences on School Hygiene in 1904 and 1908, and – far more ubiquitous – in the policy of what Rose calls 'neo-hygienism'. The latter, in opposition to eugenics, meant solving problems related to 'physical deterioration' with programmes of environmental reform, parental education, and the medical examination of pupils. And there is no doubt that the Service was intended to be an agent in the hygienist strategy, at least within the debate over national physique.[11]

Social historians of the period regularly and justifiably refer to

the campaigns for 'national efficiency' and eugenic reform, as well
as to the impact of the Boer War and the subsequent report on
physical deterioration. With respect to children, the report was
especially important for two reasons. First, it implicitly rejected
the strict eugenist thesis concerning degenerate stock, in favour of
a more optimistic – neo-hygienist – analysis; secondly, it echoed
the calls of numerous investigators in making a number of specific
recommendations for improvements in the care and protection of
young people, notably provision of school meals and school medical
inspection. The report stipulated that the 'Juvenile Population' had
to be given urgent consideration if the problems associated with
the 'condition of England question' were to be solved. In other
words, it recognized the social and racial relevance of children and
adolescents. No matter that some of these topics had been discussed
since the 1880s, 'the quest for national efficiency', of which the
report was a part, 'gave social reform what it had not had before
– the status of a respectable political question'.[12]

II

Despite all this interest and activity, 'child labour' was relatively slow
to emerge as a distinct social question. Except among a minority of
socialist and Labour reformers, the matter was seen as a nineteenth-
century problem, which had been more or less resolved through
factory legislation and compulsory education. In several respects,
the worries expressed by many observers may well have been seen as
those of unfinished business. All the same, they were uncomfortable
reminders of the failure of sections of the working class to conform
to approved notions of family respectability: child labour detracted
from home-centredness; confused dependent relationships between
adult and child; threatened morality; interfered with schooling; and
in certain forms and conditions, was unhealthy. Total abolition,
however, was rarely seriously considered. By and large, observers
viewed *some* degree of labour, either paid or unpaid, as desirable.
It was said to be 'positively beneficial' in terms of moral and social
teaching; and, given that the alternative often meant spending time
in 'public thoroughfares or in the penny music-hall', was 'a useful
part of a boy's education', if only because it taught 'habits of
industry'.[13] Consequently, reform was usually limited to calls for
greater controls, raising the minimum age, and limiting hours of
employment.

Apart from socialist and trade union agitation, the first specific and in any way formal public pronouncement on wage-earning schoolchildren came from a government committee on *Conditions of School Attendance and Child Labour* (1893–4), which was primarily concerned with the half-time system. The committee reported that thousands of parents, after obtaining half-time status for their children, were then sending them to work other than in the textile mills for which the exemption had been allowed. It went on to question whether children street-selling, or working as shop assistants, milk boys, errand boys, office boys, and domestics could be termed either 'necessary' or 'beneficial'.[14] But the most consequential development was the decision of the Women's Industrial Council to conduct a London-based inquiry, under the direction of Mrs F. G. Hogg, which turned attention away from the half-timer (there were hardly any in London), towards employment before and after normal school hours.[15] Indeed, Frederic Keeling, the well-known Fabian labour exchange manager and 'expert' on juvenile labour, claimed that 'little attention' was given to the problem of school wage-earners until Hogg's inquiry.[16]

In 1897 Mrs Hogg summarized her findings in an influential article, and at a second attempt persuaded the Education Department to receive a deputation on the subject.[17] According to Sir John Gorst, the sympathetic Tory MP and social reformer, there was a lack of sympathy at government level for further investigation, but a Parliamentary Return demanded by an opposition MP, estimated that approximately 144,000 pupils worked for wages in England and Wales. The usefulness of the Return (1899) was limited by its narrow focus on children in regular out-of-school employment, so that seasonal and casual workers were excluded. Furthermore, it ignored those in employment not deemed 'prejudicial' to health; those whose wages were paid direct to parents, and those who worked illegally during school hours. In the same year, however, the London School Board published a report on child labour, emphasizing the danger of 'physical incapacity', and this helped to consolidate opinion in favour of a more searching inquiry.[18]

Within a few months of the Parliamentary Return the government appointed a joint committee of the Home Office and the Board of Education to consider the whole matter and advise on legislation. In its Report (1902) the committee found that the largest numbers of working children were in shops, agriculture, and domestic service, with half-timers in factories and workshops, followed by street trading, home industries, and miscellaneous employment. The size of the child labour force was said to be in the region of 300,000 (Keeling's more detailed and reliable survey, published in 1914, suggested a total for the UK which was 'possibly considerably over 600,000'). Although the members agreed that the danger of particular employments to health and to education was hardly 'in question', their refusal to abrogate part-time child labour put a premium on identifying a reasonable number of hours, which appeared to be around twenty a week. But the important consideration was not so much the total hours worked, as the *length* of each shift – witnesses agreed that a 13-hour shift, for example, was 'excessive' and, therefore, damaging to the child's development.[19]

Several months later the Employment of Children Act, 1903, was passed. The Act allowed, but did not compel, local authorities to make bye-laws prescribing for children a limited number of daily and weekly working hours, and the age below which employment was illegal. It also permitted the prohibition of their employment in any specified occupation, and the curtailment of street trading. This was the first and only piece of comprehensive legislation during the Edwardian period to attempt regulation of child labour. Where the half-time system was concerned, there was no mention of bringing it to an end, and the government showed little inclination to confront the issue.

III

But what influence had medical opinion brought to bear on the legislative process up to this time? And to what extent had that opinion shaped the debate? Before 1900, the answer to both questions must be very little. It is true, as has been shown, that since the 1880s the condition of children was of interest to various groups of reformers, including a number of doctors.[20] But with regard to part-time child labour (as distinct from half-time) and its link to ill health, vocal and public medical consideration was minimal prior to the turn of the century.[21] There was a certain medical awareness in the *Report of the Inter-departmental Committee on the Employment of School Children*, (1902), which described working weeks of 30, 40 or 50 hours for children, as 'detrimental to their health, their morals, and their education'.[22] There was also the occasional notice in the *Lancet*. In September 1898 it had drawn attention to the 'demoralising tendency' of street trading, and the following year, in an editorial

51

on the London School Board's report (which drew on medical opinion), it sounded the danger of physical incompetence arising from the problem. A couple of months later the journal carried a piece arguing that the future of 'a large section of the community' depended upon making the lives of labouring children 'healthier and better'; and again in 1901 it warned that such children were prone to 'fatigue, restlessness and incapacity'. Reform, therefore, would be of benefit 'to the race in the next generation'.[23]

One of the clearest statements came from the authoritative figure of Crichton-Browne in his opening address on 'Physical Efficiency in Children', given in 1902 to an international congress on the welfare and protection of children. It was important, he said, to keep in view their 'well-being', and 'the physical development of our adult population' because they were 'mutually dependent on each other.' After calling for more 'precise scientific data', and claiming that 'physical decadence' was 'going on', he emphasized the deleterious effects of underfeeding, but drew particular attention to child labour, since 'its influence [on 'physical impairment'] is direct and obvious'. The danger was not that of the 'atrocities' of past employment, but of 'putting burdens heavier than they [children] can bear on young shoulders'.[24]

Following these examples, several witnesses appearing before the inquiry into physical deterioration (1904) commented on the prevalence and consequences of child labour. While Charles Booth thought half-time domestic work for girls was 'very desirable' (as did others who gave evidence), Dr Alfred Eichholz, Medical Inspector for Schools for Lambeth, stressed the need to keep girls away 'from the ugly circumstances of overstrain of their homes'. They were, he said, 'ruined' in health and constitution by the excess of work. But it was left to Sir Lauder Brunton, Physician to St Bartholomew's Hospital, and executive member of the National League for Physical Education and Improvement, to broaden the issue when he said that generally speaking, *all* extra-curricular wage-earning 'wearied' the child.[25]

So, despite the long-standing interest in the half-timer, not until around 1900 did doctors start to perceive part-time child labour, whatever its form, as a feature of the social problem, and in particular of the concern over 'the condition of the people' and the prospects for national health. And even then, they were little more than occasional voices, briefly raised. With the coming of the Edwardian Liberal reform programme after 1906, however, a much more sustained and public medical intervention was about to begin.

IV

In his *The Health of the State*, (1907), George Newman, soon to be the first Chief Medical Officer (CMO) at the Board of Education, noted that out-of-school employment 'plays havoc with the health and physique of children'.[26] This was by no means a casual remark since, in common with a growing number of reformers and doctors, he saw such employment in the context of comprehensive health considerations. Looking back a few years later, in his first annual report on the School Medical Service, Newman captured the mood of unease about child health when he identified it as 'the English Problem'. He wrote that, by 1900, it was clearly insufficient to deal only with children suffering from 'some obvious mental or physical defect'. It had come to be seen that 'a close and vital connection exists between the physical conditions of the normal child and the whole process of its education'. This suggests that not only did Newman intend to consolidate the medical authority implicit in the relationship between children's physical life and their life in the school, but also that he claimed the authority in respect of defining the 'normal' developmental process, rather than the clinically 'abnormal'.[27] Equally important for the future of the Service, as he saw it, was his conclusion that the larger question concerned 'national health' and the 'standard of national physique'. Here was a definite sign of his ambition to seek a broader (and possibly an easier and cheaper) role for the SMO.[28]

While Newman's first annual report of 1908 said nothing specific about child labour, the second included a footnote to the effect that several SMOs were reporting on wage-earning schoolchildren, and the matter would be dealt with 'more fully' in the future. The following year there was an 'addendum' on the 'Employment of School Children', in which the medical officer for Halifax, Dr D. M. Taylor (who seems to have had a high profile), made the familiar contention, especially with reference to half-timers, that among children who did not work the average height was 59.8″, weight was 81.5 lb. and chest expansion was 1′8″, whereas among those who were wage earners, it was 54″, 67 lb., and 1′2″, respectively. Other groups of child workers, even when 'no adverse influence' on their general health could be found, were said to be 'tired . . . dull . . .

[and] mentally stale'. Elsewhere, Taylor urged that weaker children in particular needed protection from overstrain, since in addition to tiredness they were already 'anaemic . . . and often with muscular tremor' all of which was made worse by the long hours, lack of proper sleep, monotony, and an unhygienic environment. All forms of child employment, he charged, were 'detrimental in one or more aspects – physical, mental, moral or social'. During 1910, in their initial appearance before a Parliamentary Committee, SMOs (two of them) gave evidence on the ill-effects of child labour, stressing the injuries caused by excessively long hours.[29] Clearly, doctors, who as SMOs now had a platform, in speaking out publicly on the issue, and providing specific and apparently scientific detail, were beginning to claim a competence in this and other areas of child welfare.

The report for 1911 contained a separate section on the employment of children and adolescents. Evidence was drawn from eleven medical officers, the *Report of the Home Office Departmental Committee on Accidents*, and three other government inquiries, all of which exposed part-time child labour as leading to 'overstrain' (through the carrying and lifting of heavy weights); spinal curvature (in newsboys and milk boys); loss of weight; anaemia; heart stress, and tiredness.[30] Tiredness was of special importance owing to the 'keen and growing anxiety' of psychologists and physiologists 'on the subject of the [*sic*] deficient sleep', which 'directly conduces to mental instability, physical inefficiency and emotional excitability'. Sleep was deemed to be essential for the needs of the nervous system, and for the regeneration of the organism as a whole. This medical 'fact' made it extremely difficult to contradict the widespread view that 'premature employment', and excessively long hours of labour were 'physiologically detrimental'.[31]

In general, warned Newman, these young workers were 'being spoilt physically, mentally and morally'; they suffered the 'evil effects' due to insufficient control. Here was the mixture of themes (medical, educational and moral) to which he would return annually, drawing on the views of local medical officers. For example, one SMO lamented, 'Unfortunately, there is on all sides ample evidence of the serious injury to health and education which may arise from wage-earning'. Others described the moral results as the 'contagion of the street' and the 'aping [of] manhood'; and claimed that the children's 'moral nature is liable to be warped'. In their minds, there was no doubt that such employment 'saps the vitality of the growing child . . . the great majority . . . are ill developed, badly nourished, and anaemic . . . they are so often mentally dull and backward'. It was foolish, cautioned Newman, to ignore the creation of such ill health, since medical care of children concerned 'the physical equipment and preparation of the child for its industrial life'. But no one, he said, could read the local reports without realizing the 'impracticability' of 'improving the health or the mental and moral equipment of a child subjected to toils and strains of the character implied in these long hours of unproductive labour'.[32]

Let us be clear as to the nature and the extent of medical mediation. On the basis of combined diagnostic and prognostic practices (which often confused evidence, analysis and assertion), doctors, notably SMOs, confidently expressed their opinion that the malevolent effects on children of 'excessive' labour were fatigue, strain (including of the heart) and physical deformities. And they were able to propagate their views through a School Medical Service which was doing so much to focus attention on wage-earning pupils.

As we have seen, from the 1880s to the early 1900s, child labour received only scattered references in the medical press. Similarly, doctors who appeared before government committees exhibited few signs of professional interest in the problem, despite the long-established debate on the consequences for health of the half-time system. In the closing years of the nineteenth century, there were medical figures (such as the MOHs cited by Margaret McMillan) who warned against various forms of employment as damaging to the physical and mental development of children, but in the circumstances of poverty, malnutrition, disease and bad housing, the majority of reformers looked on this as a matter of lesser consequence. Moreover, although Booth and Rowntree had pointed to the social significance of young people, it was only when social reform achieved its new status after the Boer War that the condition of children (and adolescents) came to be *popularly* regarded by *politicians* as in any way necessary for national health and welfare. Not until then did 'the rather casual public interest in the health of schoolchildren suddenly become a widespread fear over the apparent physical deterioration of the British working class'.[33]

V

This helps to explain why the intervention of SMOs was so explicit and sustained, for they were a new breed among the professionals most directly involved with the sweeping manifestations of poverty.

Or, to be precise, they determined to involve themselves. School medical inspection is usually said to have begun in 1893 with the appointment by the Bradford School Board of Dr James Kerr (the very first SMO was appointed in London in 1890), but it was 1907 before the Education (Administrative Provisions) Act formally established the Service. By this time, forty-eight local education authorities (LEAs) were providing some form of medical inspection, which in many areas was performed by the local MOH (compulsorily appointed under the Public Health Act, 1872), and this practice was allowed to continue under the terms of the new legislation.[34]

The social policy historian, Bentley Gilbert has claimed that these early years were dogged by political intrigue and professional rivalries. Neither the National Union of Teachers' oligarchy in London nor the BMA, he says, had much affection for the school doctors. The teachers and their supporters were antagonistic because they foresaw the new service coming under the control of the MOHs, thereby marginalizing the LEAs. The BMA, which was hostile to the MOHs, and to Newman, regarded the SMOs as upstarts and accorded them little or no status. Much of the BMA's opposition, it seems, arose out of an exaggerated fear that 'a Fabian-planned school medical service' would grow into a complete State health service over which neither they nor LEAs would have any control.[35]

Given that child welfare was a developing specialism, however, the school was obviously the arena where medical interests were most conspicuous, and the reports demanded by the Service provided Newman, and presumably his local staff, with the means publicly to record clinical examinations, assessments, opinions, and recommendations. In this respect, the child labour issue, along with others, gave these low-status doctors two related opportunities to participate in neo-hygienist practice and to enhance their prestige: first, to increase the scope and responsibilities of the Service (though this appears to have had little effect on salaries, and even less on career structures); second, by assuming further duties, to compete effectively with the teachers and the psychologists, for control of the health of the classroom.[36]

The increasing importance attached to child labour was signalled by Newman's elevation of the subject in his annual reports from a footnote to several pages. What began as a reference grew within three years to a fully fledged section: 'Relation of School Medical Service to juvenile employment', which was subdivided into Factory

Certificates, half-timers and other school wage-earners; examination of leavers; inspection of young workers above the age of fourteen; and supervision of children unfit for employment. The significance of this expansion needs to be appreciated. The remit of doctors was being enlarged to include the entire field of juvenile labour. The word 'juvenile' referred not just to children, but to a range of provisions in the newly emerging Juvenile Employment Service for adolescents aged 14–17, which included the medical examination of school leavers, and the system of 'after care'. Noting the statutory machinery (the 1903 Act, the Labour Exchanges Act, 1910, and the Education [Choice of Employment] Act, 1910), 'the question', commented Newman, 'arises how best to bring into relation with it the school medical service'.[37] This has all the signs of a piece of professional imperialism. There was little or no necessary reason why such a question should arise, since the teachers (not to mention the Board of Trade) had equal claim to monopolize the machinery themselves.[38] Of course it was hoped that the desired new relationship would enable the Service to extend its mandate beyond the classroom, to include the health and welfare of the wage-earning adolescent.

Newman pressed his intention by suggesting that 'new' arrangements were now required between the medical and the employment services. There were, he said, several groups involved in LEA activities: doctors, school nurses, teachers, and attendance officers (and very soon juvenile labour exchange officials). And, therefore, 'the chief burden must inevitably rest upon the school medical officer' who should be responsible for a comprehensive programme of inspection and management.[39] The following year, 1912, he called for all employed children to be registered by the LEA and examined periodically by the SMO.[40] In claiming this potentially enormous area for his doctors, Newman felt he had support from the Board of Education circular 813 which dealt with the medical records of school leavers and, in specifically citing his suggestions, recommended further action between medical personnel and the LEAs, while leaving the matter open for discussion.[41]

Some development occurred along these lines as the annual report of 1913, in what was now a thirteen-page section, described the extension of the SMOs' duties in relation to the whole area of child and juvenile employment. Newman observed that nationally the SMO 'is turning his attention in increasing degrees to this aspect of his work'. One can imagine Newman's sense of satisfaction when he declared that these changes represented 'the development of the School Medical Service'.[42] Furthermore, by the end of 1911, after a legal ruling, the long-standing political opposition to MOHs in London came to an end with the agreement of the London County Council (LCC) Education Committee to commit all 'school medical work' to the MOH for London County, thereby accepting the 'principle of unification of all children's medical services'.[43] Moreover, the LCC brought SMOs into closer co-operation with the LEA through the work of the Children's Care Committee system which included, among its varied duties, the supervision of the employment of school leavers. The committees were to proceed under the guidance of a memorandum, written by the MOH, which detailed 'the Disabilities from a Medical Point of View attaching to certain Employments'.[44]

The Education Act, 1918, elaborated circular 813 and consequently extended the work of the Service. The Act not only encouraged the examination of wage-earning children, with a special recommendation that those in certain occupations should obtain a medical certificate from the SMO (many LEAs introduced a new bye-law to accommodate this); it was also made a 'duty' of LEAs to provide medical examination of adolescents under 18 years of age on admission to certain institutions, including the proposed day continuation schools. By 1919 Newman could summarize the SMO's principal responsibilities for juvenile employment as follows: examination of all children under fourteen when they began work, and at regular intervals over the next three to four years; examinations of all 'leavers', together with treatment where necessary; and medical advice given to parents with regard to future employments of their children. The SMO was also expected to attend relevant educational conferences and meetings, and to act in close co-operation with teachers and local juvenile employment committees.[45]

To some extent all this may be said to explain why these doctors promoted themselves in the child labour debate. Professional status was undoubtedly of crucial importance. It has just been shown that Newman, as CMO, openly articulated his ambitions for the Service. In terms of the growth and expansion of the medical profession, by 1918 child welfare was a source of legitimation, income and advancement.[46] One has only to think of the developing inspection and treatment services, providing work for doctors, dentists, opticians and nurses, and the increasing number of infant welfare clinics and health visitors (without suggesting that there was a unity of interest between these different professions). Besides providing posts, the welfare of the schoolchild offered doctors the chance to become specialists of a kind, even though their career possibilities, and their salaries, remained a subject of dispute well into the 1930s. Indeed, in 1928 a Ministry of Health official confessed that being a SMO was regarded as a 'blind alley'.[47]

All the same, this group of doctors was in a position to become knowledgeable and 'expert', and so further to consolidate their position. We should distinguish between the admittedly low status of the Service and its staff within the medical profession and among civil servants, and its political importance in the social politics of the period. Prestige in the former was not necessarily a prerequisite for significance in the latter. There is no doubt that the relationship between the BMA, the Service, and the development of social welfare programmes was extremely complex. Notwithstanding this complexity, broadly speaking, school doctors correctly saw that through 'neo-hygienism', the school was about to become a central area in public health policy and, with the help of 'child labour', they grasped the opportunity to claim an indispensable role in the establishment and inspection of socio-health standards (environmental and moral as well as medical), in the treatment of those who failed to meet those standards, in the psycho-medical aspects of defective and epileptic childcare, and in the measurement of intelligence.[48]

History, however, can rarely be written in terms of naked professionalism. School doctors, like other professionals, were unable to divorce themselves from either contemporary anxieties, or political loyalties. This is not to deny the convenience of these anxieties in relation to responsibilities, job satisfaction, and career structure. And while the social and political dramas familiar to Edwardian Britain were often consciously exploited for group interests, they were too pervasive to be confined in this way. One of the principal reasons for the political interest in child health in general, and medical inspection in particular, was 'the progress of the race'. This is what R. L. Morant, the influential Permanent Secretary at the Board of Education, hinted to Margaret McMillan, and made clear at the annual dinner of the Society of Medical Officers of Health in 1909: 'we have now to think of the English people in competition with other races, and if we neglected the health of the race . . . we should lose in the racial competition of this world'.[49] Newman had also written in the same spirit: 'The Child is father of the man, and the children of today are the nation of tomorrow. If we would rear a race of strong men we must first breed healthy children.'[50]

Of course, this could be seen as an example of a determined civil servant using racial rhetoric to dupe his opponents. If it were true, then at the very least it would show the power of this theme in contemporary British politics. But it cannot be held to be true of all school doctors, many of whom, it is reasonable to suppose, accepted the validity of the racial question for reasons to do with imperialism, national efficiency, and social engineering, as much as out of a concern for personal advancement. We should not need to remind ourselves that, in practice, ideology and professionalism are rarely found unmediated.

VI

How, then, are we to assess the impact of medical involvement? For our period, it is extremely difficult to prove the extent of its influence, except at the level of circumstantial evidence. After the passing of the Employment of Children Act, 1903, there was no new relevant legislation until 1918. In fact the situation worsened with the outbreak of the First World War when child labour was widely used. Nor did all local authorities exercise their powers under the 1903 Act. Out of a total of 329 authorities, 98 were still without any regulatory bye-laws for general employment by 1914, and nearly two hundred had no restrictions on street trading. Moreover, the passing of a bye-law did not lead automatically to its enforcement, except in cities such as London, Bolton, Bradford, Bristol, Leeds, and Liverpool. Nevertheless, Frederic Keeling estimated that, between 1903 and 1914, the decline in the number of wage-earning children was somewhere in the region of 10 to 15 per cent.[51] But the law could do little for the majority of employed school children, especially those who laboured at housework for their parents (usually girls, known as the 'drudges') and the thousands of shopworkers, delivery and messenger boys. In 1913–14, R. D. Denman, the Liberal MP and chairman of the London juvenile advisory committee, introduced a bill to abolish exemptions for children under thirteen, to raise minimum ages for employment and effectively to tighten up the law, but it was talked out.[52] It would seem that, in this context, the influence of school doctors on national and local government was marginal.

Perhaps their prestige is better displayed in helping to shape the

debate: in assisting child welfare reformers to construct a framework
for their campaigns, as well as changing the nature of them. Once
MOHs and SMOs began to examine child labour they started to
accumulate a body of references on which reformers could draw
and exploit in relating 'labour' to 'health', and this no doubt
attracted a wider audience than might otherwise have been the
case. Besides Margaret McMillan, Sir John Gorst was prominent
among the reforming politicians who stressed that 'overwork'
among schoolchildren tended to 'the serious deterioration of public
health'.[53] Alexander Paterson, teacher, youth worker and later influential penal reformer, wrote of child work being 'injurious to body
and mind', and of 'white faces and weak hearts'.[54] In his extensive
survey of half-timers, Arthur Greenwood, lecturer, writer on child
and juvenile labour, and eventually a Labour cabinet minister, cited
the Oldham school medical officer's report to argue that not only
was there a relative decline in the physique of children in half-time
towns, but also they showed defects of eye, nose and throat, were
'not so bright or responsive in appearance', and were 'less clean
and tidy'.[55] Similarly, Grace Paton, a Student Christian Movement
author, used references from Newman's reports to substantiate her
claim that next in importance to malnutrition 'in its effect upon the
health of the child is the excessive work done in many cases out of
school hours'.[56]

And what effect did the amassing of this form of medical capital
have on the School Medical Service itself? Over the years in question
the doctors turned themselves into 'experts' on various aspects of
child life, and while the extent of medical interest in child labour
should not be exaggerated (since it was only one among many
child-medical foci), by 1918 it had almost certainly helped them to
establish their authority across much of the spectrum of the health
and welfare of young people. The SMOs were gradually creating a
separate corpus of knowledge on labour and related subjects which
implicitly took account of the social and physical constitution of
'childhood', as it was developing conceptually during the period.
A brief look at the contents of the annual reports will instruct us
in the evolution of the Service.

The first report was confined to dealing with the physical condition of children, sanitation of the premises, and special schools for
defective children. In 1909, however, not only did the chapter on
'Special schools' have a subsection headed 'Duties of SMO', which
was obviously meant to reflect their ambitions, but also there was

a new chapter entitled 'Following up', in which the roles of parents, teachers, attendance officers, nurses and care committee workers were described. The next year, further specification occurred in another new subsection where the roles 'played by the doctor and parent' in 'Following up' were carefully delineated. In a measured understatement, Newman asserted that 'the first person responsible in this matter is the medical officer. He holds the key to the position'. By 1911, the work of the MO in 'Following up' was treated separately from that of 'the parent', leaving little doubt as to who was the senior partner. Furthermore, the increasing specificity of the labour question in the reports was accompanied by the identification of other new areas – hygiene, mothercraft, education and infant welfare, and co-ordination of provision of meals – which the Service successfully claimed as part of its portfolio. The life of the child and adolescent at school was now procedurally perceived in relation to the family, the home and, more comprehensively, to public health.[57] Clearly, Service personnel were involved in much more than merely orthodox medical commentary.

Under the leadership of Newman and Morant, the SMOs successfully began a very limited form of treatment, as well as the inspection of children; and they fought off bids by psychologists, and the teachers, to organize facilities for the feeble-minded.[58] According to Nikolas Rose, the victory of the doctors derived from their long-standing view of the school as a place which was 'as much medical as pedagogic'. And if 'victory' is too strong a term, he is surely correct to remind us that from 1910 there was 'a formidable apparatus, legally enforced, with School Medical Officers in every authority, with every schoolchild compulsorily inspected, the whole enterprise supported by public funds, exploiting the existing conceptual and technical resources of clinical medicine, and linked in to the statutory established system of public health'.[59] Moreover, the BMA lost some of its initial hostility to the Service, and in 1908 recommended the creation of school clinics where children could be treated as well as inspected.[60] With the passing of the Local Authorities (Medical Treatment) Act, 1909, clinics began to open in increasing numbers so that, by 1914, 241 of 317 LEAs were giving some form of medical treatment. From the perspective of social politics, if not from medical status, these were significant developments for the prerogative of medicine, and for the school doctors whose responsibilities and *social* influence continued to grow.

VII

Finally, it is worth remembering that the consequences of medical intervention went well beyond the immediate issues of child labour and welfare, and into other processes necessary for a new construction of childhood. As the sociologist David Armstrong has suggested, towards the end of the nineteenth century the child becomes 'object and problem'; its 'body' was 'fabricated' by medical discourse and moral and educational concerns. The significance of medicine being that, in conjunction with education, it 'manipulated' and 'transformed' childhood. In this circumstance, says Armstrong, the School Medical Service was a link between educational and medical surveillance.[61] Leaving aside for the moment whether or not 'surveillance' is the most apt word, we saw earlier how the Child Study movement of the late 1890s, with a membership of doctors, psychologists, educationalists, teachers and parents, focused both on individual children and on the child population as a whole. The movement concerned itself with the range of issues and policies designed to deal with social and economic problems. During the period 1880–1914 these were gradually attended to by a combination of voluntary and governmental agencies, and by legislation.[62] One important result of all this activity was compulsorily to attribute to children (and adolescents) a calendar of characteristics which conformed to the bourgeois 'domestic ideal'. The child was to be vulnerable, ignorant, immature, irrational, irresponsible, dependent, incompetent, innocent and generally in need of 'care and protection'.[63] Thus we should speak not merely of 'surveillance', which emphasizes close observation, but of 'intervention' which refers to the prevention and modification of behaviour.

Throughout the Victorian years there had been uncertainty as to the 'nature' of childhood – what it was, and what it should be – an uncertainty which was partially illustrated by the ambiguities and contradictions in attitudes toward wage-earning children. At mid-century, Mary Carpenter, in her reconception of juvenile delinquency, had been one of those who strived to impose 'childhood' on the delinquents who were 'independent, self-reliant . . . and devoid of reverence for God or man'. Margaret McMillan, perhaps the foremost child welfare reformer of our period, echoed this sentiment. 'Should child labour cease', she wrote with respect to the half-time system, 'children may become less precocious, but more promising; less independent, but more loving'.[64] Educationalists shared this ambition. The *Report of the Committee on Partial Exemption*, (1909), recounted how a witness had been told by teachers in rural areas 'that they had to give their biggest half-timers a thrashing regularly each October'.[65] Reformers, of all political hues, looked to the tightening up of juvenile labour legislation to create the docile and obedient child. Despite this anxiety, we know that few commentators, including doctors, were prepared to argue for the complete abolition of child labour, preferring instead to propose reducing 'excessive' hours and regulating the most (morally) dangerous occupations, such as street trading.

Medical opinion, however, increasingly stressed its developing view that children's part-time employment, for an 'indecent' number of hours and in particular conditions, tended to damage their health and, apart from any considerations of national interest, this was an infringement of their special 'nature'.[66] Considerations of this 'nature' also served to emphasize the *normal* child, rather than what was abnormal or 'sick'. The Service was in a position to do this because as it assembled a specialized knowledge (albeit of limited scientific accountability), not least through the enquiries of SMOs, it could argue the importance of sufficient sleep and exercise, define and describe the effects of strain, suggest other probable ill effects on health and physique, and assess the likely consequences of poor working environments. So it could assert its authority through definitions of normal developmental progress.

In effect, through its ability to describe normal growth and the obstacles erected by immoderate toil, medicine gave children a *physical* and *material* identity. This may be described as a form of *medicalization*, a *mentalité* which internalized an understanding derived from medicine (and psychiatry and psychology).[67] The inherent awareness of this *mentalité* with respect to children was 'real' in two senses. The child as a maturing person, observable to the eye, who could be physically damaged – the idea objectifies the child (and annexes its body) – by stress and strain; and, second, it saw the child (or childhood) as a phenomenon which in part could be understood only by reference to medicine, and other categories of 'expertise'.[68] The identity bestowed upon children was one which confirmed their special 'nature', whose existence nineteenth-century opinion had first conceded, however ambiguously and ambivalently.[69]

64

VIII

Granted that during the debate, for the majority of participants, with the exception of the socialists and their allies, the issue was never child labour *per se*, the difficulty lay in identifying unhealthy occupations and conditions, in establishing relevant criteria, and in suggesting practical solutions. The SMOs, through inspection and treatment, sought to bring within their jurisdiction ever larger areas of juvenile employment, while at the same time incorporating this specialist interest into their comprehensive concern with health and hygiene, of family and home. In both contexts the doctors moved rapidly to a position where they could demonstrate their growing expertise through practical experience, accumulated knowledge, and (rather less impressively) legislative connections. In the name of the child, then, 'child labour' was one of the subjects which made it possible for them to appropriate a certain amount of professional, medical, and social authority.

ACKNOWLEDGEMENTS

I wish to record my thanks for comments, criticisms and suggestions to Anne Digby, David Martin, Margaret Pelling and John Stewart. I am especially grateful to Roger Cooter.

NOTES

1 For a survey of constructions of childhood in the nineteenth and twentieth centuries, see my 'Past and present constructions and reconstructions of childhood: an interpretative survey', in A. Prout and A. James (eds) *Constructing and Reconstructing Childhood*, Basingstoke: Falmer Press, 1990: 35–59.
2 Comprehensive and stimulating histories of the Service are available in J. David Hirst, 'The origins and development of the School Medical Service, 1870–1919', Ph.D. thesis, University of Wales (Bangor), 1983; Bernard John Harris, 'Medical inspection and the nutrition of schoolchildren in Britain, 1900–1950', Ph.D. thesis, University of London, 1988; and John Welshman, 'The School Medical Service in England and Wales, 1907–1939', D.Phil. thesis, Oxford University, 1988. See also Bentley B. Gilbert, *The Evolution of National Insurance in Great Britain*, London, Michael Joseph, 1966: ch. 3, and Deborah Dwork, *War is Good for Babies and other Young Children. A history of the infant and child welfare movement in England, 1898–1918*, London: Tavistock 1987: 184–207. For the development of school

medical inspection prior to the establishment of the Service, see *Inter-departmental Committee on Medical Inspection and Feeding of Children Attending Public Elementary Schools, Report*, XLVII, 1906.

3 George K. Behlmer, *Child Abuse and Moral Reform in England, 1870–1908*, Stanford: Stanford University Press, 1982; Gilbert, *National Insurance*: ch. 3; Nikolas Rose, *The Psychological Complex: psychology, politics and society in England, 1869–1939*, London: Routledge, 1985: chs 4, 5; Gillian Sutherland, *Ability, Merit and Measurement: mental testing and English education, 1880–1940*, Oxford: Clarendon Press, 1984: ch. 2; John Stewart, 'Children and social policy in Great Britain, 1871–1909', M.Phil. thesis, University of London, 1988.

4 Sutherland, *Merit and Measurement*: 6; see also 7, 9, 11–13.

5 Ibid.: 6–13; J. S. Hurt, *Elementary Schooling and the Working Classes, 1860–1918*, London: Routledge & Kegan Paul, 1979: chs V–VI; Gilbert, *National Insurance*: ch. 1.

6 F. B. Smith, *The People's Health, 1830–1910*, London: Croom Helm, 1979: 183.

7 Sutherland, *Merit and Measurement*: 5–13; A. Wooldridge, 'Child study and educational psychology in England, *c.* 1850–1950', D.Phil. thesis, Oxford University, 1985: 21–2; *Lancet*, 5 April 1890: 743.

8 Sutherland, *Merit and Measurement*: 7–8; Hurt, *Schooling*: 106–8. But for the 'sanitary influence' on the 'emergence of interest in the health of the child', see Hirst, 'School Medical Service': ch. 1.

9 Sutherland, *Merit and Measurement*: ch. 1; Wooldridge, 'Child study': 22, 33–4, 51; A. G. Caws, 'Child study fifty years ago', *Bulletin of British Psychological Society*, 1949, 1: 104–9; Francis Warner, *Report on the Scientific Study of the Mental and Physical Conditions of Childhood*, London: Royal Sanitary Institute, 1895.

10 Wooldridge, 'Child study': pp. 43–4, 52–4; Caws, 'Child study'; Sutherland, *Merit and Measurement*: 93, 128–9; Gillian Sutherland and Stephen Sharp, '"The fust official psychologist in the wurrld": aspects of the professionalization of psychology in early twentieth century Britain', *History of Science*, 1980, 18: 181; Rose, *Psychological Complex*: 131–8.

11 James Kerr and E. White Wallis (eds) *Second International Congress on School Hygiene*, London, 1908; Rose, *Psychological Complex*: 84–9, 132–5. For confirmation of doctors' importance in relation to teachers, see Sutherland and Sharp, 'The fust': 182.

Eugenics never figured prominently in the references to child labour. The MOHs who supported school medical inspection and the arguments of the *Report of the Inter-departmental Committee on Physical Deterioration*, XXXII, 1904 (hereafter *Report, 1904*), were far more interested in public health provision within the framework of an integrated public health service, than in any kind of eugenics programme. For MOHs, see Harris, 'Medical inspection': chs 2, 4. Discussions of eugenics can be found in Greta Jones, *Social Darwinism and English Thought. The interaction between biological and social theory*, Sussex: The Harvester

Press, 1980: ch. 6; G. R. Searle, *Eugenics and Politics in Britain, 1900–1914*, Leyden: Noordhof International, 1976; and M. Freeden, *The New Liberalism. An ideology of social reform*, Oxford: Clarendon, 1978: 185–94.

12 Gilbert, *National Insurance*: 60. The 'national efficiency' movement is discussed in G. R. Searle, *The Quest for National Efficiency*, Oxford: Basil Blackwell, 1971. *Report, 1904*: 44–76. For the importance of this report in relation to the direction of public health, see Harris, 'Medical inspection': 18–30. See also lead article in the *British Medical Journal*, 25 July 1903: 207–8, which, in calling for an inquiry into physical deterioration, declared that if the *stunting effect of work upon children* (my emphasis) were combined with lack of fresh air, sunshine and outdoor exercise, and if family income was insufficient for proper maintenance, then it was conceivable that the British race would deteriorate.

13 Parliamentary Paper (P.P.) *Report of the Inter-departmental Committee on the Employment of School Children*, XXV, 1902, (hereafter *Report, 1902*): 10–19. For a sample of the conflicting views on the desirability of child labour, see *Physical Deterioration Committee, Minutes of Evidence*, XXXII, 1904: Qs 719–20, 729, 1094, 1824–6, 8286–96, 10253–5; V. Butler, *Social Conditions in Oxford*, London: Sidgwick & Jackson, 1912: 79; and Alexander Paterson, *Across the Bridges*, London: Edward Arnold, 1911: 19–21.

14 On the views of socialists and trade unionists, see David Howell, *British Workers and the Independent Labour Party, 1886–1906*, Manchester: Manchester University Press, 1983: 343–85; John Stewart, 'Some aspects of the British Labour movement's attitude to child welfare, 1880–1914', unpublished paper, and his 'Children and social policy': 87–116, 202–35. For the role of the ILP-er Margaret McMillan, see Carolyn Steedman, *Childhood, Culture and Class in Britain. Margaret McMillan, 1860–1931*, London: Virago, 1990: 108–10. For the committee's response, see *Report of Departmental Committee on Conditions of School Attendance and Child Labour*, LXVIII (1893–94) (hereafter *Report, 1893–94*): 21–4.

15 Mrs Hogg was a founder member and Secretary of the Committee on Wage-earning Children. See its *First Report*, London, 1900.

16 Frederic Keeling, *Child Labour in the United Kingdom*, London: P. S. King, 1914: 26. The *Report, 1902* also credited her with drawing attention to the problem.

17 Edith Hogg, 'School children as wage earners', *The Nineteenth Century*, 1897, 42: 235–44; Sir John Gorst, *The Children of the Nation*, London: Methuen, 1906: 92.

18 Gorst, *Children*: 92–4; House of Commons Paper *Elementary Schools (Children Working for Wages)*, LXX (1899) (hereafter *Return, 1899*): 5–9; London School Board Report quoted in the *Lancet*, 11 March 1899: 707.

19 *Report, 1902*: 10–19; Keeling, *Child Labour*: xxviii; Grace M. Paton, *The Child and the Nation*, London: Student Christian Movement,

1915; 80–4; Thomas Burke, 'Wage earning children in England', *Forum*, 1902, 33: 286.

20 Hurt, *Schooling*: chs V–VI; Sutherland, *Merit and Measurement*: chs 1–2.

21 Socialist and trades union arguments focused on the half-time system. See above, note 14, and Margaret McMillan, *Child Labour and the Half-Time System*, London: Clarion Newspaper Co., 1896. McMillan drew on the work of Dr Kerr and his colleagues in Bradford. Steedman, *Childhood*: 110. For medical views on half-timers since the 1870s, see Marjorie Cruickshank, *Child and Industry*, Manchester: Manchester University Press, 1981: 97–101.

22 *Report, 1902*: 18.

23 *Lancet*, 24 September 1898: 821; 11 March 1899: 707; 13 May 1899: 1309; and 16 March 1901: 806.

24 Sir William Chance (ed.) *Third International Congress for the Welfare and Protection of Children*, London: P. S. King, 1902: 6–14.

25 *Physical Deterioration Committee, Minutes of Evidence*: Qs 719–20, 1094, 2453. See also Qs 1824–6, 1924, 8286–96, 10253–5, 11939.

26 George Newman, *The Health of the State*, London: Methuen, 1907: 147

27 I am grateful to Margaret Pelling for drawing my attention to the importance of 'normal' in this context.

28 *Annual Report for 1908 of the Chief Medical Officer of the Board of Education*, (hereafter *CMO Report*), XXIII, 1910: 6.

29 *CMO Report for 1909*: 80–1. Citing reports from Essex, Brighton, Wolverhampton, Yeovil, Liverpool, Leamington, Southport and Old-ham. *CMO Report for 1910*: 117. Citing reports from Halifax, Barnstaple, Bromley, and Ashton-under-Lyne. D. M. Taylor, (SMO, Halifax) 'The school child worker', in T. N. Kelynack (ed.) *School Life*, London: National Health Manuals, 1911: 49–54. *Departmental Committee on Employment of Children Act, 1903, Evidence*, XXVIII, 1910: Qs 9533, 9791–5.

30 *CMO Report for 1911*: 248–54. This report quoted Dr C. J. Thomas (LCC) who had examined 384 wage-earning boys in London, of whom 233 showed signs of fatigue, 140 were anaemic, 131 had severe strain, 64 were deformed through carrying heavy weights, and 51 had severe heart signs. See also Clive Riverie, 'Heart strain in boys', *School Hygiene*, 1910, 1: 155; Eric Pritchard, 'The physiology of the child', *Child Study*, 1909, 1: 6–14. The government inquiries cited were the *Departmental Committee on Accidents in Places under the Factory and Workshop Acts, Report*, XXIII, 1911; *Committee on Employment of Children Act, 1903, Report*, 1910; *Inter-Departmental Committee on Partial Exemption from School Attendance, Report*, XVII, 1909; and the *Report, 1902*.

31 Alice Ravenhill, 'Some results of an investigation into hours of sleep among children in the elementary schools of England', *Child Study*, 1909, 1: 116–22, and C. Rivière, 'On sleep', *School Hygiene*, 1912, 3, no. 2: 108–18. He also quotes a letter on the matter written by prominent medical figures to *The Times*, 22 December 1905. For

a European perspective on the cultural significance of tiredness and energy, see Anson Rabinbach, 'The body without fatigue: a nineteenth-century utopia', in Seymour Drescher, David Sabean, and Allan Sharlin (eds) *Political Symbolism in Modern Europe. Essays in Honour of George L. Mosse*, New Brunswick/London: Transaction Books, 1982: 42–62. My thanks to Roger Cooter for this reference.

32 *CMO Report for 1911*: 248–54; *CMO Report for 1912*: 316–17; *CMO Report for 1913*: 280; and Taylor, 'School child': 55.

33 Gilbert, *National Insurance*: 120. Given the political and ideological interests within the ambit of the 'national efficiency' movement, this seems to be a reasonable conclusion. However, the post-Boer War alarm should be seen less as a causal factor and more as a symptom of these interests, albeit an influential one. But see Harris, 'Medical inspection', for school medical inspection before 1907: 32–43; Hirst, 'School Medical Service' for the influence of sanitary matters and the 'over-pressure' controversy on concern for the health of the schoolchild: 5–42, and p. 153 for an argument in favour of the influence of the Education Act, 1902, as against that of the physical deterioration debate.

34 For discussion of the role of the MOH see Harris, 'Medical inspection': 66–78.

35 *CMO Report for 1908*: 9; Gilbert, *National Insurance*: 132–54. The BMA was not opposed to the Service in principle.

36 Gilbert, *National Insurance*: ch. 3; Rose, *Psychological Complex*: 131–8; Sutherland, *Merit and Measurement*: 46–50. On salaries and careers see Welshman, 'School Medical Service': 35, 45–6, 374, and Harris 'Medical inspection': 77–8.

37 *CMO Report for 1911*: 260. See also Welshman, 'School Medical Service': 46.

38 On the squabble between the Board of Trade and the Board of Education as to who should control the juvenile employment system, see Jose Harris, *William Beveridge. A biography*, Oxford: Clarendon Press, 1977: 159–65; and my *Images of Youth; age, class, and the male youth problem, 1880–1920*, Oxford: Clarendon Press, 1990: ch. 7.

39 *CMO Report for 1911*: 261–4.

40 *CMO Report for 1912*: 375.

41 *CMO Report for 1912*: appendix G.

42 *CMO Report for 1913*: 271–2.

43 Gilbert, *National Insurance*: 143. For a thorough account of the dispute see Hirst, 'School Medical Service': 303–54, and Harris, 'Medical inspection': ch. 4.

44 *CMO Report for 1919*: 188. For some years SMOs had worked with CCCs and Newman was keen to use them to unify the system of treatment and inspection. *CMO Report for 1909*: 80–7.

45 *CMO Report for 1919*: 184–94.

46 I am grateful to my colleague Dr Anne Digby for pointing out to me that child health was one of the expanding areas of medical practice in an otherwise well-stocked profession.

47 Cited in Welshman, 'School Medical Service': 35, 45–6, 374.

48 Smith, *People's Health*: 187; Rose, *Psychological Complex*: 131–8; Sutherland, *Merit and Measurement*: chs 1, 2. Morant agreed with Newman that the life of the child at school could not be separated from the health of the family and home. On this, see Welshman, 'School Medical Service': 30. See also Gilbert, *National Insurance*: 128–9.

49 Quoted in Gilbert, *National Insurance*: 148. This, Morant wrote to McMillan, was far more important than the attention given to 'what and how much' children were taught. See also Gorst, *Children*: 1. Racial progress was perhaps *the* theme of the 'national efficiency' movement. Gilbert, *National Insurance*: 72–7, 107, 124–5; Sidney Webb, 'Lord Rosebery's escape from Houndsditch', *Nineteenth Century*, 1901, L: 366–86.

50 Newman, *Health of State*: 134, though at the end of his life he repudiated the thesis that medical inspection grew in response to fears about physical and racial deterioration, arguing instead that it was primarily an educational concern. Sir George Newman, *The Building of a Nation's Health*, London: Macmillan, 1939: 194–5. For a discussion of the issues, see Gilbert, *National Insurance*: 123–36, and Hirst, 'School Medical Service': 483–5.

51 Keeling, *Child Labour*: 31–2, 57–9. Probably due to the effect of bye-laws in several cities and to the removal of very young traders.

52 Paton, *Child*: 95–6.

53 Gorst, *Children*: 91.

54 Paterson, *Bridges*: 104–5.

55 Arthur Greenwood, *The Health and Physique of School Children*, London: P. S. King, 1913: 30, 33, 57–8.

56 Paton, *Child*: 79.

57 *CMO Reports 1908–14*, *passim*; and Welshman, 'School Medical Service': 30.

58 Sutherland, *Merit and Measurement*: 46–9; Sutherland and Sharp, 'The fust': 182; Rose, *Psychological Complex*: 123–34.

59 Rose, *Psychological Complex*: 131, 135.

60 Gilbert, *National Insurance*: 148–54; J. David Hirst, 'The growth of treatment through the School Medical Service, 1908–1918', *Medical History*, 1989, 33: 318–42.

61 D. Armstrong, *Political Anatomy of the Body*, Cambridge: Cambridge University Press, 1983: 13–15.

62 For example, the Child Study movement, the NSPCC, children's care committees, juvenile employment committees, and numerous youth organizations. In addition to school medical inspection and treatment, the areas covered by legislation included cruelty to children, feeble-mindedness, juvenile delinquency, child labour, school feeding, infant life protection, and the comprehensive consolidating 1908 Children Act.

63 R. Dingwall, J. M. Eekelaar and T. Murray, 'Childhood as a social problem: a survey of the history of legal regulation', *Journal of Law and Society*, 1984, 11: 207–32; Anna Davin, 'Child labour, the working-class family, and domestic ideology in 19th century Britain', *Development and Change*, 1982, 13: 633–52. See also A. Prout

and A. James, 'The emergent paradigm: origins and obstacles', in James and Prout, *Constructing Childhood*; and my 'Past and present constructions and reconstructions of childhood', in same.

64 Mary Carpenter, *Juvenile Delinquents, their condition and treatment*, London, Cash, 1853: 292. McMillan, *Child Labour*: 11–12. See also her *The Child and the State*, London: National Labour Press, 1911: 9, and Stewart, 'Some aspects': 9–10.

65 Quoted in Hurt, *Elementary Schooling*: 203.

66 On 'nature', see Hugh Cunningham, 'Slaves or savages: some attitudes to labouring children, 1780–1870', unpublished paper, 1986; Peter Coveney, *The Image of Childhood*. Harmondsworth: Penguin, 1967: ch. 1. See also my *Children in Twentieth-century Britain. A social history*. London: Routledge, forthcoming: ch. 1.

67 I have taken the definition from Harold J. Cook, 'Policing the health of London: the College of Physicians and the early Stuart Monarchy', *Social History of Medicine*, 1989, 1: 3.

68 For example, those who worked in the organizations cited above, n. 62.

69 Cunningham, 'Slaves'; M. May, 'Innocence and experience: the evolution of the concept of juvenile delinquency in the mid-nineteenth century', *Victorian Studies*, 1973, 17: 7–29.

3

'WONDERLANDS OF BUTTERCUP, CLOVER AND DAISIES'

Tuberculosis and the open-air school movement in Britain, 1907–39

Linda Bryder

The open-air school movement for debilitated children began in Britain in 1907 and was adopted with great enthusiasm over the following decades. At its peak in the late 1930s some 16,500 children were being catered for. Historians have usually placed the movement within the 'progressive' public health framework of the early twentieth century. The late Marjorie Cruickshank, for example, claimed that the schools marked a new era in preventive medicine.[1] This chapter challenges this interpretation, arguing that, far from being progressive, the open-air school movement in fact harked back to a sentimental pre-industrial Golden Age,[2] and essentially sought to inculcate Victorian notions of self-help and self-discipline. Acknowledging, however, that the movement was believed to be 'scientific' at the time, this chapter will also discuss how the movement came to be placed within the remit of scientific preventive medicine. It will be argued that preventive medicine in this instance aimed to prevent deviance as well as disease, and in addition had the effect of relegating food to a position of secondary importance in relation to fresh air in the treatment of malnutrition.

'PRE-TUBERCULOUS CHILDREN'

Open-air schools were primarily an offshoot of the early twentieth-century anti-tuberculosis campaign. The latter was itself a relatively recent development which stressed the therapeutic value of open air.

72

Tuberculosis was regarded as a disease of civilization, the treatment of which required a return to Nature. Open-air sanatoria were set up in Britain from the 1890s by a new group of tuberculosis specialists who made great claims for this form of treatment.[3] The institutions catered for those suffering from pulmonary tuberculosis, the major form of the disease. Pulmonary tuberculosis was primarily a disease of adults, and was spread by coughing or spitting. When children contracted tuberculosis it was generally bovine tuberculosis, caused by drinking infected milk. Some attention was paid in the anti-tuberculosis campaign to improving the milk supply to combat bovine tuberculosis, but the primary focus of the campaign was on pulmonary tuberculosis.

Despite the low death rates from pulmonary tuberculosis among children, attention was also directed to them after the isolation of the tubercle bacillus by Robert Koch in 1882. Koch's 'tuberculin test', which was refined in the early twentieth century and widely used, showed that a large number of children, while they did not display signs of having tuberculosis, were in fact infected. According to a famous tuberculosis specialist in Edinburgh, Sir Robert Philip, this threw a new light on the anti-tuberculosis campaign. He cited the work of various tuberculosis researchers from the Continent who showed that most working-class city children had been 'tuberculized' by the age of fifteen.[4] He claimed that 30 per cent of the schoolchildren (aged 6 to 14 years) examined by him showed 'tuberculosis stigmata', and argued, 'If the conclusion which seems forced on us be correct, that in the majority of instances infection occurs in childhood, we are faced with a problem of totally different complexion and proportion from that which was previously conceived.'[5] In other words the focus of the anti-tuberculosis campaign, in his opinion, should not be on adults suffering from the disease but on children exposed to infection. The medical officer for the Paddington and Kensington Dispensary for the Prevention of Tuberculosis in London noted this new emphasis in 1913: 'We find that the importance of the tuberculous child as a factor to be dealt with has of late years rapidly come to the front.' He quoted Philip's description of these children as the 'seedlings' of tuberculosis, and claimed that 'it is of the utmost importance to the nation to discover these "seedlings" while they are but seedlings, and to deal with them effectively, if tuberculosis is to be stamped out'.[6]

There were wide discrepancies in estimates of how many children actually had tuberculosis. As two tuberculosis specialists pointed out in 1911, 'the divergence of opinion as to what percentage of children are tuberculous is indicated by figures which range from 0.3 to 80 per cent'.[7] It was the interpretation of the tuberculin tests which led to the confusion. The significance of infection as shown by the tuberculin test was far from clear. Some thought that infection and tuberculosis were one and the same thing. One American tuberculosis specialist, the paediatrician Alfred F. Hess, concluded that as a result of the tests, there was a new 'realisation that tuberculosis [was] essentially a disease of childhood'.[8] Others, such as R. C. Wingfield, stated firmly that tuberculosis was not a disease of childhood. Nevertheless, Wingfield added, 'we cannot help wondering if some more decisive steps could be taken during this quiet period of tuberculosis, between the ages of 7 and 15, to influence the chances of pulmonary tuberculosis appearing later in life'.[9] In other words, whether children actually had tuberculosis or not, they were still claiming attention in the anti-tuberculosis campaign.

Doctors claimed an ability to identify the type of child at risk from tuberculosis. While it was no longer believed that tuberculosis was hereditary, a common belief in the nineteenth century, it was still generally held that a predisposition to tuberculosis could be inherited, that there existed a 'tuberculous diathesis'. M. S. Fraser, Assistant Medical Officer of Health (MOH) for Cumberland, referred in 1914 to the 'phthisical type' of child, who 'in many instances will develop phthisis [pulmonary tuberculosis] in later life'. In his opinion, 'The proper treatment of children of the phthisical type is most important, and offers one of the most effective means of attacking the problem of pulmonary tuberculosis'.[10] In 1911 two tuberculosis specialists, Halliday Sutherland and W. E. Goss, quoted Philip's 1909 statistics on childhood infection:

> No one has ever suggested that 30 per cent of children should be removed from school to be placed in sanatoria, but we do hold that as each of these children is a *potential case* of advanced pulmonary tuberculosis, the conditions of childhood, and particularly of school life, should be such that resistance against the disease is increased, and the child strengthened against the time when he enters the critical age periods of life.[11]

A new clinical category was introduced to label these potential cases of tuberculosis, 'pre-tuberculous'. 'Pre-tuberculous' children

had not even necessarily been infected, but showed certain characteristics. The most common one was being underweight, but there were
others. The Leicester school medical officer (SMO) described some
of the signs: 'stunted growth, loss of muscular tone, dryness of the
hair, dark rings round the eyes, long silky eyelashes, inflammation of
the eyelids, enlarged glands, anaemia, feeble circulation, and shallow
breathing'. He explained, 'Some of these children are listless and
apathetic, whilst others are of a highly nervous temperament. In a
large proportion of cases, excluding those who are neglected, there
is a history of consumption [pulmonary tuberculosis] in the near
relatives.'[12] A further description was given by James Kerr, Medical
Officer to the London County Council (LCC): 'children with easy
fatigue and exhaustion, poor colour, earthy-greenish complexions
and various catarrhal conditions, ill nourished, with poor appetite,
losing weight and so on'. He added, 'they, and in fact nearly all
town children, require to have their immunity to tubercle raised as
much as possible.'[13]

SMOs were responsible for classifying this type of child. School
medical inspections became an integral part of the School Medical
Service set up in 1907. Indeed, the Service showed a particular
addiction to the classification of children, perhaps to compensate
for the inability to make more positive contributions.[14] By 1935
SMOs were performing two million routine inspections and more
than one million special inspections each year. In their inspections of
the school population these SMOs were finding many children with
the characteristics outlined by the tuberculosis officers, children
who were not actually suffering from a specific disease but were
undernourished, pale, debilitated. In fact many children from
the slums fitted the bill. The term 'pre-tuberculous' became an
extremely useful clinical category, to categorize that amorphous
mass of sickly undernourished children. One SMO developed an
even more elaborate set of categories: 'Phthisis', 'Very Suspicious
Phthisis', 'Suspicious Phthisis', and 'Phthisical Type'.[15] A full 10
per cent of the school population was estimated to fall into
the 'pre-tuberculous' category in the first two decades of the
twentieth century.[16] This amounted to 600,000 children in 1916,
according to the Chief Medical Officer to the Board of Education,
Sir George Newman.[17] Newman explained in 1917 that from
the administrative point of view there was no definite line of
demarcation between those children with incipient tuberculosis
and the delicate, anaemic and 'pre-tubercular' children. All of them

were, he believed, suitable candidates for the newly founded open-air schools.[18]

DEVELOPMENT OF OPEN-AIR SCHOOLS

A new medical category of 'pre-tuberculous' children had thus been created, and open-air schools were to provide the treatment for their condition. An open-air school set up in Berlin, in 1904, attracted much attention in Britain following the first International Congress on School Hygiene at Nuremberg in that year. The first open-air day school in Britain was founded by the LCC at Bostall Wood, Plumstead, Woolwich, in 1907. The first open-air residential school was set up at Halifax in 1911, by which time there were nine open-air day schools in existence. By 1937 there were 155 open-air schools, catering for approximately 16,500 children.

Some schools were established by local voluntary 'after-care' committees attached to tuberculosis dispensaries or by local branches of the National Association for the Prevention of Tuberculosis (NAPT), a voluntary organization which had been set up in 1898. The Oxfordshire branch of the NAPT reported in 1914, 'A very satisfactory part of the work has been sending delicate – so-called "pre-tuberculous" children to the sea or the country.'[19] The branch subsequently set up two small country homes at Hermitage, on the Berkshire Downs, for open-air treatment for 'delicate and predisposed children'.[20] The Kensal House open-air school was set up by the Paddington Tuberculosis Dispensary in 1911, and taken over by the LCC in 1913.

While much of the impetus for open-air schools came initially from the tuberculosis specialists and the anti-tuberculosis campaign, it gained momentum because the SMOs took it up with enthusiasm. It provided a form of medical intervention for those children found on inspection to be malnourished and debilitated. Inspections unaccompanied by treatment possibly proved a source of frustration for the SMOs and even trivialized their role. Singling out children who would benefit from attending an open-air school was one line of action they could take, albeit restricted by the availability of facilities.

Additional facilities were provided by individual benefactors. For example, Mr and Mrs Barrow Cadbury donated an estate to the Birmingham local education authority for an open-air school at Uffculme in 1911. Margaret McMillan set up three camp schools in

Deptford from 1911 to 1914.[21] Many of the residential as opposed to the day schools were private institutions (32 out of 54 in 1937). The Cambridgeshire Education Committee sent 'pre-tubercular' children to open-air residential schools managed by the Invalid Children's Aid Association and the Ogilvie Charity.[22]

In his annual reports as Chief Medical Officer to the Education Board, Newman constantly urged local authorities to set up or expand existing open-air schools. In 1918 he asserted: 'The slow growth in England of the open-air school method seems scarcely creditable to our national good sense.'[23] Newman and others who wished to promote the cause of open-air schools took advantage of the lessons learned during the First World War. The beneficial effects of army life on former slum dwellers had already been widely commented on. For example, the senior medical officer of the Education Committee for the City of Nottingham said of a local returned soldier that one could 'hardly recognize the bronzed and stalwart young fellow . . . from the weedy, immature, town-bred youth, a little overgrown perhaps, with narrow chest and sloping shoulders'. He explained that the youth had been to 'Lord Kitchener's Open-air school'.[24] In his account of life in Salford in the early twentieth century, Robert Roberts similarly recorded that after the first few months of hostilities the recruits 'astonished us all. Pounds — sometimes stones — heavier, taller, confident, clean and straight, they were hardly recognizable as the men who went away'.[25]

Pointing to the physical benefits for urban dwellers of camp training in the Army, Newman argued,

> No one can measure the national gain that will accrue from this increased physical well-being, even as no one can estimate the loss in defective and devitalized man-power which the nation has sustained for many years, due to the lack of appreciation, and even systematic neglect, of the value to the human body of fresh air and sunlight. The open-air school is a simple and economical way of applying a method of natural education to the susceptible body and mind of the child.[26]

The heightened premium attached to manpower during the war was used as ammunition to extend the open-air school movement. In 1917 one advocate of open-air schools wrote in response to the objection that the cost of open-air education was excessive: 'Surely not, when by the children's restoration to health we rescue them from the industrial scrap heap, and fit them to become the parents of future British citizens. . . . Shall Imperial Britain, with her fast declining birth rate, neglect her chiefest [sic] weapon?'[27] Thus, the national efficiency movement which had played a part in the launching of both the anti-tuberculosis campaign and the School Medical Service earlier in the century, was now used to promote open-air schools.

Those involved in the anti-tuberculosis campaign itself also kept up the pressure on local authorities for the establishment of open-air schools after the war. The NAPT attempted to promote these schools by including information on open-air schools in its *Handbook on Tuberculosis Schemes in Great Britain and Ireland* from 1919, updated approximately every five years. Each local authority was asked to supply information on the provision of open-air education in its area, and where none was provided this was noted in the handbook. The NAPT also produced a film called *Air and Sun* in 1921 to publicize the benefits of open-air schools.

THE FUNCTIONS OF OPEN-AIR SCHOOLS

The open-air school movement was given scientific backing not only by tuberculosis specialists but also by Dr L. E. (later Sir Leonard) Hill, Director of the Department of Applied Physiology of the newly established National Institute for Medical Research. Hill's special interest, for which he attracted a great deal of attention, was the value of ventilation in health. He invented a special instrument to measure the cooling power of air, which he called a 'katathermometer'. His work on ventilation led him to take an interest in open-air schools. Pointing out that 21 per cent of children in the county boroughs of the north of England died before 5 years, while 9 per cent did so in the rural districts of the south, Hill expounded his theory that 'the cooling and evaporative powers of the air are closely connected with the causes of high infant mortality, these acting on the skin and respiratory membrane'. He explained that he had estimated that a man camping out of doors in cool weather, and taking several hours' hard exercise, might have almost ten times greater flow of blood and secretion through his respiratory membrane than one living in a warm humid tenement. In the latter the infection from dust and saliva spray from carriers of disease was very great, in the former nil. He concluded,

It is the lack of windage which largely explains the correlation between density of population and high morbidity and mortality.

The tenement baby, over-clothed and confined indoors by the mother – for fear of its catching cold and to save trouble under the difficulties of tenement life – dies from digestive, nutritive, and respiratory troubles, brought on largely by lack of adequate cooling and evaporative powers of the air. It is surrounded with a tropical, still, humid atmosphere. Nothing is done to secure the natural massage of its belly organs by outdoor exercise and the deeper breathing excited thereby, to maintain the capillary venous circulation, by the pumping action of the muscles during such exercise, and by the hard tone of the body which results from such exercise, and to stimulate combustion of food, and a full utilization of the products of digestion, and so a clean bowel and keen appetite which will secure enough of the many rarer 'building stones' required in the food for growth and health.[28]

James Kerr thought the salutary effects of fresh air might explain the higher tuberculosis rates among schoolgirls than boys, with boys taking more exercise out-of-doors. He also advanced a scientific rationale for open-air schools: 'Fresh cool moving air with its qualities of heat removal and nerve stimulation takes a high place in promoting the metabolism, and . . . helps the development of auto-immunity.'[29]

Fresh air was seen to have beneficial effects on the children's character as well as their physical condition. An article on the School Garden Association of America which had been founded in 1910 to bring the child 'more intimately into connection with Mother Earth' appeared in the British journal, *The Child*, in 1914. The Association reported that the children were 'made better, more thrifty, and more interested in life's normal problems. . . . The red cheeks of the school garden child form a flower we must not fail to cultivate'.[30] The analogy with plants was a constant theme. When Dr Rollier's Sun Cure Station at Leysin, Switzerland, was described in *The Child* in 1914, the children were said to be 'disporting themselves in their natural element – from which civilized life tends to exclude them more and more – hence the marvellous results'. It was explained that light and air were as necessary to the child as to the plant, that the child covered in dark clothing was the same as a plant placed in a dark, airless environment. The conclusion was that: 'The effect on the whole organism of the delicate child, on its nerves, spirits and mentality, of bathing in air and sun, is truly miraculous.'[31]

The NAPT council described its film, *Air and Sun*, as showing 'the benefit to be derived from air and sun, not only as a means of special treatment for the diseased, but generally in strengthening and hardening the delicate and weakly, by a return for a time to a natural life, which, owing to the restrictions of modern conditions has been largely lost'. The film was set in an open-air school in Switzerland, although the methods were said to be equally applicable to Britain. The boys were shown ice-skating, wearing only shorts: 'By direct contact with Air and Sunlight, the skin which clothing has made tender like a hothouse plant, recovers its natural functions. By systematic training the children become so hardened that even in the depth of winter they can play naked in the sun. Their bronzed skin is a natural clothing.'[32]

In 1915 a 'new experiment in open-air education and hygienic management of delicate children . . . children in whom the germs of all fatal diseases of adult life are to be found in their incipient forms', was described in the *Child*. This was an open-air residential school on the hillside of West Malvern, opened in 1914. An example was given of one particular 'town-sick' child. After eight weeks in a 'wonderland of buttercup, clover, and daisies':

> this child had returned home a bonny, merry child, hungry and health-coloured, 14 lb heavier, with firm little muscles that could pull up her weight on a bar, or 'swing her up' on the swing without anyone to push her, able to dig a little, weed carefully, keep places and bright things very clean, wash cups and saucers without breaking them, brush and comb a smaller child's hair *thoroughly*, keep her own little body, nails, fingers, and teeth clean, mend her clothes, help the cook, and bear adversity in the shape of a wet day or a dismal letter from home with philosophy and unselfish behaviour. She was able to do sums in her head for the practical everyday needs of life. She was equal to narrating a good story, and singing a pleasant song; willing to tell you quietly what the 'Travellers Psalm' (cxxi) meant to her. She was weather-wise and house-wise, and health-wise, a possible little missionary of untold value to her own community at home.[33]

The benefits of open-air schools were clearly seen to extend beyond the restoration of physical health. The general rules of life in open-air school apparently included: 'respect for order and food and sleep, love of sunny, moving air and pure water, dutiful habits, gentle manners, the power of keeping silent, the self-control of ordered play, the concrete practical lessons which really develop brain agility in a way that books *alone* never do.'[34]

The medical superintendent of the East Anglian Children's (tuberculosis) Sanatorium, Jane Walker, modelled the sanatorium school on the scout movement which had been set up in the early twentieth century, itself having the aim of inculcating the values of self-discipline and fresh air.[35] At Kensal House, an open-air school run by the LCC, it was reported that 'scoutcraft' was popular and (proudly) that ten 'old boys' had subsequently joined the army or navy.[36] Instruction in gardening, according to one SMO, was in particular 'likely to have far-reaching results', by creating a permanent interest in outdoor life.[37]

An important part of the open-air school regime was the teaching of personal hygiene and good habits. Newman believed that open-air education provided a tremendous opportunity of 'encouraging people to work out their own salvation in regard to some of the problems of domestic sanitation'.[38] His successor as Chief Medical Officer in 1935, A. S. MacNalty, discussing 'the teaching of personal hygiene' in open-air schools, advised that children should have a shower at least once a week.[39] The children were also to take part in domestic work at the open-air school, 'even at some inconvenience to the adult staff' for the sake of their education.[40] F. A. Sharpe, SMO for Preston, held in 1926 that the meal times were important in inculcating habits of behaviour and table manners. He added, 'even our failures have their direct propaganda value'.[41]

Children were to be 'health missionaries', they were to take the lessons they had learnt at the open-air school back into their homes, and influence their parents. The Halifax SMO maintained in 1912,

> The educative influence of the Home is important, and children who have for some months passed through the routine of residence ought to carry the lessons of personal and house hygiene back to their homes and help to raise the standard of personal living, one of the main helps in all our efforts against disease.[42]

The managers of Kensal House were also concerned about home

3.1 The slum playground v. the open-air schoolground
Source: Annual Report, Council of the National Association for the
Prevention of Tuberculosis, 1928: 7 (by kind permission of the Bodleian
Library, Oxford).

conditions. They appointed a voluntary worker for the 'family of every child, [who] does her best to see that the child gets a suitable breakfast and tea, and suitable dinners during the weekends and holidays'. The medical officer drew up a model diet as a guide.[43]

Health visitors were felt to be an important adjunct to open-air schools, indeed they were considered by some to be essential to their success.[44] In the 'Lincoln experiment', an open-air school in Lincoln, a 'lady health visitor' was appointed for each child, to visit the home and instruct the parents. It was reported that as a result of these visits, various 'improvements' had been made, such as windows kept open at night, the front sitting-room or parlour converted into a bedroom, separate beds and special clothing provided for the children attending the school, and care taken at the weekends that the food was 'simple but of the proper quality'. Where parents failed to co-operate, children were expelled from the school as a lesson to the parents. Yet it was reported perhaps defensively that the visitors 'afford[ed] the most complete evidence of the gratitude and satisfaction of the parents'.[45]

It was not always possible to influence home environment, and it was for that reason that open-air residential schools were advocated. Lewis Williams, Medical Officer to the City of Bradford Education Authority, maintained that the disappointing results were accounted for by home conditions, that 'conditions conducive to good health are absolutely impossible in some of the homes in which they live'.[46] The solution was to keep the children away from their homes as long as possible. Many of the residential schools were summer schools only. Yet Newman advocated the 'whole-year' open-air school for those who could not 'withstand the winter, home life in the slums, and the stress of school routine'.[47]

Discussing the origin of the Halifax Open-air School for 'pre-tuberculous and early tuberculous' children, opened in 1911, D. M. Taylor, the local SMO, explained, 'It [was] very discouraging to find, as the writer has experienced, an open-air scholar playing late on a Saturday night round the rubbish-heaps of the public market.' The open-air residential school was to prevent such occurrences.[48]

The main benefits of the schools were thus seen to be derived from the educational aspects as well as from the fresh air itself. Fresh air was not only more 'natural' and health-promoting, but prevented deviancy as children could be under constant supervision. There was no privacy. Children, once educated, were to take their lessons into their homes, assisted by health visitors. The open-air movement would thus reach the wider community through the children. Open-air schools were yet another channel for the invasion of homes and family life by medical 'experts'.[49]

FOOD VERSUS FRESH AIR

At an open-air school in Chicago in the USA an 'experiment' was conducted in 1913 to assess the comparative benefits of fresh air alone and fresh air accompanied by food. It was found that 'children in fresh air rooms improved in haemoglobin, even though they received no food, but they did not make a corresponding gain in weight unless food was given'. As a result of these experiments the Chicago schools decided to provide a hot dinner at noon.[50]

In Britain too, the provision of meals was an important part of the open-air school system. Newman reported in 1913 that 'In view of the fact that practically all the children suffer from some degree of under-nourishment it is extremely important to ensure that they are being properly fed while they are attending the open-air class'. He added that the need for feeding the children was so often overlooked that it was necessary to lay special stress on its importance, and reminded his readers that the local authority could now recover half the cost of the food provided.[51] MacNalty also stressed the importance of the provision of meals in the schools, and recommended that a diet should be drawn up under medical influence.[52] The 'Lincoln experiment' included three substantial meals a day.[53] At the Halifax open-air school, treatment consisted of 'skilled supervision, abundant fresh air day and night, *wholesome plain food*, absolute cleanliness, strict personal hygiene, long hours of sleep, pure milk supply, protection from infection, cod-liver oil in some cases, but little medicinal treatment is given except in emergencies, and no surgical treatment is provided'.[54]

While Hill placed most emphasis on the benefits of 'cooling air', he also referred to the provision of food. At the open-air school he described, the children were 'fed to meet their energy demands, [so] they did extraordinarily well, but going back to the slums they would relapse again, becoming thin and pale from the caged life and ill-feeding'.[55] While he placed most emphasis on metabolism which would be increased by 'mere exposure to cooling winds', he asserted: 'It is open air and exercise, *good feeding* and well regulated rest, which have converted weedy citizens into robust soldiers, which restore the weakly in open-air schools, and the consumptive in sanatoria.' Yet the conclusion he drew from his studies was: 'It is imperative that all children should receive the education that public school boys obtain on the playing fields.' Fresh air rather than food was his preoccupation.[56]

All descriptions of the open-air schools referred to the provision of 'good food', even though it was usually mentioned second only to 'open air'. It was the provision of food which in all probability accounted for the improved health noted by the medical officers, as they were dealing with a population of children whose main medical problem was often being 'deprived of the basic diet required to sustain normal life and development', estimated by Charles Webster to include between 25 and 50 per cent of the child population.[57] The same could be said of army life in the First World War. While Newman and others had extolled the virtues of outdoor living, Robert Roberts pointed out that 'some men after joining the forces were delighted to find that it meant a full stomach – "meat every day!" as the recruiting sergeants had truly said'. He quoted John Burnett, in *Plenty and Want*: 'The nation which went to War in 1914 was (still) so chronically undernourished that for millions of soldiers and civilians war-time rations represented a higher standard of feeding than they had ever known before.'[58]

Catering for no more than 16,500 children at their peak, the open-air schools only touched the tip of this iceberg of malnutrition. It was the cost of providing substantial meals which probably hindered the further development of open-air schools despite the great enthusiasm of medical officers. In 1926 Newman suggested that cost was an obstacle in the development of open-air schools.[59] He calculated that the cost per annum for each child in an open-air day school was about £30 compared with £12 in an ordinary elementary school.[60] In any case, it was argued that once 'open-air principles' had been applied to all schools the need for special open-air schools would disappear.[61] It was constantly urged that all schools should be open-air schools. Yet when it came to discussing the transfer of these 'open-air principles' to ordinary schools it was not the provision of extra nourishment that was implied.

When open-air schools were being discussed by the Society of MOHs in 1912, one participant asked the speaker, Dr Auden, whether he could estimate roughly the amount of benefit derived by children from the open-air system, compared with that derived from healthy meals, supplied under ordinary conditions of teaching. It was recorded that Auden replied,

With regard to the relative value of air and the food in producing the satisfactory results in the children, his own impression was that the fresh air itself was of the greater value. He was one of those who held that in England we are apt to put too much faith in food and to eat too much. In fact he believed that the fresh air had an importance which was double that of giving a meal.[62]

In 1937, the SMO for Mansfield, J. E. Wilson, reported that the cases at Mansfield Open-air School which showed the most dramatic improvement were those with malnutrition, anaemia and bronchitis. Wilson explained that fresh air conditions and instruction in the art of proper breathing had in a great many cases provided a definite cure, and concluded, 'I know of no other means whereby these conditions can be cured . . .'.[63] It seemed that fresh air itself could cure malnutrition. A debate was concurrently being waged concerning the relative importance of sunlight and vitamins in the deficiency disease of rickets.[64] In both instances there were implications for local education authorities' policies. The interest was not purely academic.

'ALL SCHOOLS SHOULD BE OPEN-AIR SCHOOLS'

In his report for the year 1934, MacNalty maintained that the reports of the SMOs of the more 'progressive' local education authorities were 'unanimous in their opinion of the high value of the open-air school as a factor in the cure of malnutrition'. Yet when he came to describe the way in which open-air schools influenced general education he wrote in the same report that the open-air school had had 'a valuable effect on the planning of ordinary *school buildings* for, in a large proportion of plans of elementary schools submitted to the Board, classrooms are now provided where children can be taught under open-air conditions'.[65]

The advantages for 'ordinary' children of the open-air regime had been discussed as early as 1915. The editor of the *Child* stated: 'The benefits of out-door living and the wonderful restoration of the sick and debilitated to health and vigour have conclusively demonstrated the wisdom of making use of the recuperative powers of fresh air in the management of so-called normal children.' He reported that many new schools had been constructed on more hygienic lines, and referred specifically to the Derbyshire Education

Committee's 'experiment in lighting, ventilation and heating', the North Wingfield Open-air School.[66] Derbyshire schools were to become a model for almost every new school building during the inter-war period.[67]

In the nineteenth century, school buildings had generally been in the form of a central hall. However, as a result of this new emphasis on open air, schools were being built as pavilions to allow cross-ventilation.[68] The first of the new type was reported to be that built by the Staffordshire Education Authority in 1910 at the suggestion of the MOH, George Reid, sanctioned by the Board of Education 'very much as an experiment'.[69] It attracted much attention in educational, architectural and medical circles and periodicals.[70] The City of Lincoln Education Committee also planned a new school in 1915 for 1,000 children, 'designed on the open-air principle, and every one of the 21 classrooms can be effectively turned into an open-air classroom'.[71] The Nottingham Local Education Authority was reported in 1916 to have adopted, 'as a result of much serious consideration . . . a marked progressive "fresh-air" policy in their elementary schools, and with the most encouraging success as regards the children's health'. This included shelters and awnings in the playgrounds, and a greater use of public parks and recreation grounds.[72]

At a conference on open-air schools and education in 1927, held in conjunction with an International Child Welfare Congress in Paris, it was agreed that the open-air movement should be applied to general education.[73] In 1930 the Medical Research Council and Industrial Health Research Board published a study by N. H. Vernon and T. Bedford on heating and ventilation in schools. It was argued in the report that the construction of all schools should be based on 'physiological principles'.[74]

From 1916 Newman had constantly urged in his annual reports to the Board of Education that 'all elementary schools should be so constructed or managed as to provide the advantages of the open-air system'.[75] He was 'extremely disappointed' in 1918 to find that there were probably less than 50 out of 318 local education authorities which ran open-air classes in their schools, maintaining that 'effectual ventilation is as necessary as effectual instruction'.[76] He found it 'incredible' in 1919 that so few authorities had made arrangements, given the acknowledged value of open-air education in 'combating the adverse effects of town dwelling' and, perhaps more importantly, given that arrangements were 'so simple and inexpensive to effect'.[77] In 1920 he again stressed the cheapness of open-air provision, pointing out that the recent cutbacks in education as a result of retrenchment could not have affected this area.[78]

By 1928 Newman was reporting with satisfaction that 80 per cent of the plans submitted to the Board for approval included proposals for throwing open to the outside air whole portions of the classrooms. He also reported an increase in open-air classes in the playground, school journeys and school camps. He concluded, 'This sort of progress exerts far greater effect in the long run than the building of special open-air schools for sick and defective children.'[79] In 1932 Newman claimed the advances which had been made in open-air provision for school children during the last twenty-five years were 'so profound that it is almost entitled to the term revolution'.[80]

Scotland too was making some open-air provision for school children. Forty out of 221 schools in Glasgow, as well as portions of 21 others, had been constructed on 'open-air principles' by 1935, with classrooms designed with open verandahs and sliding doors. It was reported that year that all new schools in Glasgow were being constructed in this way.[81]

The application of the open-air school movement to ordinary schools showed how medical influence was extended to general education and not confined to those children with medical problems. Some SMOs wanted to extend their mandate over schools even further, advocating what amounted to a 'medicalization' of school life. In this scheme, the influence of the SMO would override the teacher. School attendance would apparently improve the health of all children so that 'the careful mother will say "My child seems ill, I must send him to school", for the school will stand for health and vigour and life'.[82] It was argued:

> The school is, in fact, a recognized place for medical treatment, but it is also a place of education, and this two-fold aim should be emphasized in every way possible. The primary object of the school is not education, but establishing the health, and consequently . . . the medical side ought to have the last word. In Lincoln this principle has been very fully adhered to [leading to a] correlation of the medical and educational issues, not only in open-air schools, but in all schools.[83]

3.2 An open-air classroom in Nottingham, 1930

Source: British Journal of Tuberculosis, October 1930, 24: 233 (by kind permission of the Bodleian Library, Oxford).

While the provision of fresh air was carried over from open-air schools to ordinary schools, the provision of food was not. In 1939 in England and Wales, 2.8 per cent of the school population received free meals and free milk, 1.2 per cent received free solid meals only, and 11.5 per cent received free milk only.[84] The cost was a possible hindering factor, as well as the ideology of self-help which permeated the whole public health movement at that time. There was an entrenched belief that free school meals would take away parental responsibility for feeding their children. Likewise, in the infant welfare movement in the early twentieth century, milk depots had been set up to provide milk for mothers and babies, but these were soon abandoned in favour of 'mothercraft' classes and the appointment of health visitors to advise mothers on how best to manage.[85] In the anti-tuberculosis campaign too, after-care committees were attached to the dispensaries but they were instructed not to become another charity but rather to help their clients to help themselves.[86] In the open-air schools food was provided, but it was not this factor which was seen to be most significant. Rather the schools were seen as character-building institutions, training in 'natural' living, and it was this emphasis on fresh air or 'communion with nature' which was carried over to general education despite the fact that it did not in all probability account for the improvements noted as a result of attendance in open-air schools. Fresh air was moreover, as Newman noted, cheap. Through open-air provision the School Medical Service and local education authorities could be seen to be doing something positive and 'progressive', and thus deflect attention away from inadequacies in other areas. Fresh air was far cheaper than food.

Thus, this article has challenged Cruickshank's thesis that the open-air school movement marked a new era in preventive medicine. The emphasis on escape from the urban environment for the promotion of health can be traced back to the nineteenth century, as can the attempts to inculcate good habits and self-help. Cruickshank's assertion that open-air schools were abandoned after the Second World War because they had outlived their usefulness, because children were now healthier than ever before, must equally be questioned.[87] By the 1930s the number of articles extolling the virtues of open-air schools in the medical and educational press had already declined.[88] Attention had been diverted away from special schools to the provision of open-air conditions and recreational facilities for general schools (given legislative expression in the

1937 Physical Training and Recreation Act).[89] This article does not attempt to explain the demise of the open-air school movement. For this, the social and political conditions of the 1930s and 1940s must be examined. Yet it is suggested that the change in emphasis may have been related to the mounting attacks on the government's public health policies by nutritionists and social investigators.[90] Special schools for a minority no longer seemed a realistic solution. Victorian sentimentality and 'wonderlands of buttercup, clover and daisies' perhaps seemed less appropriate in the harsh realism of the 1930s.

NOTES

1 Marjorie Cruickshank, 'The open-air school movement in English education', *Paedagogica Historica*, 1977, 17: 62–74; John Welshman, 'The School Medical Service 1907–1939', D.Phil. thesis, Oxford University, 1988: 297–305.

2 See also Roy Lowe, 'The early twentieth century open-air movement: origins and implications', in N. Parry and D. McNair (eds) *The Fitness of the Nation: physical and health education in the 19th and 20th centuries*, Leicester: History of Education Society Conference Papers, December 1982, 1983; D. Turner, 'The open-air school movement in Sheffield', *History of Education*, 1972, 1: 58–78.

3 L. Bryder, *Below the Magic Mountain: a social history of tuberculosis in twentieth-century Britain*, Oxford: Clarendon Press, 1988: 24–6.

4 Sir Robert Philip, *Collected Papers on Tuberculosis*, Oxford: Oxford University Press, 1937: 198 (from speech given in 1912). See also Clive Rivière, *The Early Diagnosis of Tubercle*, London: Oxford University Press, 1914: 180.

5 *British Medical Journal*, 31 July 1909: 258; Philip, *Papers*: 70

6 D. J. Williamson, 'An open-air school for London children', *Child*, 1913, 3: 443. See also T. N. Kelynack (ed.) *Tuberculosis in Infancy and Childhood: its pathology, prevention and treatment*, London: Baillière, Tindall and Cox, 1908: 1.

7 Halliday Sutherland and W. E. Goss, 'Open-air schools', in H. G. Sutherland (ed.) *The Control and Eradication of Tuberculosis: a series of international studies*, Edinburgh and London: William Green & Sons Medical Publishers, 1911: 142.

8 A. F. Hess, 'The tuberculosis preventorium for children: a new weapon in the anti-tuberculosis campaign', *Child*, 1913, 4: 189.

9 R. C. Wingfield, *Modern Methods in the Diagnosis and Treatment of Pulmonary Tuberculosis*, London: Constable, 1924: 109.

10 M. S. Fraser, 'The control of tuberculosis in children', *Child*, 1914–15, 5: 132.

11 Sutherland and Goss, in Sutherland (ed.) *Tuberculosis*: 145.

12 A. Warner, 'Open-air schools by the seaside', *Child*, 1912, 2: 825.

13 J. Kerr, 'Tuberculosis and schools', *Child*, 1919–20, 10: 149. See also J. Kerr, *The Air We Breathe*, London: Faber & Gwyer, 1926; J. Kerr, *The Fundamentals of School Health*, London: Allen & Unwin, 1926.

14 C. Webster, 'The health of the school child during the Depression', in Parry and McNair (eds), *Fitness*: 74.

15 Fraser, 'Control of Tuberculosis': 128.

16 T. N. Kelynack (ed.) *Defective Children*, London: J. Bale, Sons, 1915: 356; R. C. Minton, 'Open-air day schools: the story of a successful experiment in Lincoln', *Child*, 1915, 5: 455.

17 *The Health of the School Child. Report of the Chief Medical Officer of the Board of Education for 1916*, London: HMSO, 1917: 103 (Newman was Chief Medical Officer to the Board of Education from 1909 to 1935, and Chief Medical Officer to the Ministry of Health from 1919 to 1935). There were an estimated 40,000 such children in London alone: 'Metropolitan open-air schools', in Kelynack (ed.) *Tuberculosis in Infancy and Childhood*: 333.

18 *Report of the Chief Medical Officer of Board of Education for 1917*: 96.

19 NAPT Oxfordshire Branch Annual Report for 1914: 10.

20 NAPT Oxfordshire Branch Annual Report for 1923: 10; ibid. 1935: 6.

21 Carolyn Steedman, *Childhood, Culture and Class in Britain: Margaret McMillan, 1860–1931*, London: Virago, 1990: 115.

22 *NAPT Handbook of Tuberculosis Schemes in Great Britain and Ireland*, 5th edn, London: NAPT, 1927: 6.

23 *Report of the Chief Medical Officer of Board of Education 1918*: 122.

24 E. M. Wyche, 'Open-air education for ailing children', *Child*, 1916, 7: 511.

25 Robert Roberts, *The Classic Slum. Salford life in the first quarter of the century*, Harmondsworth: Penguin Books, 1973: 189.

26 *Report of the Chief Medical Officer of Board of Education for 1916*: 103.

27 Wyche, 'Open-air education': 513.

28 Leonard E. Hill, 'Infant mortality and garden cities', *Child*, 1918–19, 9: 489.

29 J. Kerr, 'Tuberculosis and schools', *Child*, 1919–20, 10: 149, 150.

30 Van Evrie Kilpatrick, 'The School Garden Association of America', *Child*, 1914, 5: 20–2.

31 K. E. Behnke, 'The sun and air cure for delicate and nervous children', *Child*, 1914, 4: 634.

32 British Film Institute Archives, *Air and Sun* (1921); *NAPT Historical Sketch*, London: NAPT, 1926: 32; see also August Rollier, trans. A. E. Gloyn and M. Yearsley, *The Healer, how to fight against tuberculosis*, London: The People's League of Health, 1925: 6.

33 C. F. Stevens Burrow, 'An experiment in open-air education of school children: the Worcestershire residential open-air school', *Child*, 1915, 5: 682.

34 Ibid.: 686.
35 Jane Walker, 'The open-air life for tuberculous children: an account of the work of the East Anglia Children's Sanatorium', *Child*, 1917–18, 8: 124, 127.
36 H. Hagon, 'Kensal House London County Council School for Tuberculous Children', *Child*, 1917–18, 8: 423.
37 Minton, 'Open-air day schools': 454.
38 *Report of the Chief Medical Officer of Board of Education for 1910*: 221.
39 Ibid., *1934*: 110.
40 Ibid., *1908*: 126.
41 F. A. Sharpe, 'Medical administration of the open-air school', *Child*, 1926–7, 17: 261–2.
42 D. M. Taylor, 'Residential open-air schools for delicate and tuberculous children', *Child*, 1912, 2: 854.
43 D. J. Williamson, 'An open-air school for London children', *Child*, 1913, 3: 445.
44 G. A. Auden, 'The open-air school and its place in educational organization', *Public Health*, 1912, 7: 253.
45 Minton, 'Open-air day schools': 444–6.
46 L. Williams, 'Open-air schools and residential schools for defective children', in Kelynack, *Defective Children*: 366.
47 *Report of the Chief Medical Officer of Board of Education for 1910*: 232.
48 Taylor, 'Residential open-air schools': 849.
49 On the 'invasion' of homes and family life by medical 'experts', see, for example, Jane Lewis, 'The working-class wife and mother and state intervention, 1870–1918', in J. Lewis (ed.) *Labour and Love: women's experience of home and family 1850–1940*, Oxford: Basil Blackwell, 1988: 99–120.
50 S. C. Kingsley, 'Open-air schools in America', *Child*, 1913, 3: 1087 (he did not state how long the experiments lasted).
51 *Report of the Chief Medical Officer of Board of Education for 1913*: 220. This was different in Scotland where the powers of local authorities were not so clear; see Department of Health for Scotland, *Committee on Scottish Health Services Report*, Cmd 5204, Edinburgh, 1936: 190.
52 *Report of the Chief Medical Officer of the Board of Education, 1934*: 109.
53 Minton, 'Open-air day schools': 440.
54 Taylor, 'Residential open-air schools': 852 (my emphasis).
55 L. E. Hill, *The Science of Ventilation and Open-air Treatment*, Medical Research Council Special Report Series no. 52, Part 2, London: HMSO, 1920: 200.
56 Hill, 'Infant mortality and garden cities': 490 (my emphasis).
57 Webster, 'Health of school child': 79.
58 Roberts, *Classic Slum*: 189; John Burnett, *Plenty and Want: a social history of diet in England from 1815 to the present day*, London: Scolar Press, 1966.

59 *Report of the Chief Medical Officer of Board of Education for 1926*: 28.
60 Ibid., *1925*: 17.
61 Williams, 'Open-air schools': 365–6.
62 *Public Health*, 1912, 7: 258.
63 *Report of the Chief Medical Officer of Board of Education for 1937*: 77.
64 Greta Jones, *Social Hygiene in Twentieth Century Britain*, London: Croom Helm, 1986: 73–7.
65 *Report of the Chief Medical Officer of Board of Education for 1934*: 112 (my emphasis).
66 Editorial, *Child*, 1915–16, 6: 84.
67 Lowe, 'Open-air movement': 91.
68 See also M. Seaborne and R. Lowe, *The English School – its architecture and organisation, ii, 1870–1970*, London: Routledge & Kegan Paul, 1977: 65, 77, 81.
69 Ibid.: 91.
70 *Report of the Chief Medical Officer of Board of Education for 1925*: 63–8.
71 Minton, 'Open-air day schools': 446.
72 Wyche, 'Open-air education': 511.
73 *Report of Chief Medical Officer of Board of Education for 1927*: 29.
74 Ibid., *1930*: 37.
75 Ibid., *1916*: 108.
76 Ibid., *1918*: 116–18.
77 Ibid., *1919*: 138, 144.
78 Ibid., *1920*: 133.
79 Ibid., *1928*: 27–8.
80 Ibid., *1932*: 112.
81 *NAPT Handbook*, 8th edn, 1935: 95; *Edinburgh Medical Journal*, 1931, 38: 157.
82 M. E. Nath, 'Open-air education for well-to-do children', *Child*, 1914, 4: 439.
83 Minton, 'Open-air day schools': 442.
84 *Report of the Chief Medical Officer of Board of Education for 1938*: 22.
85 Jane Lewis, *The Politics of Motherhood*, London: Croom Helm, 1980; Deborah Dwork, *War is Good for Babies and Other Young Children: a history of the infant and child welfare movement in England 1898–1918*, London: Tavistock, 1987.
86 Bryder, *Magic Mountain*: 87–96.
87 Cruickshank, 'Open-air school movement': 73, 74.
88 One exception is the Wytham open-air school, near Oxford, the virtues of which were extolled by Raymond Ffennell: 'To them it was, as one of the teachers wrote, a dream come true – a visit to fairyland', *Times Educational Supplement*, 18 January 1936. See also the *British Journal of Tuberculosis*, 1933, 27: 64.
89 See also Sir George Newman, *The Building of a Nation's Health*, London: Macmillan, 1939: 229–30, 262–4.

90 Celia Petty, 'Primary research and public health: the prioritization of nutrition research in inter-war Britain', in J. Austoker and L. Bryder (eds) *Historical Perspectives on the Role of the MRC. Essays in the history of the Medical Research Council of the United Kingdom and its predecessor, the Medical Research Committee, 1913–1953*, Oxford: Oxford University Press, 1989: 59–82.

4

ORPHANS AS GUINEA PIGS
American children and
medical experimenters, 1890–1930

Susan E. Lederer

In the decades between 1870 and 1930 the social and economic value of children in American society underwent a profound transformation.[1] The sentimentalization of children and the greater sensitivity to child mortality contributed to campaigns to promote child welfare, to the creation of a number of specialized institutions to enhance the physical and emotional well-being of American children, and to the development of a new medical specialty, paediatrics. The commitment to child health also spurred physicians to undertake researches that involved the use of both sick and healthy children, many of whom were inmates of orphanages or public hospitals, as experimental subjects. This chapter examines the use of children in medical research in the late nineteenth and early twentieth centuries. Although institutionalized children were more likely than their more prosperous counterparts to be reported as subjects of medical experiments, I will argue that physicians' decisions to experiment on these populations reflected the intersection of competing professional obligations and personal commitments, rather than the uncomplicated exploitation of accessible children.

One revealing source of information on professional attitudes toward experimentation with children is the controversy in the first two decades of the twentieth century over non-therapeutic human experimentation or 'human vivisection'.[2] In response to criticism from American anti-vivisectionists and vivisection reformers, for whom the 'vivisection of children' was the inevitable result of medical science grounded in animal experimentation, several paediatric experimenters offered explicit justifications for their use of institutionalized children in clinical trials of new vaccines and diagnostic tests.[3] All parties active in the debate over vivisection agreed in theory on the necessity of therapeutic human

96

experimentation in which experiments were performed with the expectation of benefiting individual patients. In practice, however, the distinction between therapeutic experiments and non-therapeutic research protocols designed to enhance medical knowledge proved problematic. Discussions about trials of new vaccines and diagnostic tests reveal the considerable ambiguity that invested both professional and public responses to using 'orphans as guinea pigs'.

Paediatric experimentation, both therapeutic and non-therapeutic, was more extensive than some historians have allowed.[4] Some experiments in which children participated involved substantial risks, yet to assume that physicians were unconcerned with risks is mistaken. Evaluation of risk and discomfort from untried drugs and procedures and the potential of therapeutic benefit were critical considerations for most physicians. In some cases experimenters misconstrued the nature of the risks and dangers for child participants. In the development of vaccines, for example, a major focus of research in this period, physicians sometimes exposed children to greater risks from the vaccine than the potential risk of acquiring the disease in the institution. As in the introduction of the Salk vaccine for polio in the 1950s, investigators were not always the best judges of the safety and efficacy of a biological product.[5]

Experimentation with child subjects did not begin in the late nineteenth century. Perhaps one of the most famous incidents in the history of American medicine, the introduction of variolation for smallpox, involved initial testing on children. In 1721, at the instigation of the Puritan divine Cotton Mather, Zabdiel Boylston first attempted variolation against smallpox on those close at hand, his six-year-old son and his two slaves.[6] After three weeks, presumably satisfied with the success of the procedure, Boylston variolated his second son.

Smallpox outbreaks provided the occasion for continued experimentation with institutionalized children. In the introduction of vaccination with cowpox for smallpox, children in almshouses and the offspring of physicians were again among the first to receive the vaccine. When Benjamin Waterhouse, who played a leading role in the introduction of vaccination in the United States, received his initial shipment of vaccine from London, he first administered it to his own son.[7] In Philadelphia in 1802 when smallpox again visited the city, Thomas C. James, accoucheur to the almshouse, tested the Jennerian vaccine on forty-eight of the children under his care. He later challenged their immunity to the disease by inoculating the same children with smallpox.[8]

Similar, but unsuccessful, attempts were made to immunize children against another childhood disease, measles. In 1905 Ludvig Hektoen, director of the McCormick Institute for Infectious Diseases in Chicago, reported at least three attempts by American physicians to produce immunity from the disease. The earliest case instanced a Rhode Island physician who in 1799 inoculated 'three young persons in his circle'; the other two cases involved physicians charged with the care of orphans.[9] Nathaniel Chapman, who in medical studies abroad learned of attempts to produce immunity from measles, returned home and undertook a series of investigations in 1801 with children at the Philadelphia Almshouse. Chapman attempted in vain to inoculate children with blood, tears, and the material from skin eruptions of other children already infected with measles. Indeed, Chapman's lack of success in infecting children with the disease led him to conclude that measles was in fact non-contagious.[10]

Five decades later a Chicago physician made a series of measles inoculations involving children from the local orphan asylum where a measles outbreak had erupted. Using blood drawn from children already ill with measles, John E. M'Geer inoculated three children in the asylum. When these children developed mild cases of measles, M'Geer proceeded with additional injections, concluding that inoculation was effective in producing a milder case of measles than the children would have experienced otherwise during the epidemic.[11]

M'Geer's services to the two Chicago orphan asylums reflected a new pattern of social organization in the middle decades of the nineteenth century. Beginning in the 1830s, the number of institutions devoted to the care of children grew rapidly throughout the United States.[12] Although children had received care in the general almshouses, orphan asylums were virtually unknown in the eighteenth century. Concern about the high mortality of infants and young children in the general almshouses (in some institutions as high as 80 per cent) led social reformers and philanthropists to create foundling homes and hospitals to care for both indigent mothers and their offspring.[13]

Childhood itself became a locus of meliorist energies at mid-century. In the face of changes wrought by urbanization and industrialization, reformers and philanthropists looked to carefully designed institutions they hoped would re-educate the children of depraved, intemperate, and impoverished parents. In addition to caring for the spiritual needs of children, many child-saving institutions secured the services of an attending physician to see to the children's medical needs. Some medical superintendents, confronted with the challenges of group care and opportunities for systematic testing, reported the results of modest experiments with their young charges. These reports reflected both the nascent interest in numerical methods and the on-going conflicts between medical sectarians that characterized mid-century medical practice.[14] Concerns about the large numbers of children on urban streets and the poor quality of life for children in the almshouses continued to make construction of orphanages a priority for many social reformers. Although Charles Loring Brace's New York Children's Aid Society began in 1854 to send economically productive children to farms in New York and the Middle Western states, younger children and children whose poor health made them unattractive candidates for foster care remained a source of concern.[15] Beginning in mid-century, philanthropists and physicians jointly established the first children's hospitals in the United States. Concentrated primarily in the north-eastern United States, these specialized medical facilities, like other nineteenth-century hospitals, initially embodied the desires of reformers to provide moral training, as well as medical care, for the poor.[16]

Paediatric hospitals also provided physicians with both opportunities to study the diseases of children and occasions to secure appointments as hospital physicians. As Charles E. Rosenberg has argued, in an era before formal clinical training and board certification, hospital appointments offered invaluable experience and a means of entry into an urban clinical élite.[17] Hospitals moreover permitted a concentration of paediatric patients that offered physicians the opportunity to pursue studies of children and their diseases. Although interest in clinical studies reflected the aspirations of only a small segment of the American medical profession, these élite physicians increasingly dominated professional discourse through the establishment of specialty societies and the reorganization of medical education.

In exchange for the charitable benevolence of wealthy patrons and élite physicians, patients in nineteenth-century hospitals served as 'clinical material' for physicians and medical students. Edward Atwater has observed, 'teaching was, almost without exception, one of the reasons physicians gave for promoting hospitals'.[18] Physicians offered their services in part for the privilege of bringing medical students along for instruction. Indeed medical schools emphasized their access to interesting and 'abundant clinical material' in hospitals and dispensaries as a means of drawing students.[19] Hospital managers also exploited the educational possibilities in campaigns for funds. The Boston Children's Hospital (established in 1869) attracted wealthy supporters by appeals to the 'double interest' for patrons in the institution: 'not only on account of the great benefit it will confer on its little inmates, but also because of the advantages it offers for the study of special diseases by which their offspring may be afflicted'.[20] However, using patients for the purposes of teaching was not always unproblematic. Although conflicts between physicians and lay managers of hospitals periodically erupted over the instrumental use of patients, many physicians and hospital administrators agreed that in the United States patients were rarely subjected to the abuses suffered by patients at the hands of German physicians.[21]

Just as there was friction between the hospital's teaching function and its role in providing patient care, the pursuit of research and the care of patients in the hospital were seen as potentially in conflict. In his 1886 Boylston Prize essay, a Boston physician C. F. Withington identified some problems and solutions in the use of hospitals for both education and research. Patients, he suggested, might have to serve as subjects in therapeutic experiments, given the uncertain state of medical knowledge.[22] These same patients, he argued, had the right to expect immunity from non-therapeutic experiments in which benefit for themselves was not anticipated. He acknowledged that enthusiastic physicians occasionally violated the rights of hospital patients. Indeed his discussion was a response to an 'egregious usurpation' involving two English physicians, Sydney Ringer and William Murrell, who administered a number of drugs to hospital patients in order to study their reactions to purified dosages of commonly prescribed medications.[23] Withington's objections to the English trials stemmed from the discomfort and pain suffered by the patients, who received the medications without their knowledge or permission.

Withington conceded that not all researches involved discomfort or danger for patients. In cases in which a physician wished to obtain, for example, such benign information as thermometer readings or the normal conditions of the reflexes, he maintained that performing such measurements without permission was unobjectionable: 'If the physician were to ask these things as a favor, few, if any, patients would refuse him, and if as a matter of convenience he takes them as a right, no harm was done.'[24] In Withington's view, the obligation to do no harm to patients took precedence over all other considerations. When discomfort or harm did not pose a problem, physicians were free to pursue their enquiries.

Many American physicians shared this distinction between acceptable and unacceptable non-therapeutic experimentation, at least in theory. In cases in which a benefit was not intended for the individual patient involved, risk avoidance assumed priority, even in instances in which patients permitted experimental procedures known to possess substantial risks.[25] However, in at least some cases, the fact that a previously untried procedure or drug would subsequently prove to be harmless (and valuable) was sufficient to exonerate a physician from charges of misconduct.[26] One of the most discussed examples of paediatric experimentation at the turn of the century illustrates the considerable ambiguity that characterized interpretations of appropriate use of children as subjects of medical research.

In August 1896 Arthur Howard Wentworth, a recent graduate of the Harvard Medical School and outpatient physician to the Children's Hospital in Boston, reported results from forty-five lumbar punctures on infants and children. Wentworth explained that he first performed the operation of tapping the spinal canal on a child with a questionable case of tubercular meningitis. Although the child proved free of disease, she responded unfavourably to the puncture, leading Wentworth to suspect that the spinal tap was not as harmless as many believed. He then resolved to attempt 'control experiments on normal cases', explaining:

The diagnostic value of puncture of the subarachnoid space is so evident that I considered myself justified in incurring some risk in order to settle the question of its danger. If it proved to be harmless, then one need not wait until a patient becomes moribund before resorting to it.[27]

He subsequently withdrew spinal fluid from twenty-nine children ranging in age from a few months to a few years, concluding that although 'the momentary pain of the puncture' caused children occasionally to shrink back and cry out, the procedure itself was harmless and would prove to be a useful diagnostic tool.[28] The fact that Wentworth's prediction about the clinical utility of lumbar puncture proved accurate should not obscure the uncertainties and risks that confronted physicians in 1896.[29]

Wentworth presented his results to both the Suffolk County Medical Society and the American Pediatric Society in 1896 where he received encouraging responses. Publication of the article, however, provoked an angry editorial in the *Philadelphia Polyclinic*. John B. Roberts labelled Wentworth's procedures 'human vivisection', reminding his readers:

> It must be remembered that there were no therapeutic indications for the operation such as often lead us to justly and properly adopt operative treatment, the positive value of which is still undetermined. These operations were purely and avowedly experimental.[30]

Roberts rebuked Wentworth for using hospitalized children without explaining his plan to their mothers or gaining their permission, and thus fostering fear of hospitals, a prejudice he identified as already deeply rooted among the poor.

Wentworth's experimental procedures and, perhaps more importantly, Roberts' criticism of the lumbar punctures did not escape the attention of anti-vivisectionists and vivisection reformers. Although the relationship between human and animal experimentation may seem obscure today, late nineteenth-century animal protectionists saw the two as intimately, if not causally, related.[31] Opponents of unrestricted animal experimentation insisted that protracted exposure to animal vivisection blunted compassion for human beings. Frequently cited was the warning by an Illinois jurist, A. N. Waterman: 'To whomsoever, in the cause of science, the agony of a dying rabbit is of no consequence, it is likely that the old or worthless man will soon be a thing which in the cause of learning may well be sacrificed.'[32] Anti-vivisectionists warned that it was a short step from the animal kennels to the hospital charity wards where unsuspecting patients would be used in experiments.[33]

In October 1897 at the annual meeting of the American Humane Association, Albert Tracy Leffingwell, a prominent advocate of vivisection reform, warned the delegates that human vivisection, the use of human beings in non-therapeutic experiments without their knowledge or consent, had already begun.[34] Although his concern was provoked by the work of an Italian physician G. Sanarelli, whose inoculations of five people with the purported bacillus of yellow fever also prompted censure by William Osler, Leffingwell identified two American examples of human vivisection, including Wentworth's experiments at the Children's Hospital.[35]

In preparation for a hearing on proposed legislation to restrict experimentation involving animals in the District of Columbia, the American Humane Association in 1899 circulated a pamphlet on human vivisection in which Wentworth's 'vivisections of children' figured prominently.[36] In addition to Sanarelli's yellow fever experiments and the lumbar punctures, the circular described nine experiments involving children in institutions in Hawaii, England (Ringer and Murrell), Austria, Germany and Sweden. Perhaps the most notorious case involved a Swedish physician. When Dr Jansen of the Charity Hospital in Stockholm began experiments with 'black smallpox pus' he preferred to use calves, which were only obtainable at considerable cost. He reported that it was cheaper to use the children at a local foundlings' home.[37]

Together with newspaper accounts of experiments involving children in European hospitals, the Senate hearings and charges of 'murder in the name of science' compelled several prominent physicians to respond.[38] Alarmed by publicity generated by charges of child vivisection and fearful that such attention would lead to restrictions on animal experimentation like those enacted in Great Britain, several leading Boston physicians met to discuss the Wentworth situation. Wentworth had been scheduled to testify at a legislative hearing in Boston on animal experimentation, but he did not appear. None of his colleagues publicly defended the research, and Wentworth resigned quietly from Harvard, though he did retain his posts at the Children's and Infants' Hospitals.[39]

Wentworth's explicit identification of the lumbar puncture procedures as experiments involving 'normal cases' made him a notable target for anti-vivisectionist criticism. In the next two decades, such prominent anti-vivisectionists as Caroline Earle White, president of the American Anti-Vivisection Society, and Diana Belais, president of the New York Anti-Vivisection Society, continued to accuse the Boston paediatrician of human vivisection and to censure the medical profession for not joining in their condemnation of his work. Notable for her histrionic garrulity, Belais went so far as to accuse Wentworth of causing the deaths by spinal puncture of the children under his care.[40]

Misrepresentation of Wentworth's experiments and the recognition that the lumbar punctures embodied potentially influential propaganda for the anti-vivisectionist cause led William Williams

Keen, a Philadelphia surgeon long active in defence of research activities, to defend Wentworth on several occasions.[41] Encouraged by the case of William Bayliss, a British physiologist who won a libel suit against an anti-vivisectionist, Keen urged Wentworth to consider legal action against Caroline White and the *Journal of Zoophily*. When Wentworth declined this suggestion, Keen also wrote to John B. Roberts, author of the editorial ubiquitously cited in human vivisection tracts that criticized the lumbar punctures, asking whether the proven safety and efficacy of the procedure had modulated his views about Wentworth. Roberts, though sympathetic to the request of his former teacher, regretfully declined to retract his criticism.[42]

Although Wentworth explicitly used 'normal cases' to verify the safety of an untested procedure, lumbar puncture proved to be both safe and effective for diagnostic purposes. The fact that Wentworth did not harm his patients counted heavily in his favour, even though it was not a therapeutic procedure. Whereas physicians and most anti-vivisectionists agreed that experiments conducted to benefit an individual patient were not only ethical but necessary to continued progress in medicine, the separations between the acquisition of new information, diagnosis and treatment were frequently debated. The disparity of views on experiments conducted for the purposes of developing new diagnostic tools and vaccines loomed large in the subsequent controversy over two additional cases of 'human vivisection' involving orphans and hospitalized children: the testing of tuberculin for the diagnosis of tuberculosis and trials of luetin for the diagnosis of syphilis.[43]

In 1908 three Philadelphia physicians, Samuel McClintock Hamill, Howard C. Carpenter and Thomas A. Cope reported the results of comparisons of several diagnostic tests for tuberculosis.[44] These tests involved administration of tuberculin to different sites in the body: conjunctiva (Calmette); deep muscle (Moro); and skin (von Pirquet). Under the heading 'material used', Hamill and his colleagues described their subjects as children under eight years of age, all but 26 of whom were inmates of St Vincent's Home, 'an institution with a population of about 400, composed of foundlings, orphans, and destitute children'.[45] Hamill and his associates tested the orphans, deliberately deferring physical examinations of the children until diagnostic tests had been performed. This fuelled criticism that the children had been used merely as subjects regardless of their medical conditions.

104

The physicians explained that before beginning the conjunctival test, they were unacquainted with any adverse effects associated with the procedure. The ease of implementing the test (application of a few drops of tuberculin to the surface of the eye) and the relatively quicker results obtained thereby made it attractive to clinicians in search of an effective diagnostic tool. However, in the course of testing, several disadvantages quickly became manifest. The reaction produced a 'decidedly uncomfortable lesion' and in several cases, serious inflammations of the eye resulted. In addition, the possibility that permanent impairment of vision might result for several children worried the physicians. These disadvantages, together with adverse reports from more than fifteen other physicians, led Hamill's group to conclude:

> we are strongly of the opinion that any diagnostic procedure which will so frequently result in serious lesions of the eye, irrespective of the way in which it produces them, has no justification in medicine, especially since there are other diagnostic tests of equal if not superior value, which are applicable to the same class of cases and not attended with the same serious results.[46]

Routine tuberculin testing of the child population of St Vincent's Home revealed a large number of cases of previously unsuspected tuberculosis, an unsurprising outcome given the crowded conditions at the home and the poor nutritional status of many of the children. For these physicians, the 'experiments' thus provided an identifiable therapeutic benefit.

The dual purpose of the tuberculin testing at St Vincent's Home – both to diagnose disease in the children and to compare methods of instilling tuberculin – led American anti-vivisectionists to label the trials as examples of non-therapeutic experimentation. In response to the tuberculin tests, the Vivisection Investigation League, the New York Anti-Vivisection Society, and the Philadelphia-based American Anti-Vivisection Society issued pamphlets compiled from the extracts of reports of the tuberculin tests from the medical literature.[47] Consistent with anti-vivisectionist reliance on visual representations, two of the circulars included coloured pictures reproduced from Hamill's report of children's eyes inflamed by tuberculin. In addition, Diana Belais wrote an article for *Cosmopolitan* that described the tuberculin tests and presented photographs of Kitty Logan, 'Little Catherine' and Agnes

Morgan, three young inmates from St Vincent's Home (*see* illustrations 4.1 and 4.2).[48]

Belais challenged the therapeutic status of tuberculin testing of the children of St Vincent's. Not only had Hamill, Carpenter and Cope failed to state or even imply benefit to the children, Belais argued, their own report 'even to a layman' suggested that the tests were in 'the nature of experiments in diagnostic values'.[49] Belais also denounced the 'cold professional terms' used by physicians to describe the reactions of the children and labelled the tests of the conjunctival application unnecessary, in the light of Hamill's own citation of multiple reports of discomfort and injury from other physicians. Anti-vivisectionists consistently criticized experimental medicine on these grounds, claiming that most researchers only repeated the work of other investigators and, even then, failed to produce a useful consensus about the value of a particular procedure or experiment.

Belais's objections to Hamill's tests persisted in accusations of human vivisection against an eminent New York paediatrician, L. Emmett Holt. In January 1909 Holt, a professor of diseases of children at Columbia University's College of Physicians and Surgeons, reported results of another series of comparisons of tuberculin tests involving infants at New York Babies' Hospital.[50] The repetition of earlier experiments disturbed anti-vivisectionists, but perhaps more distressing was the perceived clinical detachment with which Holt described the results of tuberculin tests on 'dying children':

> With a callousness somewhat astonishing even to one versed in the writing of vivisectors, this particular representative of the species seems to feel no hesitancy whatever in referring to this strange use of sick and dying babies.[51]

For critics of human vivisection, issues of insensitivity to the human subjects of research and the redundancy of such experiments recurred in other reports of comparisons of tuberculin administration.[52] References to patients as 'material' and expressions of gratitude to staff physicians who allowed investigators 'use of material' led the American Anti-Vivisection Society to charge: 'quotations clearly indicate that after these tests were found to be distinctly dangerous the experiments still continued and "material" was freely furnished by authorities of various public institutions'.[53]

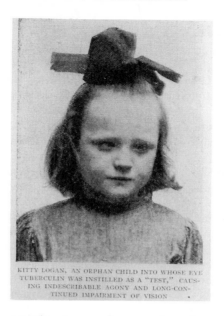

KITTY LOGAN, AN ORPHAN CHILD INTO WHOSE EYE
TUBERCULIN WAS INSTILLED AS A "TEST," CAUS-
ING INDESCRIBABLE AGONY AND LONG-CON-
TINUED IMPAIRMENT OF VISION

4.1 Kitty Logan – human guinea pig
Source: Diana Belais, 'Vivisection – animal and human', *Cosmopolitan*,
1910, 49: 271.

4.2 Experimental 'material' from St Vincent's Home, Philadelphia
Source: Diana Belais, 'Vivisection – animal and human', *Cosmopolitan*,
1910, 49: 273.

Clinical trials of diagnostic tests for tuberculosis were not the only focus for critics of human vivisection. At the Rockefeller Institute for Medical Research, a consistent target of anti-vivisectionist activity, Hideyo Noguchi's development of a diagnostic test for syphilis, similar to tuberculin, using orphans and hospital patients as subjects and controls provoked considerable outcry in the years 1912–14.[54]

Noguchi's use of children and hospital patients to test for the presence of a disease only recently mentionable in polite company angered New York anti-vivisectionists. However, they directed comparatively little criticism at the researcher, preferring to focus on the physicians and medical superintendents whose 'courtesy' allowed Noguchi access to their patient populations. Thus, both the Vivisection Investigation League and the American Anti-Vivisection Society, avid to identify the 'medical conspirators', published in full the names and hospital affiliations of the physicians who provided Noguchi with subjects.

Disturbed by Noguchi's report that he used 46 normal children between the ages of two and eighteen as controls, the president of the New York Society for the Prevention of Cruelty to Children instituted a formal complaint against Noguchi on charges of battery. Although the district attorney's office declined to prosecute Noguchi on such charges, accusations of human vivisection continued. As in the case of Wentworth and the tuberculin testers, defenders of medical research found such charges difficult to understand. Two factors influenced the medical interpretation of Noguchi's trials. First, the administration of the inactivated solution of luetin did not injure the children. Although application of the luetin did cause minor irritation, it was certainly less than that occasioned by the Calmette eye test.[55] Perhaps more important, Noguchi's defenders argued that the test application was therapeutic in intent in spite of Noguchi's use of the word 'control'. According to Noguchi's supporters, the test allowed the seemingly normal children to receive treatment for the disease, treatment which would not have been given if not for the diagnostic value of the luetin test.

The tumult over human vivisections involving tuberculin and luetin led Walter Bradford Cannon, the chair of the American Medical Association's Council on the Defense of Research, to enlist the aid of a young Philadelphia physiologist to answer the accusations of human vivisection. Richard Mills Pearce's analysis of human vivisection was the only pamphlet in the defence of research series that expressly addressed the ethics of human experimentation.[56]

Responding to charges against Hamill, Pearce explained that Hamill had conferred with other physicians before embarking on the trials, thus countering the claim that the trials were undertaken without careful consideration. He challenged the assumption that the use of orphans, foundlings, and destitute children implied that the consent of guardians had not been sought. Pearce explained that Hamill had approached the directors of St Vincent's and secured co-operation for the purposes of both determining the incidence of tuberculosis in the asylum and the simultaneous comparative study of the different methods of applying tuberculin. Hamill insisted that the sisters had readily assented to the plan, even though public criticism interfered with continued testing of the children.[57] On the issue of Hamill's conclusions about the undesirability of the ophthalmic test, Pearce pointed to the fact that the eye test continued to enjoy some support among physicians, despite the discomforts and dangers associated with it.[58]

Pearce did acknowledge as 'difficult to excuse' one set of experiments by an American physician cited by critics of human vivisection. He explained that the clinical experiments of Dr J. W. Stickler, a New Jersey physician, who in 1887 inoculated several children with 'virus' of foot-and-mouth disease in the belief that this would confer immunity to scarlet fever, were not unlike the experiments undertaken by Edward Jenner in seeking a preventive inoculation against smallpox.[59] He conceded that increased knowledge of the infectious diseases in the 1880s could not justify Stickler's methods, but expressed confidence that one isolated observation made twenty years earlier could not be held up as an indictment of current American medical research practices.[60]

Although Hamill chose not to respond to critics of tuberculin testing, L. Emmett Holt wished to address his accusers directly. Angered by newspaper reports that he injected dying babies with tuberculin, Holt consulted Simon Flexner, the scientific director of the Rockefeller Institute and an active ally of Cannon in the defence of research, about an appropriate response to the accusations. Citing the fact that the New York anti-vivisectionists had been largely discredited by revelations of inaccuracy and misrepresentation in charges of human vivisections at two New York hospitals, Flexner advised Holt not to respond.[61] Renewing the controversy over the tuberculin tests, he argued, could only serve to reopen the problematic questions of consent for non-therapeutic procedures that arose in the context of Noguchi's tests of luetin.

Perhaps more to the point, Flexner reminded Holt that his explanations of the tuberculin tests did not answer one of the primary criticisms of the tuberculin tests:

> one of their chief arguments [is] that in the beginning the test was applied to children who were not supposed to be suffering from tuberculosis. They of course overlook the fact that the application of the test discovers at times tuberculosis which is unsuspected but since your article does not discuss the question of controls they would not feel you had met the issue.[62]

Flexner's advice reflected a consistent preference on the part of defenders of medical research to avoid whenever possible discussing the ethical ambiguities of clinical research involving humans, especially in situations in which continued public support for animal experimentation without restrictions was at stake.[63]

Despite this advice, Holt chose to respond after newspapers continued to print stories on the tests at Babies' Hospital. Contrary to his research report, Holt denied both that he had tested children irrespective of their ailments and that he had tested dying children. He did not address the issue of controls.[64] If he had done so, he would have had to acknowledge that in order for a diagnostic test to be useful, it must give a negative response in tests of patients known to be free of the disease. In such cases, the test might pose little risk but neither could a therapeutic benefit be expected or defended.

Much of the discussions about the use of children in the development of diagnostic tests, new procedures, or even confirmation of the etiological status of a newly identified microbe, reflect the polemics of the controversy over animal experimentation in this period. Committed to preventing legal restrictions on animal vivisection, defenders of medical research not surprisingly directed their energies to undermining their opponents, branding anti-vivisectionist criticism as misguided and vivisection reform as unnecessary. Defenders of medical research hoped to preempt further condemnation of the use of human subjects through closer attention to research reports, the major source of anti-vivisectionist propaganda. Cannon, for example, circulated a letter among editors of medical journals asking that particular attention be directed to reporting details of anaesthetic use and post-operative care in the case of animal vivisection and the details of individual consent or the permission of guardians in reports involving human beings.[65]

Cannon continued to monitor situations in which references to experimentation involving human beings, and children in particular, could be misunderstood. In alerting the manager of the Rockefeller Institute to an advertisement of a glycerinated vaccine virus 'physiologically tested on children before being placed on the market', Cannon maintained that the public would not countenance anything that could be interpreted as experimenting on children which was not for the good of the children themselves.[66] Most of the defence of research materials promoted the idea that medical science was the only way in which progress could continue, and that any restrictions on animal or human experimentation would not be in the best interests of humanity.

Anti-vivisectionists, for their part, believed that focus on human vivisection would further their efforts to gain popular support for legislative restrictions on the use of animals in research. Thus, legislation to restrict experimentation on human subjects was introduced with the view of publicizing the link between animal and human vivisection and the necessity for restrictions on the laboratory use of animals.[67] This commitment to animal protection may explain in part the anti-vivisectionists' disinclination to produce examples of human vivisection other than the small number which were continually cited in their literature, a repetition for which they were often criticized.[68] Reiteration of such human vivisections as those of Wentworth and Holt reflected their belief that human vivisection was not commonly practised by American physicians. It may also be a consequence of their method for identifying cases of human vivisection, namely reliance on newspaper reports of new medical discoveries. Perhaps believing that Wentworth's procedures or Noguchi's tests served as compelling representative illustrations, anti-vivisectionists did not pursue systematic exploration of the extent of paediatric experimentation. Had they done so, they would have discovered that the practice was much more common than they believed. Their critics suggested an alternative explanation, namely that anti-vivisectionists were more committed to the protection of animal welfare than to that of children.

To what extent were American children used as subjects in the development of new drugs, procedures, tests, and vaccines in this period? The literature of the human vivisection controversy provides citations to child participation in the development of a

SCHOOL DAYS

NEARLY 25 million children will enter the public schools in the United States in September. The intimate contact, incident to school life, is one of the most potent factors in the production and spread of disease.

LEDERLE'S **Glycerinated Vaccine Virus** is physiologically tested on children, before being placed on the market, thus insuring an active and potent product. The LEDERLE collapsible tube affords the simplest known means for administering the virus.

Send for illustrated booklet.

Lederle Antitoxin Laboratories

Schieffelin & Co., Distributors

New York

4.3 'School Days' – advertisement for vaccine product tested on children, 1914
Source: American Journal of Public Health, February 1914: 2.

vaccine for tuberculosis (the von Ruck vaccine tested on children in a North Carolina orphanage), the use of newborn infants to discern the mechanisms of gastric hunger, the use of additional children from St Vincent's to study infection with a contagious skin disease (molluscum contagiosum), and the use of children to establish the cause of whooping cough.[69]

In addition to these reports, a survey of one paediatric journal for the years 1911–16, at the high point of controversy over the vivisection of children in hospitals, reveals sixty-eight reports describing the use of child subjects. Given an unknown rate of experiments performed but not reported, this suggests that paediatric experimentation was not a rare occurrence.[70] These reports allow limited information about the circumstances under which experiments were undertaken. Few physicians explicitly noted parental involvement. In 1912, for example, two prominent American investigators related how they obtained infants for cal-orimetric studies through the directory of wet nurses at the Boston Babies' Hospital, studies for which mothers were present the entire time.[71] Failure to mention parental permission does not necessarily mean parents were not consulted, but it may reflect the fact that many of the children used in hospitals and asylums were orphans, either literally or socially. The use of the word 'material' to describe paediatric patients, so repellent to critics of human vivisection, was not uncommon.[72] Whether this usage reflects the conventions of medical communication or the social distance between indigent patients and élite physicians is difficult to assess.[73]

Considerable attention was devoted to technical difficulties in pursuing research with paediatric patients. The collection of blood and the products of metabolism in infants and young children was impeded by their smaller size and 'unruly' behavior. Efforts to achieve compliance with research protocols in some instances may have placed children at greater risk than the experimental procedure itself. For example, when a child's activity interfered with attempts to obtain results of normal electrical response to galvanic current, investigators reported that 'constant resistance necessitated mild chloroform narcosis in a few cases'.[74] Other physicians reported that in 'unruly infants' X-ray studies of normal anatomy and physiology of the infant stomach necessitated the use of anesthesia.[75] Metabolic studies involved restraining infants and young children on a metabolic frame for a considerable period of time. In one study of a baby with a 'rather happy disposition' investigators placed the infant on a metabolic frame for a second period of 'prolonged confinement' of seven days. After the baby lost weight, the investigators removed the child from the frame despite his lack of obvious discomfort, noting they 'carried the observation as far as was advisable with a human subject'.[76]

Given the difficulties associated with experiments involving uncooperative and uncomprehending subjects, why would physicians undertake researches on children? To some extent the research problem dictated the choice of research subject. In the case of tuberculosis, the ubiquity of adult infection in early twentieth-century America led several investigators to attempt to develop a prophylactic vaccine for artificial immunity against the disease.[77] These researches necessarily involved subjects as yet uninfected, generally children. The introduction of live or attenuated vaccine into children free of the disease in the name of an anticipated, if uncertain, future immunity worried some physicians. In 1912 the respected Colorado physician Gerald Webb acknowledged his uneasiness about 'inoculating the uninfected' with a live tubercle bacillus vaccine. Only extraordinary circumstances and parental permission convinced Webb to try the experiment on the two young children (aged 9 months and 3 years) of 'a distinguished scientist dying of tuberculosis'.[78]

Researchers at times looked to child subjects for explanations of phenomena observed under different conditions in adults. For example, when the safety of chemical food additives came under investigation in 1908, the Referee Board of Consulting Scientific Experts conducted extensive clinical experiments using adult volunteers.[79] Questions about the action of the preservative sodium benzoate in young children led to clinical experiments involving infants fed artificial milk containing the additive.[80] Other investigators looked to studies of infants and children for comparisons with adult physiology. The physiologist A. J. Carlson and his group at the University of Chicago undertook extensive studies of human digestion in the first two decades of the twentieth century. In addition to auto-experiments, investigators used a 'professional adult subject' and normal infants in physiological studies of hunger in health and disease.[81]

Paediatricians, especially those entrusted with the care of institutionalized children, had additional reasons for experimentation. Confronted with high rates of morbidity and mortality, physicians sought to develop both preventive and therapeutic means to improve the health of their charges. In some cases, an interest in experimentation could not be separated from the desire for professional advancement. Medical discoveries enhanced careers. Some paediatricians no doubt hoped to have their names immortalized in an eponymous diagnostic test or vaccine.[82] These desires, and the accessibility of children for systematic experimentation, may have contributed to greater risks for institutionalized children.

The instrumental use of orphanage children is well illustrated in the work of Alfred F. Hess, a prominent New York paediatrician, who conducted extensive research involving children housed in the Hebrew Infant Asylum in New York City.[83] In several papers, Hess acknowledged the advantages of studying certain problems within the confines of a custodial institution. In reporting trials of a prophylactic vaccine for pertussis, Hess observed:

> It is probably also of advantage, from the standpoint of comparison, that these institutional children belong to the same stratum of society, that they have for the most part been reared for a considerable period within the same walls, having the same daily routine, including similar food and an equal amount of outdoor life. These are some of the conditions which are insisted on in considering the course of experimental infection among laboratory animals, but which can rarely be controlled in a study of infection in man.[84]

The availability of children at the asylum led Hess to pursue extensive studies of the anatomy and physiology of digestion in infants. In 1911 he reported the development of a duodenal tube for infants which could be used to sample gastric secretions. Although conceding the difficulty of predicting the value of any new agent, he subsequently used the instrument in a number of studies of both normal and diseased infants and children.[85]

Hess's reports of the use of balloon catheters, X-rays, duodenal tubes, and other apparatus to study the process of normal digestion in children do not contain evaluations of risks to participants. Despite the fact that dangers associated with X-ray exposure were known to practitioners, there continued to be ambiguity about what levels of exposure constituted harmful levels of radiation.[86] In fact, children were used as subjects in a number of experiments involving X-rays in which risk from participation was deemed unremarkable. In one instance, however, risk to orphans at the Hebrew Infant Asylum in Hess's researches on nutrition did generate one of the few critiques of paediatric experimentation in this period that was not associated with anti-vivisectionists.

In 1921 Konrad Bercovici, a social worker and journalist, criticized Hess and his associate Mildred Fish for using 'orphans as guinea pigs' in studies of dietary factors in rickets and scurvy.[87] Bercovici described Hess's studies on scurvy, which involved withholding orange juice from institutionalized infants until they developed the characteristic haemorrhages associated with the disease.[88] He also quoted the employment of similar methods by Hess and his associates to discover a diet that would induce rickets.[89] Although Bercovici acknowledged the importance of studying the effects of different diets on children, he explicitly rejected the methods in producing the disease in non-volunteers, especially when some of the children did not fully recover from the effects of the disease:

> no devotion to science, no thought of the greater good to the greater number, can for an instant justify the experimenting on helpless infants, children pathetically abandoned by fate and intrusted to the community for their safeguarding. Voluntary consent by adults should, of course, be the *sine qua non* of scientific experimentation.[90]

Bercovici's assessment of Hess's experiments seemingly generated no further discussion, either among physicians or among members of the public.

Bercovici's efforts to separate himself from other critics of the medical profession, 'the anti-vivisection freaks and the various cranks and fanatics', suggests by 1921 the marginalization of anti-vivisectionist critics of human vivisection. However, his analysis of the medical use of orphans at the Hebrew Infant Asylum reflected similar concerns about child welfare, namely the absence of therapeutic benefit and the potential for permanent injury for the child participants. American physicians shared in theory these commitments to therapeutic potential and minimization of risk. However, definitions of therapeutic potential in this period proved exceptionally elastic and risk assessment especially problematic. In the name of child welfare, physicians performed considerable experimentation, not always in the best interests of their child subjects.

ACKNOWLEDGEMENTS

I would like to thank V. Carchidi, D. Barnard, J. Watson and R. Cooter for their generous assistance.

NOTES

1 See V. A. Zelizer, *Pricing the Priceless Child*, New York: Basic Books, 1985.

2 See S. M. Lederer, 'Human experimentation and anti-vivisection in turn-of-the-century America', Ph.D. thesis, University of Wisconsin, 1987.

3 The American anti-vivisection movement encompassed both those adamantly opposed to any experimentation involving living animals and those who labelled themselves vivisection reformers, i.e. willing to accept vivisection with certain restrictions. See S. E. Lederer, 'The controversy over animal experimentation in America, 1880–1914', in N. A. Rupke (ed.) *Vivisection in Historical Perspective*, London: Croom Helm, 1987: 236–58.

4 See M. A. Grodin and J. J. Alpert, 'Children as participants in medical research', *The Pediatric Clinics of North America*, 1988, 35: 1389–1401, and D. J. Rothman, 'Ethics and human experimentation', *The New England Journal of Medicine*, 1987, 317: 1195–9. Grodin, Alpert, and Rothman argue that paediatric experimentation was rare before the Second World War. For an opposing view, see R. G. Mitchell, 'The child and experimental medicine', *British Medical Journal*, 21 March 1964: 721–7, and M. S. Frankel, 'Social, legal and political responses to ethical issues in the use of children as experimental subjects', *Journal of Social Issues*, 1978, 34: 101–13, who state that orphanage children were commonly used as subjects in the late nineteenth century. These articles, however, are little more than brief surveys of the history of child experimentation.

5 A. M. Brandt, 'Polio, politics, publicity and duplicity: ethical aspects in the development of the Salk vaccine', *Connecticut Medicine*, 1979, 43: 581–90.

6 J. B. Blake, 'The inoculation controversy in Boston, 1721–22', in J. W. Leavitt and R. L. Numbers (eds) *Sickness and Health in America*, Madison: University of Wisconsin, 1985: 348.

7 J. B. Blake, *Benjamin Waterhouse and the Introduction of Vaccination: a reappraisal*, Philadelphia: University of Pennsylvania, 1957: 14–15.

8 In New York, Boston and Baltimore, almshouse children were also among the first to receive the vaccine. S. X. Radbill, 'The use of children in pediatric research', paper delivered at AAHM, Pittsburgh, PA, 4 May 1979. Also S. X. Radbill, 'Centuries of child welfare in Philadelphia', *Philadelphia Medicine*, 1975, 71: 279–91, 319–27.

9 L. Hektoen, 'Experimental measles', *Journal of Infectious Diseases*, 1905, 2: 238–55. Hektoen also cites the efforts of Hungarian, Italian, German, and English investigators to produce measles immunity in

children. Dr Green of Greenwich, Rhode Island, is discussed in J. Stewart, *A Practical Treatise on the Diseases of Children*, New York: Langley, 2nd edn, 1844: 416.

10 W. P. Dewees briefly cites Chapman's lectures on the non-contagiousness of measles in *A Treatise on the Physical and Medical Treatment of Children*, Philadelphia: H. C. Carey and I. Lea, 1825: 471. See Radbill, 'Centuries of child welfare': 369.

11 J. E. M'Geer, 'Inoculation in rubeola', *Eclectic Medical Journal*, 1851, 10: 322–4. Hektoen cites him as McGirr in 'Experimental measles': 249. See J. H. Cassedy, *American Medicine and Statistical Thinking, 1800–1860*, Cambridge, Mass: Harvard University, 1984: 138.

12 See D. J. Rothman, *The Discovery of the Asylum: social order and disorder in the new republic*, Boston: Little, Brown, 1971: 208–36.

13 P. C. English, 'Pediatrics and the unwanted child in history: foundling homes, disease, and the origins of foster care in New York City, 1860–1920', *Pediatrics*, 1984, 73: 699.

14 Cassedy describes how the homeopath C. Wright in 1842 eliminated all but homeopathic treatments for the children in New York City's Protestant Half-Orphan Asylum and reported the results. Suspicious of Wright's success, James McCune Smith, the first American black with a medical degree and attending physician to the Free Negro Orphan Asylum in New York City, questioned Wright's results and accused him of turning away sick children as a means of improving the recovery rate. A decade earlier the medical director of the Albany Orphan Asylum instituted a vegetarian diet for the children after a systematic comparison of the health benefits accruing from adoption of the Graham system. See Cassedy, *American Medicine and Statistical Thinking*: 116–48.

15 Brace's society placed more than 80,000 older children. See 'The Children's Aid Society of New York: its history, plan, and results', in National Conference of Charities and Corrections (comp.) *History of Child Saving in the United States*, Montclair, New Jersey: Patterson Smith, 1971: 30.

16 S. A. Halpern, *American Pediatrics: the social dynamics of professionalism, 1880–1980*, Berkeley: University of California, 1988: 36–43.

17 C. E. Rosenberg, *The Care of Strangers*, New York: Basic Books, 1987: 174–5.

18 E. C. Atwater, 'Internal medicine', in R. L. Numbers (ed.) *The Education of American Physicians: historical essays*, Berkeley: University of California, 1980: 143–74 (quote appears on 151).

19 Announcement of the Johns Hopkins Medical School for 1893. I am grateful to John Parascandola for this citation.

20 Quoted in M. J. Vogel, *The Invention of the Modern Hospital, Boston 1870–1930*, Chicago: University of Chicago, 1980: 22.

21 Some physicians conceded that in the past 'pauper patients' had been subjected to risks which would not have been incurred in the case of wealthier patients, but that it was exceedingly rare in 1900, see 'Experimental operations in hospitals', *American Medicine*, 1904, 8: 313. Also Lederer, 'Human experimentation': 112–14.

22 C. F. Withington, *The Relation of Hospitals to Medical Education*, Boston: Cupples, Upham, 1886.

23 The Ringer and Murrell affair is discussed in R. D. French, *Antivivisection and Medical Science in Victorian Society*, Princeton: Princeton University, 1975: 320–2.

24 Withington, *The Relation of Hospitals to Medical Education*: 17.

25 For example, in the demonstration of the role of the Aedes mosquito in the spread of yellow fever, Walter Reed expressed anxiety that volunteers would perish as a result of participation in research. Reed and his colleagues took pains to ensure that volunteers understood the risks they incurred, as well as the benefits of receiving the best supportive care in the event that they fell sick with the disease, by using written contracts. See W. B. Bean, 'Walter Reed and the ordeal of human experimentation', *Bulletin of the History of Medicine*, 1977, 51: 75–92.

26 G. L. Geison makes a similar point in 'Pasteur's work on rabies: reexamining the ethical issues', *Hastings Report*, 1978, 8: 26–33.

27 A. H. Wentworth, 'Some experimental work on lumbar puncture of the subarachnoid space', *Boston Medical and Surgical Journal*, 1896, 135: 133.

28 S. Benison, A. C. Barger and E. L. Wolfe list twenty-seven children as subjects. More significant, they downplay the experimental nature of the spinal taps, an aspect that Wentworth explicitly emphasized, *Walter B. Cannon: the life and times of a young scientist*, Cambridge, Mass: Belknap Press of Harvard University, 1987: 176–7.

29 Even today the procedure is not free from risks. Although serious complications are rare, common complications include local pain and headache. See J. R. Botkin, 'Informed consent for lumbar puncture', *American Journal of Diseases of Children* (hereafter *AJDC*), 1989, 143: 899–904.

30 J. B. R. [John B. Roberts], 'Human vivisection', *Philadelphia Polyclinic*, 1896, 5: 357.

31 For a contemporary analysis of a possible correlation between animal abuse in childhood and subsequent cruelty to humans in adulthood, see S. R. Kellert and A. R. Felthous, 'Childhood cruelty toward animals among criminals and noncriminals', *Human Relations*, 1985, 38: 1113–29.

32 *Shall Science Do Murder?* (From the *Chicago Evening Post* of May 18, 1899), Providence, Rhode Island, 1899.

33 For example, see G. A. S., 'Supremacy of honest convictions over all other considerations', *Journal of Zoophily*, 1901, 10: 66.

34 *Twenty-first Annual Report of the American Humane Association*, 1897: 38–9.

35 For criticism of Sanarelli's research, see W. Osler, *The Principles and Practice of Medicine*, New York: D. Appleton, 3rd edn, 1898: 183.

36 *Human Vivisection: a statement and an inquiry*, 2nd edn, American Humane Association, 1899.

37 See *Human Vivisection: foundlings cheaper than animals*, Washington, DC, 1901. G. L. Fitch, 'The etiology of leprosy', *New York Medical*

Record, 1892, 42: 293–303. Fitch took the fact that the girls did not develop syphilis as proof of his theory.

38 See G. M. Searle, 'Murder in the name of science: experiments on children', *Catholic World*, 1900, 70: 493–504. One surprising omission in the discussion of child vivisection was the introduction of diphtheria antitoxin. In claims about the inutility of animal experimentation, the antitoxin was cited as another example of inflated claims by defenders of medical research. See A. Leffingwell, *The Vivisection Question*, Chicago: Vivisection Reform Society, 1907: 180–2.

39 Benison, Barger, and Wolfe, *Walter B. Cannon*: 177–9.

40 D. Belais, 'Vivisection animal and human', *Cosmopolitan*, 1910, 49: 267–73; for White, see 'Still more barbarity', *Journal of Zoophily*, 1910, 19: 44.

41 W. W. Keen, 'The influence of anti-vivisection on character', *Boston Medical and Surgical Journal*, 1912, 166: 651–8, 687–94. This appeared in the American Medical Association's Defense of Research Series, Pamphlet XXIV.

42 A. H. Wentworth to W. W. Keen, 22 June 1911, William Williams Keen Papers, Library, College of Physicians of Philadelphia. For Bayliss's victory in the Brown Dog libel suit, see 'An anti-vivisection leader', *Journal of the American Medical Association*, 1910, 54: 540; C. Lansbury, *The Old Brown Dog: women, workers, and vivisection in Edwardian England*, Madison: University of Wisconsin, 1985: 10–12.

43 W. J. Shultz, *The Humane Movement in the United States, 1910–1922*, New York: AMS Press, 1924: 154–7, mistakenly cites these cases as the first attention paid to human vivisection.

44 S. M. Hamill, H. C. Carpenter and T. A. Cope, 'A Comparison of the von Pirquet, Calmette, and Moro tuberculin tests and their diagnostic value', *Archives of Internal Medicine*, 1908, 2: 405–47.

45 Hamill, 'Comparison': 419.

46 Hamill, 'Comparison': 425.

47 *Tuberculin Tests on Human Beings*, Philadelphia, n.d.; *Vivisection – A Menace to Hospital Patients*, New York, n.d.; and *Vivisectors Clamor for Human Beings to Vivisect*, New York, n.d.

48 See photograph; Belais, 'Vivisection': 273.

49 Belais, 'Vivisection': 269.

50 L. E. Holt, 'A report upon one thousand tuberculin tests in young children', *Archives of Pediatrics*, 1909, 26: 1–26. For Holt's role in American pediatrics, see K. Jones, 'Sentiment and science: the late nineteenth century pediatrician as mother's adviser', *Journal of Social History*, 1983, 17: 79–96, and R. L. Duffus, and L. E. Holt, jun., *L. Emmett Holt: Pioneer of a Children's Century*, New York: D. Appleton-Century, 1940: especially 163–7.

51 *Vivisection – A Menace to Hospital Patients*: 3.

52 L. Hamman and S. Wolman reported: 'It is important that these tuberculin tests should be tried on as varied a material as possible', in 'The cutaneous and conjunctival tuberculin tests in the diagnosis of pulmonary tuberculosis', *Archives of Internal Medicine*, 1909, 3:

307–49, on 307. For staff co-operation in allowing use of 'material', see G. S. Derby and T. H. Ayer, 'A clinical investigation on the relationship of tuberculosis to certain diseases of the eye', *Journal of the American Medical Association*, 1910, 54: 1762.

53 *Tuberculin Tests on Human Beings*, Philadelphia, n.d. The pamphlet does include some misleading quotations from research reports; for example, reference to the 'Report of the committee for the study of the relation of tuberculosis to diseases of the eye' seemed to confirm professional consensus about the undesirability of the Calmette test; however, the author of the report did not agree. See W. H. Wilder, 'Report of the committee for the study of the relation of tuberculosis to diseases of the eye', *Journal of the American Medical Association*, 1910, 55: 21–4.

54 See S. E. Lederer, 'Hideyo Noguchi's luetin experiment and the anti-vivisectionists', *Isis*, 1985, 76: 31–48.

55 Noguchi described some reddening of the injection site, and in a few children, slight fever, malaise, diarrhoea and loss of appetite. Noguchi, 'A cutaneous reaction in syphilis', *Journal of Experimental Medicine*, 1911, 14: 557–68.

56 R. M. Pearce, *The Charge of 'Human Vivisection' as presented in Anti-vivisection Literature*, Chicago: American Medical Association, 1914.

57 According to Hamill's biographer, the sisters were seeking to redirect attention from their own culpability for the high mortality rate in the asylum; see J. Stokes, jun., 'Samuel McClintock Hamill', in B. S. Veeder (ed.) *Pediatric Profiles*, St Louis: Mosby, 1957: 96–7. In 1911 Hamill reported the use of children at the Baptist Orphanage of Philadelphia; see S. Hamill and K. D. Blackfan, 'Frequency and significance of albumin in the urines of normal children', *AJDC*, 1911, 1: 140.

58 Pearce, *The Charge of 'Human Vivisection'*: 20.

59 Stickler inoculated children with foot-and-mouth disease and then exposed them to scarlet fever; see J. W. Stickler, 'Foot and mouth disease as it affects man and animals', *Medical Record*, 1887, 32: 725–32.

60 Pearce, *The Charge of 'Human Vivisection'*: 6–7.

61 For loss of public credibility, see K. L. Buell, 'A campaign of lies', *Harper's Weekly*, 1914, 58: 15; 'Another anti-vivisection fiasco', *Journal of the American Medical Association*, 1914, 62: 1025.

62 S. Flexner to L. E. Holt, 2 April 1914, Simon Flexner Papers, American Philosophical Society Library.

63 For similar reservations about opening up the discussion on human experimentation in 1899, see Benison, Barger, and Wolfe, *Walter B. Cannon*: 176–8.

64 See 'Defends tests on babies', *New York Evening Post*, 10 April 1914; 'Anti-vivisection', *Journal of Zoophily*, 1914, 23: 92–3.

65 'Report of the committee on the protection of medical research', *Journal of the American Medical Association*, 1914, 63: 94.

66 See plate 5 advertisement, *American Journal of Public Health*, 1914, 4: 2. W. B. Cannon to H. James, Jun. 19 October 1914; James to

Cannon, 21 October 1914, Rockefeller University Archives, Record Group 600–1, Box 6, Folder 2. For anti-vivisection comment on the Lederle advertisement, see 'A new use for children', *Open Door*, January 1914: 11.

67 For example, a law that would require an experimenter to obtain the 'intelligent written consent' of the subject except in cases of individual benefit, and expressly outlaw experiments on children under the age of fifteen, the feeble-minded and the pregnant, was introduced in the Illinois legislature in 1905 'not in the hope of securing its passage, but of furnishing the occasion for enlightening the public'; see S. R. Taber, 'Shall vivisection be restricted?', reprinted from the Chicago *Record-Herald*, 12 May 1905, Chicago.

68 As late as 1926, the New England Anti-Vivisection Society recited the case of Mary Rafferty, who had electrodes inserted into her brain in 1874; see J. P. Morgan, 'The first reported case of electrical stimulation of the human brain', *Journal of the History of Medicine*, 1982, 37: 51–64.

69 For von Ruck, see 'A practical method of prophylactic immunization against tuberculosis', *Journal of the American Medical Association*, 1912, 58: 1504–7; reference to using gastric balloons in newborn infants, in A. J. Carlson, *The Control of Hunger in Health and Disease*, Chicago: University of Chicago, 1916; in K. S. Nicholson, 'Anti-vivisection notes', *Journal of Zoophily*, 1917, 26: 187–8; for producing molluscum contagiosum in a boy and girl at St Vincent's in 1908, see F. C. Knowles, 'Molluscum contagiosum: report of an institutional epidemic of fifty-nine cases', *Journal of the American Medical Association*, 1909, 53: 671–3, and for whooping cough, see 'Anti-vivisection notes', *Journal of Zoophily*, 1913, 22: 11.

70 Survey of the *American Journal of Diseases of Children*, which began publication in 1911. Identifying cases of non-therapeutic experimentation can be difficult, especially in the case of sick children. When, for example, is an experimental manipulation seen as directly related to diagnosis and treatment of the child? In my survey, I excluded reports of individual cases and studies involving routine tests of blood and urine in which no manipulation of the children was made.

71 F. G. Benedict and F. Talbot, 'Some fundamental principles in studying infant metabolism', *AJDC*, 1912, 4: 129–36.

72 In fifteen papers physicians explicitly referred to patients as material. For example, see E. Long and E. W. Caldwell, 'Some investigations concerning the relationship between carpal ossification and physical and mental development', *AJDC*, 1911, 1: 113.

73 For discussion of the condescension and ambivalence that marked relationships between paediatric patients and their physicians, see Rosenberg, *The Care of Strangers*: 303–4.

74 H. Wilcox, 'The diagnosis of infantile tetany', *AJDC*, 1911, 1: 393–416 (quote appears on 399). In one case, a urine collection tube on the penis of an infant caused swelling and was removed before the end of the observation period. See O. Schloss and J. L. Crawford, 'The

metabolism of nitrogen, phosphorus and the purin substances in the newborn', *AJDC*, 1911, 1: 203–30.

75 G. Pisek and L. T. Lewald X-rayed both normal and sick infants from 2 days old to 20 months; 'The further study of the anatomy and physiology of the infant stomach based on serial roentgenograms', *Transactions of the American Pediatric Society*, 1913, 25: 150–65.

76 A. W. Bosworth, H. I. Bowditch and B. H. Ragle, 'Whey in infant feeding', *AJDC*, 1915, 9: 124.

77 See Karl von Ruck and H. J. Achard, 'Specific resistance in tuberculosis', *Pediatrics* (NY), 1913, 25: 742–56.

78 G. B. Webb, 'Studies in tuberculosis', *Bulletin of the Johns Hopkins Hospital*, 1912, 23: 233.

79 J. H. Young, 'The science and morals of metabolism: catsup and benzoate of soda', *Journal of the History of Medicine*, 1968, 23: 86–104.

80 C. G. Grulee and W. H. Buhlig, 'Investigation of the action of sodium benzoate in artificially-fed infants', *Archives of Pediatrics*, 1911, 28: 849–67. L. E. Holt also did studies of infants; see Young, 'The science and morals of metabolism': 102.

81 The observations involved stomach tracings after the introduction of balloons into thirty normal breast-fed infants; see A. J. Carlson, *The Control of Hunger in Health and Disease*, Chicago: University of Chicago Press, 1916: 40, 120.

82 After his experiments on scarlet fever failed, J. W. Stickler committed suicide '"obsessed" with the idea that he was immortalizing his name and would deserve the gratitude of future generations'. See Pearce, *The Charge of Human Vivisection*: 6.

83 For Hess, see H. J. Gerstenberger, 'Obituaries: Alfred Fabian Hess, MD', *AJDC*, 1934, 47: 635–9.

84 A. F. Hess, 'The use of a series of vaccines in the prophylaxis and treatment of an epidemic of pertussis', *Journal of the American Medical Association*, 1914, 63: 1007.

85 A. F. Hess, 'A duodenal tube for infants', *AJDC*, 1911, 1: 365. See A. F. Hess, 'The gastric secretion of infants at birth', *AJDC*, 1913, 6: 264–76.

86 See D. P. Serwer, 'The rise of radiation protection: science, medicine and technology in society, 1896–1935', Ph.D. thesis, Princeton University, 1977.

87 K. Bercovici, 'Orphans as guinea pigs', *Nation*, 1921, 112: 911–13.

88 A. F. Hess and M. Fish, 'Infantile scurvy: the blood, the blood vessels, and the diet', *AJDC*, 1914, 8: 386–405.

89 For the work on rickets, see A. F. Hess and L. J. Unger, 'Dietaries of infants in relation to the development of rickets', *Proceedings of the Society for Experimental Biology and Medicine*, 1919–20, 17: 220–1.

90 Bercovici, 'Orphans as guinea pigs': 913.

5

FROM ISOLATION TO THERAPY

Children's hospitals and diphtheria in *fin de siècle* Paris, London and Berlin

Paul Weindling

During the nineteenth century, the world of the child shifted from fields and workshops to schools and the domestic environment. Although compulsory primary education had been established in most German states in the 1700s, the 1880s saw a new concern with school health with the introduction of medical inspection and greater emphasis on sports; compulsory elementary education was introduced in England in 1880, and in France in 1886. The 1880s also witnessed the rise of concern with cruelty to children both at home and in schools, and with the academic overburdening of schoolchildren in cramped and deforming classroom desks.[1] Appreciation of the distinctive features of childhood resulted in a greater degree of isolation in new institutions and professional surveillance.[2]

The question arises whether the proliferation of children's hospitals from the 1880s should be seen as reinforcing the child's world as a separate sphere, requiring special institutional facilities and custodial authorities. That many children's hospitals were intended as isolation hospitals and that many isolation hospitals were primarily inhabited by children lends some support to this view, although the process of segregation was complex. The purpose of children's hospitals changed from catering for poor children to providing therapy for children from all social classes. The following case-study of diphtheria in Berlin, Paris and London examines differing patterns of hospital provision in three major metropolitan centres. I focus on the introduction of serum therapy for diphtheria which occurred in the context of modernization of public hospital provision. Underlying this were processes of professionalization and scientifically based strategies of social reform and integration.

It is appropriate to concentrate on these expanding cities during the 1890s, as it was here especially that population growth and social tensions were acute, and where high rates of infectious diseases threatened child health. During the 1890s the population growth on the peripheries of Berlin, London and Paris meant that the concentration of hospitals in the old city centres no longer met the needs of the rapidly growing and highly mobile populations. This marked a change of priorities in public health away from water supply and sewers, and towards hospitals and dispensaries. London was by far the largest of these cities in size, with a population of around 4.2 million (according to the 1891 census), rising to 4.5 million in 1900. According to aggregate mortality statistics it had the best health, and had been pioneering in solving the problems of sanitation. The population of Berlin (excluding the burgeoning peripheral municipalities) was 1.5 million in 1890, and rapidly increased to 1.9 million in 1900. This compares with Paris's 2.4 million in 1890 and 2.7 million in 1900. According to national statistics the French had a lower mortality rate than the Germans; yet Berliners who had introduced a water supply and sewerage system in the 1870s and 1880s had a longer life expectancy than Parisians who only finalized their central sewer system in 1894. Despite the urban improvements under Baron Georges Haussmann, the incidence of infectious diseases remained high in Paris, which in 1891 had a general mortality rate of 22 per 1,000 living in comparison with 21 in Berlin and 21 in London.[3]

While mortality for adults from infectious diseases was on the decline in all three cities, there were high rates of infant deaths until about 1900.[4] Infant mortality in Berlin 1891–5 was 359 per 1,000 live births.[5] Paris with its much lower birth rate had an infant mortality rate of 170 per 1,000 live births, and the infant mortality rate was 160 for the decade 1891–1900 in London.[6] Although it is the adult–infant dichotomy in mortality rates which is generally emphasized by historical demographers, it is often overlooked that child mortality was rising during the 1880s and 1890s. This was largely because of diphtheria epidemics. Eighty per cent of all deaths from diphtheria were among children under ten. Children, moreover, were the fastest-growing age group in the expanding urban populations.[7]

It was demonstrated in Berlin in 1890 that a cure for diphtheria was possible if antitoxin serum was administered. Hitherto bacteriologists had shown how diseases were spread, but apart from the use of disinfectants there had been no successful specific cures. Koch's tuberculin cure for TB, announced in 1890, was controversial. Medical researchers at Koch's Institute for Infectious Diseases in Berlin discovered the basic principle of serum therapy. This research was taken further in Berlin and at the Pasteur Institute in Paris, so that by 1894 large-scale production of sera was possible and clinical trials in children's hospitals could be carried out. If mechanisms for the general distribution of sera could be established, the prospect of science saving children's lives was held out. Indeed, the cure for diphtheria was to be regarded as a model for all diseases presumed to be infectious, including cancer. Groups of children, such as those in poor law hospitals, thus became vulnerable to the indiscriminate experimentation of certain medical enthusiasts. Medical research became the focus of public attention, and there was a utopian sense of being on the brink of a new era of scientific medicine when disease could be eradicated.

Diphtheria serum therapy played a crucial role in changing public attitudes to the hospital, from being feared as a custodial poor law institution to admiration as a place of healing for the children of a broad spectrum of the population. While the introduction of safe surgical techniques for minor children's operations (such as the removal of tonsils) may also have played a role, serum therapy was crucial in providing a reorientation of strategies to combat infectious diseases. Efforts to promote the cause of scientific therapies and preventive measures meant to the authorities that poverty could be erased from the medical discourse. Instead of attributing disease to social deprivation – to overcrowding, malnutrition and occupational hazards – disease could be effectively prevented and cured through antitoxin sera. Socialists campaigned for higher scientific standards of care in hospitals. The saving of children's lives was a rallying cry for all political persuasions. Scientific medicine as a means of social integration drew support from a range of social interests, and was linked to professionalization and the emergence of municipal welfare schemes. Not only was the city to become a vast laboratory, but the child was dissected in terms of physiology, biochemistry and immunology. In Berlin and Paris paediatrics was to emerge primarily as a hospital specialization with university chairs. In 1879 a chair of paediatrics was established in Paris, held from 1884 by the Pasteurian physician, Jacques Joseph Grancher. In Berlin a chair was established in 1894.[8] Although not a 'social disease' such as tuberculosis, which was an indicator of malnutrition and slum housing, diphtheria as an airborne disease could be exacerbated by overcrowding, and the bacilli were known to thrive in damp conditions.[9] Compulsory schooling, and damp and ill-ventilated buildings were thus held to be important factors in its spread.

ADMINISTRATIVE CONTRASTS

The advent of antitoxin serum posed the problems of economic and geographical access to therapy, and encountered obstacles arising from the fragmentation of public health authorities. No metropolis had a unitary administration for public health and hospitals at this time. Paris came closest, and indeed it was the Parisian hospital administration that became the international model in public hospital provision. But the increase in population resulting in the growth of the peripheral *banlieue* meant a plurality of authorities.[10] Until the 1870s public health was essentially a matter of administrative policing. Thereafter a twin process of professionalization and municipalization occurred throughout France. The 1875 administrative reforms gave the municipality of Paris greater powers, but the Department of the Seine retained much authority over public health. The interlocking state-municipal relations were analogous to the establishing of the Local Government Board in 1871 in England and Wales, and the Public Health Act of 1872.[11] Paris had a unique administrative position and public health administration, since without a democratically elected mayor, it was subject to direct state control.[12] Under a *Comité Consultatif d'Hygiène Publique de France*, there were departmental committees. The internal divisions within the state resulted in the division between the prefecture of police and departmental authorities, arising from the rivalries surrounding Haussmann.[13] The prefecture of police was responsible for infectious diseases and vaccination. The Prefect of the Seine supervised a hierarchical system of councils, including a departmental *Conseil d'Hygiène Publique et de Salubrité*. Each *arrondissement* had a commission of hygiene, which met monthly and dealt with such questions as cleansing, disinfection, housing and mortality statistics.[14] However, school hygiene, mortuaries and street cleaning came under different authorities. A central bureau of hygiene – although discussed since the 1870s – was not realized. From 1889 there was a campaign to support the municipalization of hygiene by radicals and democrats.

In Germany there was a dual state and municipal system of public health. Berlin, however, had no unitary municipality: it was a city divided between the *Magistrat* – an area corresponding to central Berlin, and peripheral municipalities such as Charlottenburg, Schöneberg and Spandau. It was only in 1881 that Berlin constituted a separate administrative district (or *Stadtkreis*) of the Prussian state. The state authorities administered health through the Police Presidium in Berlin. Medical officers – known as *Kreisärzte* – were employed on a part-time basis and in an advisory capacity in the province of Brandenburg-Berlin.[15] During the 1850s and 60s a formalized system of poor law doctors emerged.[16] But by the 1890s there was much dissatisfaction with poor law medicine. The newly legalized socialist party (the SPD) campaigned against the poor law system as depriving the recipients of civil rights. Socialists in the Erfurt programme of 1892 argued in favour of municipalization of medical administration and hospitals – emulating the demands of French radicals.

In London the centralizing force of Chadwick's Board of Health had been checked, and the Local Government Act of 1871 placed public health firmly in the context of local government and the poor law. The medical officer of health was an employee of the local vestries, which tended to be obstructive when it came to expenditure on medical facilities. By the 1890s responsibility for public health was divided between medical officers of health, the vestries, local Poor law guardians, and the emergent metropolitan authorities – the Board of Works, the Board of Guardians, the Metropolitan Asylums Board (MAB) and the London County Council (LCC), as well as the central authority of the Lunacy Commissioners. Dorothy Porter (née Watkins) has undertaken a prosopographical study of metropolitan medical officers. She suggests that the Local Government Act of 1888, requiring the professional qualifications of a sanitary diploma, was a precondition for a rapid improvement in public health administration.[17] The quality of the administration improved somewhat with the Public Health (London) Act of 1891 when the LCC undertook to pay half the salary of medical officers. This resulted in a new breed of professional with knowledge of bacteriology and epidemiology. In 1892 an Institute of Public Health was established to provide professional training, and there was a new interest in preventive technologies and hospital services.

Since 1789 Paris had an innovative lead in hospital provision. In 1802 the *Hôpital des Enfants-Malades* (also known as *L'Enfant-Jésus*) was founded in rue de Sèvres. Sometimes described as the first modern children's hospital, it had 629 beds for patients aged between 2 and 15 by 1893, and was a centre of paediatric research. Among other children's hospitals in Paris were the *Enfants-Assistés* and the *Hôpital Trousseau*, the latter having over 500 beds by the 1890s. There were also convalescent homes such as that at Forges-les-Bains (established in 1859) and that for tuberculous children founded at the seaside resort of Berck-sur-mer in 1864.

During the 1860s the conviction grew that it was necessary to separate age groups and to isolate patients with different infectious diseases. By the 1870s the success of Lister's antiseptic practices and knowledge of germ theory rendered isolation a priority, and emphasized the custodial function of hospitals. The pavilion system of hospital design, introduced in France in the 1840s, was given a new importance by germ theories of contagion. The *Enfants-Malades* and *Sainte Eugénie* were provided in 1879–82 with isolation pavilions for patients with diphtheria. Defects in the system led to isolation pavilions being built at the *Hôpital Trousseau* in 1888. Thus in 1892 the surgical and medical services were rigorously separated. Although plans to build separate hospitals for specific diseases, located outside Paris to ensure total isolation, did not come to fruition, the system of isolation became yet more rigorous. J.J. Grancher introduced the system of a 'box grillage isolant' (isolation cubicles) subdividing wards, and antiseptic practices became even more stringent. The design of beds was also improved so as to permit disinfection. These measures were instituted immediately prior to the introduction of serum therapy, and it was claimed that they had a beneficial effect in reducing mortality from diphtheria. Emile Roux, Pasteur's medical disciple, was among those who in 1894 urged isolation cells for patients with diphtheria.[18]

Since 1848 there had been a single administrative authority for the Paris hospitals, the *Assistance Publique* which co-ordinated improvements. This model authority came under the Prefect of the Seine and ultimately the Minister of the Interior. The *Assistance Publique* had responsibility for the administration of hospitals, asylums, orphanages and the home care bureaux. It also had independent sources of income with investments in urban and rural properties. The increase in the value of this property in the course of the century enabled modernization of the hospital system to be financed.[19]

When Haussmann was Prefect of the Seine, hospital reform was a low priority; stress was given to developing systems of domiciliary care under the poor law.[20] By the 1890s there was much dissatisfaction with this. In order to replace the paternalistic charity dispensed by *bureaux de bienfaisance*, demands were made at a municipal level for *bureaux d'assistance*. Public assistance marked a break with the paternalistic concept of *bienfaisance*, as it was suggested that there be elected representatives rather than notables appointed by the Prefect.[21] During the 1890s there was expansion of the scope of infant welfare provisions – undertaken by the *Assistance Publique* since 1874, as single mothers became eligible for relief. Scientific hygiene eroded moralistic concerns with the depravity of the working classes. But there was a lack of a link between the hospital and the welfare offices. It was felt that this could be provided by dispensaries – analogous to the Russian *ambulatorium* or English dispensaries.[22] The culmination of these reforms came with the law of December 1892 that 'every Frenchman deprived of financial resources shall receive without charge . . . medical aid in the home and if he cannot be cared for there, in a hospital'. This law only became operational in 1897. The development of serum therapy thus occurred at a crucial intervening phase.

Whereas German municipalities lagged behind Britain as regards the appointment of full-time medical officers, municipalities like Berlin led the way in hospital provision. In 1830 the first German children's clinic was established at the state *Charité* hospital. The foundation in 1843 of the Elisabeth Hospital and in 1844 of the Louisa Hospital in Berlin were part of a wave of new children's hospitals in Germany during the 1840s. Although German municipalities were obliged to care for the sick poor, the sickness insurance system and socialist advocacy of a nationalized hospital system provided a stimulus to the building of municipal hospitals. The municipality of Berlin founded a hospital in 1874, using the pavilion system which had been introduced into Germany after the war of 1866. By 1890 Berlin had municipal hospitals at Moabit and Am Urban, as well as an asylum and a special hospital for TB. By 1900 six municipal hospitals had 3,108 beds, representing one bed per 630 inhabitants. (London achieved one bed per 1,000 in 1903.) In 1893 a single committee to direct all municipal hospitals was established, replacing the system of separate hospital boards. This combined supervisory powers over public health and hospitals in 1896.[23] From 1886 there was a disinfection centre, which from 1890 undertook disinfection of houses where there were cases of diphtheria. This was a sign of an increasingly interventionist public health policy. In 1899 a municipal health department was considered, but this was only established in 1907.[24] German socialists, arguing that hospitals were necessary to compensate for poor housing, criticized the slowness of these developments. They considered that by 1900 Berlin was short of at least 1,000 beds, despite an increasing number of hospitals and convalescent homes. They maintained that hospitals should be at the centre of a national system of public health – here taking a cue from the writings of Havelock Ellis.[25]

Berlin also had a flourishing voluntary tradition, encouraged by such leading public health reformers as the liberal politician and pathologist, Rudolf Virchow. Voluntarism was fostered by the limitations of sickness insurance which was only for the insured worker and not family dependants. The late 1880s saw an intensification of voluntary initiatives in establishing children's hospitals: the Elisabeth Hospital was rebuilt in 1887.[26] A citizens' committee, presided over by Virchow, collected funds for a children's hospital for infectious diseases – the *Kaiser und Kaiserin Friedrich* Children's Hospital, which opened in May 1890.[27] Yet funding continued to be a problem, and the hospital was taken over as a municipal hospital in 1900. The design of this hospital was on the isolation principle. There were separate pavilions for diphtheria, scarlet fever, measles, whooping cough, surgery and general medicine. The pavilions were internally subdivided into cubicles for patients, and the diphtheria pavilion contained separate operating facilities. The hospital director, Adolf Baginsky, advocated comprehensive isolation facilities, based on single-floor pavilions, each with its own medical and nursing staff, so as to prevent cross-infection.[28]

The public and voluntary division in Berlin was paralleled by the division between voluntary and Poor Law hospitals in London. The Hospital for Sick Children in Great Ormond Street was inspired by the Paris Children's Hospital, although a determined effort was made to maintain higher hygienic standards.[29] Its foundation in 1852 marked the beginning of a spate of voluntary foundations of children's hospitals. These included the Victoria Hospital for Children in Chelsea in 1866, the Alexandra Hospital for hip diseases in 1867, the Evelina in Southwark in 1869, and finally the Cheyne Hospital for Incurable Children in 1875. While late nineteenth-century commentators such as Edmund Hake contrasted the 'tenderness and care' of the voluntary hospitals to the 'government-regulated institutions' where patients could become 'subjects for scientific experiment', the muted response to serum therapy in the voluntary sector suggests that by then some of the dynamism had gone out of the voluntary system.[30] In 1892 the Charity Organization Society attempted to establish a central co-ordinating agency for the London voluntary hospitals, and put its case to a Select Committee of the House of Lords. Again the model was the Parisian *Assistance Publique*. A central hospitals council, founded in November 1897, proved to be ineffective.[31] Although the Lords report received a favourable response, it was in fact the MAB which took a series of timely initiatives.

The MAB arose from the Metropolitan Poor Act of 1867 to provide hospitals for the sick poor, and was in part modelled on the *Assistance Publique* in Paris. It aimed to provide hospital beds for patients with infectious diseases (often excluded from the other voluntary hospitals) and in particular to cater for patients with diseases such as smallpox and diphtheria. The Public Health (London) Act of 1891 extended the Board's responsibilities to non-destitute but infectious patients. By 1900, 84 per cent of MAB patients were under 15, in effect making its hospitals primarily children's hospitals.[32] The MAB drew up a comprehensive strategy to cope with the expansion of London's population in the outer metropolitan districts. Thus in London as in Berlin a central hospital authority emerged, emulating the Parisian model. Within institutions intended for paupers generally, children had come to be singled out as a constituency in need of special medical services.

RESEARCH INSTITUTIONS

During the 1890s it was hoped that large-scale research institutions could have a major impact on public health. Paris and Berlin were competing as international centres of medical research. London lagged behind: science did not occupy the same importance in the medical profession, and there was less pressure to develop research institutes and teaching posts in new medical specialisms such as paediatrics. The establishment of the Pasteur Institute in 1888 represented an innovative model of a medical research institution in a metropolitan centre. It was a private initiative, arising from the success of the anti-rabies serum, although it benefited from state and municipal grants. It was emulated in Berlin in 1891, when the Institute for Infectious Diseases was founded for Koch in order to develop his tuberculin therapy. The Institute was financed solely by the Prussian state. It was sited in the centre of Berlin, close to the *Charité* state hospital, whereas the Pasteur Institute was on the southern peripheries of Paris in the 15th *arrondissement*, owing to Pasteur's wish for a spacious site. Koch's Institute had clinical facilities, but the Pasteur Institute had only a public dispensary for anti-rabies serum.[33]

In 1889 the Lord Mayor of London chaired a fund to send cases of rabies to the Pasteur Institute (much to the horror of anti-vivisectionists who denounced Pasteur and his methods). At this time the only specialized research institute in London was the Brown Animal Welfare Institute, which had dual functions as an animal hospital and as a physiological research institute of London University. The Brown Institute was a target for anti-vivisectionists, however, as was the newly established laboratory of the Royal College of Surgeons.[34] Plans for a privately funded British Institute of Preventive Medicine in 1893, to emulate the Pasteur Institute, also foundered on protests from the anti-vivisection lobby.[35] Thus, while the Board of Trade refused to recognize it as a limited liability company, the public were reluctant to make donations.[36] Indeed mass demonstrations by anti-vivisectionists broke out in 1894 when a donation of £25,000 was received by the Institute for a bacteriological laboratory, and production of diphtheria antitoxin. The fact that the Institute was to be sited in Chelsea hardly helped matters since there were known to be high death rates there as a result of the exploratory surgery conducted at the Chelsea Hospital for Women. Protesters stated that the Institute was liable to experiment on poor hospital patients repeating 'the barbarities of the Pasteur Institute'.[37] Anti-vivisection and voluntary initiatives, characteristics of Victorian London, hampered initiatives of medical researchers.[38] Eventually, a site was secured in Chelsea Gardens, and the Institute opened in 1897 – significantly later than its French or German counterparts. The next step was a private appeal for research funds – raising only £5,700 of which £5,000 were provided by Lord Iveagh of the Guinness family. The Institute only became solvent through a further donation from Lord Iveagh of £250,000 in 1903.[39]

EPIDEMIOLOGY

It has been important to discuss administrative structures before comparing the actual incidence of diphtheria. Reports by medical officers of health provide an uncertain indication of actual health conditions. As a notifiable disease in Berlin from 1884 and in London from 1889, there were statistics on both the incidence and the mortality from diphtheria. But notification was problematic as there was a high rate of children carrying diphtheria bacilli, but not showing any symptoms of the disease. The notion of diphtheria as a contagious disease was very much a product of nineteenth-century advances in pathology and bacteriology. The Registrar-General grouped diphtheria together with scarlet fever until 1859. Opinions differed over what constituted diphtheria and whether it was distinguishable from croup – a severe form of laryngitis. It was observed that the bacillus varied in virulence in different localities and over time. Many doctors preferred to rely for diagnosis on clinical observations rather than bacteriology. Moreover, the compulsory isolation and disinfection resulting from notification of the disease meant that there were incentives not to comply with regulations. On the other hand, the apparent rise in diphtheria occurred at a time when bacteriology and serum therapy were being introduced. Medical science created the possibilities for diagnosing diphtheria as a distinct disease and then created the possibilities of a specific 'cure'.

Administrative structures varied. While local statistics of diphtheria mortality rates exist for London boroughs or Paris *arrondissements*, for Berlin there are aggregate mortality statistics by locality but no local data on specific diseases apart from those in the peripheral municipalities. Mortality rates also varied, so that contrasting trends can be discerned in different districts.[40] When mortality in London was at a high point in 1893 with 76 per 1,000 living, in Paris deaths were plunging to an all-time low. In Paris diphtheria mortality rates fell from around 77 in 1890 to 18 in 1895.[41] Deaths from diphtheria in Berlin reached 242 in 1883, but plunged to 34 in 1896.[42]

While there are statistics on the use of serum therapy in public hospitals, it is not always possible to find out about how soon the serum was administered and in what quantities. Patients often rushed to hospital suffering only from a mild sore throat. The anti-toxin sera was administered without a diagnostic test, and numbers of children who did not actually have diphtheria could boost the statistics of successful cures. A substantial proportion would in any case have recovered. Thus assertions as to the effectiveness of the serum therapy rightly encountered scepticism.[43]

INSTITUTIONAL RESPONSES

Emile Roux at the Pasteur Institute pioneered immunization of horses during 1892–3, which enabled the mass production of anti-diphtheria serum. In Paris the Council of Hygiene established a municipal hygiene laboratory, and supervised the distribution of sera. This was provided free of charge by the Pasteur Institute. The bureau of public assistance, established in July 1893, formed a network for the distribution of serum.

The Paris hospitals were used for clinical trials of the serum therapy. It was fortuitous that the Pasteur Institute was only five minutes' walk away from the Hospital for Sick Children. Alexandre Yersin, a young doctor at this hospital, had alerted Roux to the problem of diphtheria prevention, and the hospital was used for the first clinical trials from January 1894. The *Assistance Publique* strongly supported this. Indeed the President of the Republic attended an experimental immunization.[44] The *Assistance Publique* improved public access to the therapy by opening new diphtheria 'barracks' at a cost of half a million francs in 1895 at the hospital of Aubervilliers in the *banlieue*.[45] In 1896 there was an ambitious scheme to replace the Trousseau Hospital by three hospitals. This scheme involved the sale of the Trousseau site to the municipality for five million francs, the conversion of another hospital (*L'Hôpital Herold* for children) and the establishing of new hospitals in Montmartre (in the 18th *arrondissement*) and in the 12th *arrondissement*.[46] Each hospital was to have the best modern facilities, including facilities for surgery and hydrotherapy, gymnasia and facilities for dental treatment, as well as wards for contagious diseases and diphtheria treatment. There were also outpatient dispensaries. Their siting was to ensure that mothers should not have too great a distance to travel. These hospitals were to have a total of 684 beds.[47] However, the plans were too ambitious and the project had to be scaled down during the following year.[48]

Whereas the Pasteur Institute had a virtual monopoly of serum production, in Germany there was competition between the chemical manufacturers Hoechst and Schering. Because of concern that competition would reduce standards, the state health authorities and medical researchers initially agreed that a central state institution for serum testing was necessary. In November 1894 the director of the *Charité* suggested the foundation of a national institute for serum research and therapy under Emil Behring in Berlin. A committee under royal patronage was to launch a massive public appeal to finance the Institute. This plan to emulate the Pasteur Institute was only to be partially realized, as an Institute for Serum Testing and Experimental Therapy was founded with joint state, municipal and private finance in Frankfurt. It represented an important model of a national medical research institute, on a charitable basis later realized for infant welfare.

During the autumn of 1892 the first experimental immunizations were conducted at Koch's infectious diseases wards and at the children's clinic of the *Charité*.[49] In May 1894, after trials in five Berlin hospitals, it was established that the children treated on the first day showed the best rates of cure.[50] At the *Kaiser und Kaiserin Friedrich* Children's Hospital the paediatrician Baginsky conducted clinical trials for the new therapy from March 1894 for a ten-month period.[51] The municipality financed the costs of treating sick children at this hospital. The new serum of Aronson – who was Virchow's protégé – was tested here. The coincidence of Virchow's role in the founding of the hospital and the use of serum developed by a protégé should be noted. By way of contrast the Prussian authorities supported the use at the *Charité* of the Behring-Ehrlich serum manufactured by Hoechst.

It was not until 1894 that serum therapy was used in Britain. At a time when there were hundreds of horses producing serum in Berlin and Paris, a single horse was immunized at the Brown Institute; when a relative of the physiologist Charles Sherrington fell ill, the serum was quickly utilized.[52] The Local Government Board's policy was essentially voluntaristic. It decided in 1894 that while prepared to monitor the spread of diphtheria, it 'should not take any part in supplying materials for the treatment and prevention of the disease'.[53] Yet during 1894 the MAB increased the number of beds available for diphtheria patients. In October 1894 the MAB began to consider provision of facilities for the antitoxin treatment, and an experimental trial period began for six months in December 1894; this 'experimental phase' was periodically renewed until the treatment became routine in 1897. However, medical superintendents of the MAB had found that they could not obtain sufficient antitoxin sera.[54] In December 1894 the MAB accepted the offer of the royal colleges of physicians and surgeons to supply antitoxin (using three horses). The laboratories were also to carry out routine diagnoses. The aim was that comprehensive statistical trials could be conducted by the Clinical Society in order to assess the therapy.[55] The Board rejected as 'unfair' the suggestion that it should compare patients treated with antitoxin with patients not so treated. Instead it compared the records of patients not treated with antitoxin during 1894 with the rates of those treated in successive years.

Serum therapy came at a crucial time for the MAB. It had already begun to expand facilities for infectious diseases. A cholera epidemic – expected from Hamburg – did not materialize, but rates of infection from diphtheria were rising. The Board's hospitals had first admitted diphtheria patients in 1888. The opening of the North Eastern Hospital in Tottenham, Fountain Hospital in Lower Tooting from 1893, the Brook Hospital in Woolwich from 1896, Park Hospital in Hither Green from 1897, and Tooting Grove from 1899, raised the number of beds for fever and diphtheria from 2,070 to 4,544.[56] The social spectrum of those admitted broadened. As the MOH for Woolwich observed, 'all classes in the borough make use of the fever hospitals, the middle class less so than the working class, but it is by no means unusual for the professional and well-to-do classes to send their children to these hospitals'.[57] A series of MAB reports confirmed that the antitoxin serum was effective if promptly administered. Whereas in 1890 17.9 per cent of notified cases were admitted to Board hospitals, by 1900 72.5 per cent were so admitted.[58] The Webbs argued that speedy and efficient administration of antitoxin meant a financial saving to public health authorities.[59]

Laboratories symbolized the new scientific approach to therapy. On 24 May 1894 the *Assistance Publique* agreed to a laboratory for microbiology at the *Hôpital des Enfants-Malades* and one was established at the *Hôpital Trousseau*.[60] In 1895 the council of public hygiene of the 3rd *arrondissement* petitioned that the prefecture of police establish a central laboratory of bacteriology for the diagnosis of infectious diseases. This was sited in an annex of the town hall.[61]

The instituting of a municipal laboratory in Berlin was controversial as it raised the issue of whether there should be a central health office. There were also tensions within Koch's Institute which performed routine diagnostic tests. Koch was jealous of the success of Behring, and denied him research facilities. Behring and Paul Ehrlich rented an arch under the urban railway to stable horses. They required separate facilities for the manufacture and distribution of sera. Public appeals were made by Behring, Ehrlich and Wassermann to raise funds for serum research.[62] Not only was Koch's Institute cramped on its central site, it was overly rigid in structure when compared to the Pasteur Institute. In 1896 Virchow supported plans to relocate Koch's Institute next to a planned fourth municipal hospital. This was seen as a 'condominium' between state and municipality, increasing the utility of and services for medical research.

It was as a result of professional pressure arising from the British Institute for Public Health (representing the interests of metropolitan MOHs) in November 1894, that the MAB entered into an arrangement for the early diagnosis of diphtheria with the Royal College of Physicians (RCP) and the Royal College of Surgeons.[63] The MAB's aim remained the establishment of its own bacteriological laboratory. It argued for this on both scientific and economic grounds, as laboratory tests would provide a means of excluding cases of sore throat which were not diphtheria, and because isolating the centres of infection might reduce the spread of the disease.[64] In November 1896 it was decided that MAB hospitals should conduct their own bacteriological tests. The MAB continued to fund the stables at the RCP laboratory for serum production.[65] The Metropolitan Branch of the Society of Medical Officers of Health pressed for a central laboratory, but testing facilities in London continued on a decentralized basis.[66] The MAB functioned independently from the MOHs as admissions came through Poor law guardians in any district. But in November 1897 it was agreed that when there was no room for a diphtheria case, supplies of the serum should be given to the MOH or a general practitioner.[67]

PUBLIC IMPACT

The health of the child was an emotive issue, which had a strong appeal in the context of the Victorian idealization of the family and of the domestic sphere for women and children. Newspapers took a key role in sensationalizing the discovery of the diphtheria serum and in organizing public subscriptions to fund its free distribution. This was partly self-interested, as it was also a means of boosting their circulations. The model was established by *Le Figaro*, of which the editor, Gaston Calmette, was the brother of the medical researcher, Albert Calmette.[68] By the end of December 1894 Roux had raised £24,000 for the Pasteur Institute, with a further £4,000 voted by the state, and the municipality supported the costs of stabling twenty horses at a cost of £800 per annum in order to produce serum for the Paris hospitals and for the poor.[69]

Public support for experimentally based medicine boosted the position of laboratory researchers in France. Serum therapy proved to be the financial salvation of the Pasteur Institute, which until then was in an extremely precarious financial position. The popular rallying to the cause of the Pasteur Institute meant that it became a symbol of national achievement. As a national but non-governmental institution, it fitted in well with the prevailing integrationist ideologies of solidarism and mutualism. Anti-vivisectionism seems to have been less evident in France.[70]

Le Figaro's fund-raising strategy was emulated in Berlin by Rudolf Mosse, a liberal newspaper entrepreneur and pioneer of the advertising agency.[71] Mosse and another newspaper tycoon, August Scherl, organized public subscriptions – publishing details of each contribution – in order to make the new remedy available to the poor. Ehrlich and Wassermann gave public lectures in order to raise funds.[72]

There were also political undertones to scientific controversies over serum therapy. In 1892 Behring proclaimed serum therapy as the basis of a new experimental medicine in a popular article in *Der Zukunft*, a new periodical launched by Maximilian Harden, who was intellectually avant-garde but pro-Junker and pro-government. Behring took the opportunity to attack the economic and welfare-oriented approach to social medicine associated with Virchow.[73] Behring argued that his notions of the healing powers of the blood accorded with popular folk traditions.[74] This prompted Virchow to support the alternative Aronson group of researchers and producers for the municipal hospital. At the same time there was popular opposition to medical experimentation on the poor. Anti-vivisectionists protested that the poor were being treated as 'human guinea pigs'. The medical literature was systematically monitored for cases of human experimentation. The most notable case was the attempt to develop a serum therapy for syphilis, when Albert Neisser, a professor in Breslau, experimentally infected a group of children.[75] The anti-vivisection movement, which had close links with the anti-semitic parties, sought to extend its appeal by extending its arguments to the protection of children. Thus while medical researchers and anti-vivisectionists competed for the role of saviours of children, the success of serum therapy boosted the prestige of medical research and legitimized animal experiments.

In contrast to Paris and Berlin, popular enthusiasm for serum therapy was conspicuously lacking in London. The 'new treatment for diphtheria' was given only a single major article in *The Times* on 26 October 1894. This in itself seemed to confirm the view of the President of the Chemical Society, who in responding to the article, commented that 'British laissez faire' was a poor contrast to German 'industrial enterprise'.[76] Nevertheless, the Goldsmiths Company gave £1,000 to the Laboratory of the Royal College of Physicians.[77] Such giving – from one venerable London corporation to another – was typical of the more traditional civic structures of London. Certainly, the antitoxin discovery did little for the floundering British Institute of Preventive Medicine. Lister wrote to *The Times* requesting contributions to a special antitoxin fund. But the amount collected was paltry, and the Institute's aim of providing therapy was never realized.

The MAB's reliance on the rates meant that it did not need to make public appeals, and it made generous sums available for the building of children's hospitals. More important to it was the need to convert the medical profession and medical officers who were resistant to scientific medicine. Here the *Lancet* played a crucial role, observing that 'medical practitioners as a body, in this country, have not used the new remedy in the very general and extended way in which it has come into operation abroad'. This it ascribed to a distrust of bacteriology in the wake of disappointment over Koch's tuberculin therapy and to 'the conservative instincts of our countrymen'. In July 1896 it published an evaluation comparing the results of imported sera with British-produced sera. The German and French sera were found to be of a much higher strength than the much cheaper British product of Burroughs Wellcome.[78]

British voluntarism and private enterprise contrasted to centralized regulatory systems in France and Germany, which maintained higher standards. In each city there was a culturally distinctive ideology by means of which the profession and public could be mobilized to augment state resources. Whereas the French and German public were persuaded to contribute to medical science because of concern for children, in London public attitudes to science were distinctly unenthusiastic. Indeed, the British scepticism of science as having a coercive ethos surfaced in opposition to the expansive activities of the MAB. In March and April 1895 the Boards of Guardians of Hackney, Mile End, Islington and Stepney protested to the MAB 'against diphtheria patients being required to submit to the antitoxin treatment without their consent, or in the case of some children without the consent of their parents, and stating that they are in full sympathy with these views'.[79] On 27 April 1895 there was a petition from 480 ratepayers 'asking the Managers to put an end to the antitoxin treatment of the diphtheria patients in their hospitals'.[80] A further eight Boards raised similar protests in May of that year. The protests underlined the hostility of many Londoners to medical research though they did not prevent the MAB from providing children's hospitals.

In the absence of significant numbers of notable paediatricians or microbiologists in London, the capital's capacity for scientific-medical innovation in the area of child health was not promising. If an analysis is conducted at the level of the vestry or of individual medical officers, then the record of innovation in anti-diphtheria measures is uneven. Certain vestries were highly obstructive, and the capacity of medical officers greatly varied. At the same time the pluralistic local government structures allowed for a degree of innovation. The new breed of public health professionals and medical researchers made common cause. They found the bureaucracy of the MAB to be responsive, and a reforming momentum was initiated. Despite a fragmented Victorian structure of boards and local authorities, the dynamic activity of the MAB compares well to Paris and Berlin, which were innovative centres for medical research.

All three metropolitan centres had mixed state and voluntary systems which shaped approaches to child health. Although Paris had the most centralized system of public health and hospital administration, massive voluntary donations were necessary to support serum therapy. While charitable donations were conspicuously absent in London, much dynamism was evident in the state sphere. Berlin had a mixed state and municipal system, and here the state encouraged both voluntary and municipal initiatives. These developments show that welfare structures had an intrinsic complexity. Serum therapy indicates that it was possible for poor law structures to be modernized so as to provide modern children's hospitals and therapies. Existing structures of local government were bedevilled by problems of propertied interests, opposing public health reforms. This was particularly so in London, but there is also evidence of this in Paris, such as the householders' resistance to improvements in the installation of a radial sewerage system during the 1890s. In Berlin there was a restricted franchise based on property qualifications, although the civic authorities were keen to support public health initiatives from the mid-1890s, and spent one tenth of the city rates on hospital building. All three cities managed to overcome administrative and financial obstacles to providing therapeutic facilities.

In the longer term the medical researchers' bid for public admiration and funds in a fight to combat disease met with considerable success. Children's hospitals and isolation hospitals inhabited mainly by children were transformed into places of therapy, and public access was broadened. The public health laboratory and children's hospitals as centres of child health marked a contrast to approaches based on self-help or domestic welfare measures. The advent of mass immunization reinforced the scientific approach to child health. The next phase of public health was to focus on tuberculosis and infant welfare measures. These placed greater reliance on education and welfare measures such as dietary supplements and housing improvements in order to promote the body's physical capacity to resist infections. Serum therapy – although markedly different in scale and organization – was a crucial stage in bringing together the state and medical researchers, and in going some way to removing the stigma of poverty from public hospital care. It established that child health as a medical specialism was to be primarily hospital-based and to draw on a combination of voluntary and state financial and administrative resources.

NOTES

1 E.g. G. Behlmer, *Child Abuse and Moral Reform in England 1870–1908*, Stanford: Stanford University Press, 1982: 44.

2 C. Heywood, *Childhood in Nineteenth-century France: work, health and education among the 'classes populaires'*, Cambridge: Cambridge University Press, 1988: 1–3; M. F. Morel, 'Reflections on some recent French literature on the history of childhood', *Continuity and Change*, 1989, 4: 323–37.

3 B. R. Mitchell, *European Historical Statistics 1750–1975*, London: Macmillan, 1980: 86–136. *London Statistics*, 1909–10, 20: 54.

4 The infant mortality rate for France in 1890 was 174, in Germany 226, and in England and Wales 151.

5 W. R. Lee, 'Germany', in Lee (ed.) *European Economic and Population Growth*, London: Croom Helm, 1979: 187.

6 G. Ayers, *England's First State Hospitals and the Metropolitan Asylums Board 1867–1930*, London: Wellcome Institute for the History of Medicine, 1971: 123. *London Statistics*, 1909–10, 20: 53.

7 Behlmer, *Child Abuse*: 46.

8 H.-H. Eulner, *Die Entwicklung der medizinischen spezialfächer an den Universitäten des deutschen Sprachgebietes*, Stuttgart: Enke, 1970: 202–21.

9 A. Baginsky, *Diphtherie und diphtheritischer Croup*, Vienna: Hölder, 1898: 42–3.

10 L. R. Berlanstein, *The Working People of Paris, 1871–1914*, Baltimore and London: Johns Hopkins University Press, 1984: 56–65.

11 L. Murard and P. Zylberman, 'De l'hygiène comme introduction à la politique expérimentale (1875–1925)', *Revue de Synthèse*, 1984, 3rd series, 115: 313–41, 321.

12 M. Garet, *Le régime spécial de la ville de Paris en matière d'hygiène*, Paris, 1906.

13 Concerning Pietri since 1859.

14 The records of many of these are in the Archives de Paris.

15 *Dritter Verwaltungsbericht des königlichen Polizei-Presidiums von Berlin f. d. Jahren 1891 bis 1900*, Berlin, 1902.

16 Berlin Stadtarchiv Rep. 00/1407 betr. Armenkrankenpflege.

17 D. E. Watkins, 'The English revolution in social medicine 1889–1911', Ph.D. thesis, University of London, 1984: 80.

18 G.-R. Siguret, *Histoire de l'hospitalisation des enfants malades à Paris*, Paris, 1907: 68–87. A. Herbert and W. Douglas Hogg, 'Isolation wards and hospitals for contagious diseases in Paris', in J. S. Billings and H. M. Hurd (eds) *Hospitals, Dispensaries and Nursing*, Baltimore and London: Johns Hopkins and Scientific Press, 1894: 162–70.

19 Jean Imbert, L'Assistance publique à Paris de la Révolution française à 1977', *L'administration de Paris*: 79–109 (cited as offprint).

20 L. C. Groopman, 'The internat des hôpitaux de Paris: the shaping and transformation of the French medical élite, 1802–1914', Ph.D. thesis, Harvard University, 1986: 94–6.

21 J. H. Weiss, 'Origins of the French welfare state: poor relief in the Third Republic, 1871–1914', *French Historical Studies*, 1983, 13: 47–78. P. J. Weindling, 'The modernisation of charity in nineteenth-century France and Germany', in J. Barry and C. Jones (eds) *Medicine and Charity Before the Welfare State*, London: Routledge, 1991:190–206.

22 Report by Bompard, *Conseil municipal de Paris. Rapport au nom de la 5e commission sur le project pour réorganisation du services de secours à la domicile*, Paris, n.d: 23–4.

23 *Bericht über die Gemeinde Verwaltung der Stadt Berlin 1889 bis 1895*, Berlin, 1900: 162.

24 Berlin Stadtarchiv Rep. 00/1812.

25 A. Labisch, 'Das Krankenhaus in der Gesundheitspolitik der deutschen Sozialdemokratie vor dem Ersten Weltkrieg', in *Medizinische Soziologie, Jahrbuch*, 1981, 1: 126–51. H. Ellis, *The Nationalization of Health*, London: T. Fisher Unwin, 1892.

26 Berlin Stadtarchiv Rep. 00/1964 Elisabeth Kinder Spital.

27 Berlin Stadtarchiv Rep. 00/1936.

28 A. Baginsky, 'Ueber den Bau von Kinderkrankenhäusern, Isolierung und Verhütung der Uebertragung von Infektionskrankheiten, Verpflegung der Kranken', in Billings and Hurd (eds) *Hospitals*: 353–62.

29 J. Klosky, *Mutual Friends. Charles Dickens and Great Ormond Street Children's Hospital*, London: Weidenfield & Nicolson, 1989: 49.

30 A. E. Hake, *Suffering London*, London, 1892: 48.

31 G. Rivett, *The Development of the London Hospital System 1823–1982*, London: King Edward's Hospital Fund for London, 1986: 152.

32 Ayers, *State Hospitals*: 110

33 P. J. Weindling, 'Scientific élites and laboratory organisations in *fin de siècle* Paris and Berlin: the *Institut Pasteur* and Robert Koch's *Institut für Infektionskrankheiten* compared', in A. Cunningham and P. Wilson (eds), *Laboratory Medicine in the Nineteenth Century*, Cambridge: Cambridge University Press (in press).

34 R. D. French, *Anti-vivisection and Medical Science in Victorian Society*, Princeton: Princeton University Press, 1975: 274; M. A. Elston, 'Women and anti-vivisection in Victorian England', in N. A. Rupke (ed.) *Vivisection in Historical Perspective*, London: Croom Helm, 1987: 259–94.

35 *The Times*, 6 June 1891: 11.

36 *The Times* 28 April 1894: 12, for £25,000 donation for a bacteriological laboratory.

37 *The Times* 20 August 1894: 8.

38 A. Miles, 'The Lister Institute of Preventive Medicine 1891–1966', *Nature*, 1966, 212: 559–62.

39 R. J. Godlee, *Lord Lister*, London: Macmillan, 1917: 497–501. P. Alter, *The Reluctant Patron. Science and the State in Britain 1850–1920*, Oxford: Berg Publishers, 1987: 42.

40 A. Newsholme, *Epidemic Diphtheria*, London: Swan Sonnenschein, 1900: 57.

41 Newsholme, *Epidemic Diphtheria*: 32, 62–4.

42 Newsholme, *Epidemic Diphtheria*: 79.

43 Ayers, *State Hospitals*: 117.

44 Assistance Publique, *Conseil de surveillance*, 1894–5: 9–10.

45 *Conseil de surveillance*, 21 March 1895.

46 *Conseil de surveillance*, 1896: 291, 421.

47 *Conseil de surveillance*, 1895–6: 606, 610. Archives de Paris, Cote V. 36. M1 *Programme pour la construction de deux hôpitaux d'enfants. Concours d'avant-projet*, Montévrain, 1896.

48 *Conseil de surveillance*, 1896–7: 716–21.

49 H. Zeiss and R. Bieling, *Behring. Gestalt und Werk*, Berlin: Bruno Schultz Verlag, 1941: 102. P. J. Weindling, 'From medical research to clinical practice: serum therapy for diphtheria in the 1890s', in J. Pickstone (ed.) *Medical Innovation*, London: Macmillan, 1992: 72–83, 222–4.

50 *Behring*: 111.

51 A. Baginsky, *Serumtherapie der Diphtherie*, Berlin: Hirschwald, 1897.

52 T. Tansey, 'Charles Sherrington and the Brown Animal Sanatory Institution', *St Thomas's Hospital Gazette*, 1986 (cited as offprint). G. Wilson, 'The Brown Animal Sanatory Institution', *Journal of Hygiene*, 1979, 82: 155–76, 337–52, 501–21; 1979, 83: 171–97.

53 *The Times*, 2 November 1894.

54 *Metropolitan Asylums Board Minutes* (hereafter *MAB*), 1894–5, 28: 543.

55 *MAB*, 1894–5, 28: 542, 610.

56 Ayers, *State Hospitals*: 125.

57 Quoted in B. and S. Webb, *The State and the Doctor*, London: Longmans, Green, 1910: 158.

58 Ayers, *State Hospitals*: 119.

59 Webb and Webb, *The State and the Doctor*: 165.

60 *Conseil de surveillance*, 1893–4: 718.

61 *Conseil d'hygiène publique et de salubrité*, 1896: 286.

62 *Comite zur Beschaffung von Heilserum für Unbemittelte*.

63 *The Times*, 1 August 1895: 9.

64 *MAB*, 24 November 1894, 28: 517–20.

65 *MAB*, 1896–7, 30: 609, 704; 1897–8, 31: 773.

66 Ibid: 189.

67 *MAB*, 20 November 1897, 31: 626.

68 *Le Figaro*, 12 October 1894.

69 *The Times*, 4 January 1895: 6.

70 P. Elliott, 'Vivisection and the emergence of experimental physiology in nineteenth-century France', in Rupke (ed.) *Vivisection*: 48–77.

71 W. E. Mosse, 'Rudolf Mosse and the house of Mosse 1807–1920', *Leo Baeck Institute Yearbook*, 1959, 4: 237–59.

72 *Comite zur Beschaffung von Heilserum für Unbemittelte*.

73 E. Behring, 'Das neue Diphtheriemittel', *Die Zukunft*, 1894, 3, no. 3: 97–109; 1894, 3, no. 6: 249–64.

74 E. Behring, 'Einleitende Bemerkungen über die ätiologische Therapie von ansteckenden Krankheiten', *Gesammelte Abhandlung zur ätiologische Therapie von ansteckenden Krankheiten*, Leipzig: Georg Thieme, 1893.

75 B. Elkeles, 'Medizinische Menschenversuche gegen Ende des 19. Jahrhunderts und der Fall Neisser', *Medizinhistorisches Journal*, 1895, 20: 135–48.

76 *The Times*, 30 October 1894: 3.

77 *The Times*, 26 November 1894.

78 'Report of the Lancet special commission on the relative strengths of diphtheria antitoxin serums', *Lancet*, 1896, 2: 182–95.

79 *MAB*, 1895–6, 29: 6, 38, 109.

80 Ibid: 38.

6

CLEVELAND IN HISTORY
The abused child and child protection, 1880–1914

Harry Ferguson

Of all the policies and practices that have emerged in the name of the child over the past century none now compels attention with such strength and poignancy as those focused on child abuse. Arguably, it is *the* social problem of our time, and in Britain the name Cleveland has become its synonym.

Cleveland, a county in the north-east of England which includes the towns of Middlesbrough, Stockton-on-Tees and Hartlepool, became a centre of attention in 1987 when what were regarded as unprecedented numbers of children were diagnosed by doctors as the victims of sexual abuse. The children were removed from parental custody by social workers for the purposes of further investigation. Following the social and political reactions to these events, what became known as the 'Cleveland affair' or the 'Cleveland crisis' unfolded.[1] Central to the controversy were interconnected questions over the way in which professionals in the employ of the state gained access to suspected abused children, how the process of referral to doctors operated, and what actually were the duties and responsibilities of the medical profession. Cleveland doctors appeared to go beyond established conventions by taking initiatives in the examination of suspected cases; furthermore, they appeared to use new medical criteria for selecting *which* children to examine. Of the children who were examined, further questions were raised over the nature of the medical interventions: what parts of the children's bodies could legitimately be examined? How reliable were the diagnostic methods in relation to child sexual abuse? And how were signs of abuse to be defined and interpreted? All such questions became a part of the Cleveland affair.[2]

Nor was this all; complexities at the professional and technical levels were compounded by those at the social level (so far as the two can be separated). Thus, while some mothers welcomed the interventions of the state in protecting their children, others appeared to support the men who were suspected of sexually abusing children – usually their sons and daughters. Support groups gained powerful advocates among local (male) members of parliament who challenged the power of the state to define abuse and to intervene to remove children from families.[3] The 'sanctity of the family' was exploited in the courts and in popular demonstrations aimed at resisting the power of the state, and these responses were spurred by mass media who orchestrated support for the parents. Judges dealing with abuse cases were berated in the popular press for 'relying on the "paper qualifications" of psychologists – instead of trusting the judgement of trained social workers',[4] while elsewhere in the media the competence and trustworthiness of social workers (as well as doctors) were called into question.[5] Thus the floodgates were opened for struggles between the respective rights and powers of parents, children, doctors, psychologists, social workers, politicians and the courts in the arbitration of definitions and meanings of child abuse and legitimate protection policies and practices. Through it all, Cleveland *the place* was turned into 'Cleveland' the *metaphor* for controversies of national and international importance. In effect, 'Cleveland' was rendered a symbol of the powerful ambivalences surrounding child abuse: over whose construction of 'abuse' holds truth, and over the power of class, gender and national and local cultures in the determination of appropriate policies and practices.

A CALL TO HISTORY

Lord Justice Butler-Sloss in her (government-sponsored) *Report of the Inquiry into Child Abuse in Cleveland in 1987* fully acknowledged that the context of the affair was one in which awareness of child abuse had greatly increased. What the report neglected to consider, however, was whether there might also be a history both to the awareness of child (sexual) abuse and to the ambivalences raised by it and child protection. Unwittingly, it only confirmed the tendency noted by George Behlmer in the afterword to his *Child Abuse and Moral Reform in England, 1870–1908* (1982) – that one of the major effects of the recent interest in child abuse was a foreshortening of historical perspectives and a belittling of the child protection work done in the past.[6] Ironically, however, not only were the tensions surrounding Cleveland not new, but within

Cleveland itself were some of the richest sources for assembling a history of 'Cleveland'. As it happened, it was while I was in the course of researching this local material that the Cleveland affair broke. As a study of local practices, this chapter's perspective on the history of the abused child and child protection is therefore even more heavily informed than was originally intended by key issues surrounding the contemporary politics, policies and practices of the social regulation of parent–child relations. But, for this, no apology seems necessary. Nor, given the symbolic significance that Cleveland has acquired, is special pleading now required for the geographical focus, even if, strictly speaking, Cleveland the county did not exist as such in the period 1880–1914.[7] As for my chronology, this is simply accounted for in that it was the period, as I will elaborate, in which the modern concept of 'child abuse' was socially constructed, and in which the mapping out and standardization of procedures and policies for child protection took place. But the grounding of the modern concept of child abuse and child protection was far from simply accomplished, nor was it a once-and-for-all event. To investigate it at the level of local practices is to expose a construction which was far more plastic and contested than many – more policy-oriented – histories and child welfare texts would lead us to believe.[8]

PUTTING CHILD PROTECTION IN PLACE

In the years between the 1880s and the First World War (indeed, to the Second World War), the balance of influence in child protection practices between state agencies and the National Society for the Prevention of Cruelty to Children (NSPCC) was almost the opposite of that existing today. Whereas in the *Report of the Inquiry into Child Abuse in Cleveland* the NSPCC was given a minor role in child protection, in the period that concerns us here, the Society was uniformly recognized as the primary organization in the formulation of child-protection policy and practice. As with the child guidance movement in the inter-war period (discussed in this volume by Deborah Thom), the model for the NSPCC came from the United States, where societies of this sort were organized in 1875, the first of them in New York.[9] In Britain the first society was established in Liverpool in 1883, and this was quickly followed by the London Society for the Prevention of Cruelty to Children. The latter, under its charismatic first director, the Congregationalist Revd Benjamin Waugh, was that from which the national movement arose in 1889.[10]

The NSPCC had two broad aims: to press for the reform of the criminal law surrounding the social regulation of parent–child relations, and to develop an inspectorate that could investigate cases of suspected cruelty to children. By 1889 crucial steps had been taken towards fulfilling both these objectives. The Prevention of Cruelty to Children (PCC) Act of that year made it an offence punishable by fine and imprisonment for any person who had custody, control or charge of a child to ill-treat, neglect, abandon, or expose them in a manner likely to cause unnecessary suffering. The Act also placed further restrictions on child-employment and child-hawking, rendering the accountable adult punishable rather than the child. Provisions were made in the Act for children suspected of being abused to be taken into custody until the case was determined, and for this purpose warrants could be obtained to search for suspected victims of cruelty and to have them medically examined. Finally, the Act enabled children who had been cruelly treated to be taken out of the custody of parents and be delivered by order of the court to designated persons or sheltering institutions.[11]

Upon these legal foundations a national network of twenty-nine NSPCC inspectors was established. By 1914, there were 258 inspectors investigating some 55,000 cases per annum. Over the whole of the period from 1884 to 1914, 812,682 complaints were investigated, involving some 2,260,292 children and 1,073,088 parents. Some 3,141,445 visits of supervision were made to the homes of children suspected of abuse. Prosecutions took place in 55,292 cases.[12] By the end of our period the PCC acts of 1894 and 1904 had widened the definitions of cruelty and refined the state powers to enforce them. The Children's Act of 1908 further consolidated these powers and provisions, and established children's courts within which they could be administered. In the same year, for the first time in British history, incest was criminalized through the Punishment of Incest Act.

Although the organization of the NSPCC has been relatively well documented, little is known of its branch aid committees through which child protection actually came to be practised in localities. The decision to establish such Committees was taken by the London SPCC in June 1888 with a view to 'extending its Prevention of Cruelty to Children to every place and victim in the land'.[13] In Middlesbrough a branch aid committee was formed in June 1888 after a public meeting had been convened to hear an address by Benjamin Waugh. Waugh had been invited to speak by the local Sunday School Union – then one of the most carefully organized and powerful voluntary bodies in the town – which, at an earlier meeting, had worried over 'the condition of the children of Middlesbrough, especially those in the streets of the town at night'.[14] Other aid committees were soon established in the area – being among the first twenty in the national network. Stockton and Thornaby joined together to form one in December 1888, their explicit objective being 'to detect and bring to justice those parents who treat their children in an inhuman manner'.[15] Hartlepool established its committee in January 1889 in response to a letter of encouragement from Waugh. Thus within in a short space of time the Cleveland area was covered with child protection societies, each of them conducting public relations, fund-raising and selective casework management. Executive committees were formed to carry out these duties, and their members met monthly to manage affairs. For them and their supporters the annual general meetings of the branches were the high point on the child protectors' calendar.

Members of the branch aid committees were drawn from the local élites and were dominated by clergymen and members of the judiciary. Typical was the Middlesbrough branch whose first secretary was the Revd Henry Crane, of the Cannon Street Congregational chapel. Out of the first forty-seven subscribers to the Stockton and Thornaby branch, eight were church ministers and four were JPs, while in the Hartlepool branch, six out of sixteen members of the executive in the first year were JPs. These interests continued to dominate the executive committees of the branches throughout the period, despite the fact that by the turn of the century the participation of 'working men' in the NSPCC had been formally written into the constitutions of local branches.[16] Hugh Bell, the region's major industrialist, supported the movement from the start and eventually became a vice-president of the branch.[17]

For women, though they were active in the branch aid committees from the outset, space was rationed. The 1893 constitution of the Stockton and Thornaby branch, for example, stated that its executive was to consist of not more than fourteen members, 'four of them to be ladies'.[18] In practice, women's duties largely revolved around fund-raising. The major exception was the central role that women played in maintaining the NSPCC's children's shelters which were established in the early 1890s. Each of the shelters employed a matron for the day-to-day tasks, and each had a managing committee of ladies who regularly visited. In Stockton each of the women on the managing committee undertook a fortnight's responsibility for the shelter twice a year.[19] Most of these women were the wives, daughters, or sisters of the men involved in the branches and should therefore be seen as extending into the public domain the philanthropy, domestic management and business acumen that they developed in conjunction with them.[20] Some of the women established public identities of their own, the best example being Lady Florence Bell of Middlesbrough, the wife of Hugh Bell, who was a member of that branch's committee from the early 1900s until the First World War, and who became a leading philanthropist, social investigator and woman writer of the period.[21]

Although the scope of the work that child protectors performed does not appear to compare with that of other Victorian moral reformers who took to the streets to rescue 'street arabs',[22] in their localities they were discreetly effective in providing referral information leading to the investigation of suspected cases of cruelty.[23] But casework, while performed by inspectors and administered and controlled locally, was ultimately under the central management of the Society's London headquarters. Committees were obliged to follow a strict administrative procedure, particularly with regard to the most serious cases of suspected child cruelty in which case files were forwarded to the Society's legal department in London, who made the final decisions on how to proceed.[24] Since it was the NSPCC-influenced local judiciary who usually heard the cases, it was commonplace in the 1890s for child protectors who were JPs to address the annual branch meetings with praise for the quality and scale of NSPCC casework brought before them on local benches.[25]

After branch aid committees were established it was often a few years before the function of these committees became apparent. When asked in May 1889 whether there was in fact much cruelty in the area, the Revd Henry Crane confessed that:

> Our experience has not been very large as yet. We really want an officer here, and are waiting for one now. It is impossible for us to ferret out details unless we have a skilled man . . . If we had a man here I have no doubt there would be work for him to do; in fact, I think not one of the committee has any doubt about it.[26]

In some respects, these remarks are surprising in playing down the possible prevalence of child cruelty. But they do indicate the presence of a nationally informed local optimism about the possibility of discovering child abuse. As such, they display a significant disjuncture with the past.

Hitherto there had been few interventions into domestic relations for the purpose of protecting children or preventing cruelty. Local police court records and newspapers for the 1870s and 1880s suggest that Poor Law officials and the police dealt with only a handful of cases of parental neglect and/or physical and sexual abuse of children.[27] Moreover, the character, meaning, and effects of these interventions were such that they barely penetrated to the core of domestic relations. No real attempts were made to reform offending parents. The social function of mid-Victorian penal and welfare systems was largely to repress crime through an ideology of deterrence and retribution which took its meaning from the political economy of *laissez-faire* capitalism and the system of legal jurisprudence upon which it was built.[28] Such an outlook went hand in hand with efforts to deal with all aspects of childhood as a social problem, including juvenile delinquency and non-attendance at school. In only a minimal sense were children who were the victims of parental cruelty the subjects of legal and social welfare practices. A highly restricted notion of 'child protection' existed to the extent that children were seen as in need of protection by the state from their own incipient criminality, and society was in need of protection from these children in so far as they might pose a future threat to social order.[29]

Against this background, the initial caution and ambivalence of the child protectors was well placed. It amounted to a recognition that 'child protection', as they were now wishing to define it, would require putting into practice new conceptions of abuse that would demand an intimate knowledge of and access to hitherto largely private domestic relations between parents and children. The protectors would have to construct new forms of child protection, and work to discover the 'abused child' *sui generis*. They had a sound practical sense of what was required. Besides the employment of inspectors, it was recognized as essential to obtain the co-operation of professional groups. Thus the child protectors in Cleveland sought the support of local police forces and distributed circulars to all police superintendents and officers 'setting forth their powers under the new Act'.[30] Local Poor Law Boards were also informed, and magistrates were enlightened as to the new 'place of safety' procedures provided by the legislation of 1889. Schools were visited and the interest of local coroners enlisted.[31]

To facilitate communication with the general public, notice cards were distributed in shops, post offices, workmen's clubs, common lodging-houses and other public places. 'Ill-reputed neighbourhoods' were specifically targeted with 'brief notices of cases showing what has been done to cruel users of children by magistrates and judges'.[32] Copies of the Society's populist journal, *The Child's Guardian* were placed in the reading-rooms of the Middlesbrough Free Library and the Cleveland Literary and Philosophical Society.[33] Above all, the local press was a crucial outlet for the Society's objectives. Typically, the Liberal *North-Eastern Daily Gazette*, the locality's major daily paper, proclaimed in 1889 how:

> The Middlesbrough Branch for the Prevention of Cruelty to Children is doing good work in the Town. . . . The Inspector employed by Middlesbrough & Stockton finds his hands full enough. There is unfortunately great need for such a Society, and extended efforts are necessary.[34]

In June 1889, the first NSPCC inspector arrived in Cleveland. His job was to cover both the Middlesbrough and Stockton districts. At first, the committees' sense of time and space led them to believe that one inspector could cope with the demands of this large area.[35] Not until 1892 (a time of great expansion in the NSPCC nationally),[36] did they come to realize that the 'combined area was too big for one man', and in August of that year another inspector was 'sent down from London to be the "children's man" in the Stockton district' – the original inspector remaining at work under the Middlesbrough committee.[37] The Hartlepool branch acquired its first inspector in January 1892.[38] By the end of 1892, therefore, the area was not only covered by child protection organizations, but was under the surveillance of three full-time inspectors.

An active child protection practice now began. Within a month of the arrival of the first inspector, thirteen cases were reported to the Middlesbrough committee 'from various parts of the town'.[39] By the end of its first year with an inspector the committee had investigated 100 cases.[40] The Stockton and Thornaby committee, after eighteen months with the inspector, investigated 99 cases,[41] and there was no letting up. Between 1892 and 1899 this branch dealt with 1,238 suspected cases, and the rate of investigation increased by 13 per cent over the next eight years. Between 1907 and 1914 the number of cases investigated in the district reached 1,703, constituting an increase of 17 per cent over the casework rates of the previous eight years, and 27 per cent over the years 1892–9.[42]

It was not, however, simply as a result of the acquisition of inspectors that the number of cases increased. After all, from 1892 to 1914 the number of inspectors remained constant. More cases came forward partly because of increased local knowledge of the work of the NSPCC, and partly because of shifts toward surveillance in society generally over the period. This was reflected in the process of referral through which suspected child abuse cases came to the attention of the NSPCC. The referral process was of crucial importance; arguably, without it the practice of protecting children could not have begun in Cleveland, let alone have gained cultural legitimacy.

Sources of referral information were divided in NSPCC classifications among three groups: the 'general public', penal and welfare 'officials', and NSPCC inspectors. A systematic analysis of the records for the Stockton and Thornaby district between 1893 and 1914 reveals that out of nearly 4,000 cases of suspected child abuse, 58 per cent were reported by the general public, 32 per cent by officials, and 10 per cent by NSPCC inspectors. The figures disguise, however, that the 'public response' was itself partly a consequence of the successful strategies conducted on the part of the child protectors to win the confidence of the public in the disclosing of abuse. To this end the role of the inspectors was well understood from the outset. They were to be outsiders who could tactfully negotiate their way around the crowded intimacies and intricacies of modern urban environments in a way that local lay persons could not. As the secretary to the Middlesbrough branch observed in mid-1889,

> One of the difficulties of the Society here – and I suppose in other places too – lies in the reluctance of people to be at all mixed up in proceedings that may be taken. I suppose in the abstract they object to cruelty to children, but they think very much of standing well with their neighbours. Even if a woman knows that her neighbour occasionally beats her children very brutally, or is a bad mother to them in other ways, she will keep her tongue quiet lest, if anything happen to the children or happen to the mother, the neighbour should 'call' her for having informed against the delinquent mother.[43]

Typically, a town like Middlesbrough – a mid-Victorian creation, whose population rose from a mere 5,000 in 1841 to 90,000 by

1901[44] – was a place where alienation rubbed shoulders with communalism, where social relations were both near and distant, and where needs for secrecy and trust were great.[45] That child protectors took these tensions into account is further reflected in the NSPCC recommendation that the 'names of informants will be kept strictly private'.[46] In abiding by this, NSPCC inspectors went some way towards implementing a new kind of social practice in which the professional practitioner acted as a skilled cultural intermediary working between the interests of local child protectors and the working people who wanted to protect children at the same time as preserve the social distance essential to the maintenance of their own privacy and integrity. In providing such an outlet for the channelling of information, the Society's uniformed inspectorate became a vital resource through which the public's concern for children could find expression.

But many cases were also referred by other professionals in the penal-welfare network. Penal-welfare, or 'official' sources were always classified separately in the NSPCC records, and it is clear from them that upon the arrival of an NSPCC inspector in a locality, the inspector immediately became a resource for the existing network of professional agencies. Of the first ten cases reported to the Stockton and Thornaby inspector, three were referred by the local Poor Law Union's relieving officer.[47] And the reporting of cases from official sources increased over the period: from 19 per cent between 1893 and 1903, to 40 per cent between 1904 and 1914. Partly this reflects the growth in official agencies working in the name of the child: by 1914, penal-welfare sources included probation officers and health visitors as well as the traditional sources – the police, school board, and Poor Law relieving officers. But it also reflects the different nature and greater scope of the surveillance activity of these agencies. In 1908 the NSPCC identified the School Medical Service in particular as significant in accounting for overall national increases in referrals from official sources, and this was viewed as 'largely due to the effects of the medical inspection of school children'.[48]

As public and 'official' referrals increased, the proportion of cases initiated by NSPCC inspectors declined in both relative and absolute terms. In 1894, inspectors initiated 27 per cent of cases within the Stockton district, but a decade later they were responsible for reporting only 2 per cent of cases, and this percentage was maintained thereafter. Although by the end of the period third-party referrals came to constitute the majority of cases, in the early years of establishing practices locally, the NSPCC refused to entrust child protection to the community. In their eyes a crucial part of installing an effective child protection practice depended on initiatives being taken by the inspectors without prior referrals from a third party. As the secretary of the Middlesbrough branch put it in 1889, 'It is like the R.S.P.C.A., if it depended on private individuals to report cases of cruelty to animals first then I don't think it would be going on at all'.[49] Without such an approach, it was felt, the entire problem of cruelty to children would fail to be seen to exist.

While the referrals I have examined suggest that child protection practices in Cleveland operated within various consensual norms about child abuse and legitimate forms of social regulation within local communities, from the perspective of the child protectors this was still insufficient. An uneducated, apathetic and at times even hostile social body was seen as needing further help to move beyond its traditional outlook. But while these methods were seen as indispensable to establishing child protection as a social practice, they were too arbitrary and ill-defined to survive in the long-term as legitimate forms of gaining access to cases. It was in response to increasing demands for clearer boundaries to welfare practices, accompanied by major controversies over and resistance to such methods, that the number of inspectorate referrals fell away.[50] By 1914, the gathering of information on cases was more or less evenly divided between official penal-welfare sources and the general public. Legitimate channels of access into the lives of suspected abused children were now defined in a manner that appears to have persisted largely unaltered in this locality and nationally to the present day – or, rather, until 1987, when the question of the boundaries of professional access to suspected victims of child (sexual) abuse became a focal point in the Cleveland affair.

Concerns over the boundaries to child protection practice had their complement in concerns over geographical boundaries. Although the NSPCC had in principle been a national organization since 1889, it was only around 1900 that it began to feel that it had established a truly nationalized system of child protection *practices*. Ironically, it was at this point that its rhetoric took on a more localized colour with comparisons being made between national and local levels of child cruelty. By 1902, assessments of 'Cruelty In Counties – England And Wales' were being produced to illustrate the national scope of practice and, also, to reinforce the notion that there were no local variations in the rates of child abuse. The 'root of cruelty is in people, not in places', the Society insisted.[51] But differences according to place were palpable, arising out of the fact that different regions had different numbers of inspectors reporting with different degrees of zeal. Thus, then as now, it would be difficult to argue that Cleveland had more or less child cruelty.[52] What can be said, though, is that by the turn of the century the relationship between the national and the local in child protection had changed. Within a nationalized system of laws and practices, it was now possible to identify and speak of the abused child and child protection in relation to the social, administrative and geographical boundaries of Cleveland the place. The form and meaning of these localized practices can now be examined more closely.

CLEVELAND IN PRACTICE: 1889–1914

From the outset the use of legal powers to protect suspected abused children had enormous significance in constituting the objectives and cultural meanings of child protection. Among the very first wave of referrals that were made to the Cleveland NSPCC committees, cases were brought before the courts. The Middlesbrough committee's first prosecution (in July 1889, a month before the Prevention of Cruelty to Children Act reached the statute book) resulted in a 'neglectful' shipyard labourer – a lone parent of four children – being sentenced to three months' imprisonment with hard labour.[53] The case, which was brought by the NSPCC in collaboration with Middlesbrough Poor Law guardians, is interesting not least for its gender implications. Here, indeed, was a sign of local variation: Middlesbrough, a town that had come into existence for the purpose of producing iron and nothing else (as Lady Bell put it in 1907),[54] was demographically unusual in having a 'preponderance of the male sex'.[55] In Cleveland as elsewhere, childcare was regarded as women's work and 'neglectful mothers' in particular were to be subjected to persuasion and discipline oriented toward their education and reform (such as incarceration in inebriate reformatories).[56] However, the ways in which the unfolding objectives of child protection intersected with the local character of the Cleveland area meant that men were less likely than in other places to emerge from encounters with child protectors with their parental competence, dignity and public image untarnished.[57]

There was, therefore, much at stake for parents in their encounters with child protection workers. This was especially so once the 1889 Act was on the statute book, for the NSPCC then had the legal power to act with a certain amount of institutional autonomy. Within weeks several new cases were brought before the courts by the Cleveland committees. But, again, it would be misleading to characterize the Society as acting independently in constituting the meanings and form of 'child protection'. Not only were all its legal actions brought in collaboration with the NSPCC's central legal department, but they were also mediated through the wider network of penal-welfare institutions and practices. The point can be illustrated by focusing on a single case – in fact, the first to be taken up in Cleveland after the passage of the 1889 legislation.

In September 1889, a woman described as a 32-year-old widow and mother of four children was referred to the Stockton and Thornaby branch NSPCC by the relieving officer of the Stockton Poor Law Union. It was the tenth case ever reported to the branch and already the third by this same relieving officer.[58] His complaint was that the widow had 'neglected' her children, especially the two youngest, a girl aged 2 years and a boy aged 5. Both children, it was emphasized, had been born since the woman's husband had died 6 years previously. On investigation, the NSPCC inspector found them 'much emaciated, and the youngest covered with sores', for which no medical aid had been sought. The inspector was concerned about the 'most deplorable condition' of the family home, 'the only sleeping accommodation [being] a mattress on the floor'. Medical advice was sought, and ten days later the workhouse medical officer 'visited the house and found matters slightly improved'. The NSPCC's legal decision was that the case should be 'dismissed for the present, but . . . carefully watched'. Some two months later, when the inspector paid another home visit 'at the request of the relieving officer' and in the company of the workhouse doctor, the 2-year-old girl was found 'lying dead on the table'. Another baby was in the woman's care, and the 5-year-old boy was discovered hungry and in a 'most neglected state'. The inspector removed the boy to the Stockton workhouse, where he was judged to be 17 pounds underweight for his age. With the support of this medical evidence testifying to the 'grossly neglected' state of the child, the Society was granted a warrant under Section 4 of the 1889 Act for the 'detention of the child . . . in the Workhouse, pending proceedings against the mother'.

Two court cases quickly followed. The first was a 3-hour inquest into the death of the 2-year-old girl, which was attended by the house surgeon of the Stockton hospital, the workhouse medical officer, the relieving officer of the Poor Law Union, the police and the NSPCC inspector. The hearing revealed that the widow was destitute and had been so throughout the 3 months of the NSPCC's surveillance. The relieving officer had not been aware of her means, yet 9 days before he had reported the case to the NSPCC the widow had applied to the Union for medical relief for the child who was dying. The relieving officer's response had been an order for the workhouse, which the woman refused. The NSPCC inspector, after his visits, had recommended the child be placed in the workhouse infirmary. The inspector understood that the widow had lost her parish relief by having illegitimate children, that she had no other means of support, and that she could not work because of her responsibility to her children. He had therefore 'advised her to go into the Workhouse, but she did not relish the idea'. Other welfare practitioners had similarly exhorted the woman to go into the workhouse. Indeed, such was the unitary theme of the evidence given at the inquest that the coroner himself was moved to upbraid her for not taking the advice, or rather, for taking it too late, for upon the child's death she had finally moved into the workhouse with her remaining children. Heavily influenced by the expert testimony of the workhouse medical officer, the coroner's jury returned a verdict that the child had died from natural causes, accelerated by lack of sufficient food, 'but that the mother was not to blame'.

A week later, however, a rather different verdict was reached when those involved with the inquest returned to the Stockton police court for the NSPCC's prosecution of the mother on grounds of child neglect. While the death of the child figured at this trial, the charge of neglect centred on the 5-year-old boy. The NSPCC solicitor reminded the bench that this was the fourth case that the Stockton and Thornaby branch had brought before the court, and that they viewed it as the worst thus far. For this reason it was the first case brought under the 1889 legislation which involved the use of emergency child protection powers. The evidence of 'neglect' was elaborated on much the same lines as at the inquest. Now, however, the mother *was* found guilty of 'cruelly neglecting her children' and was sentenced to one month imprisonment with hard labour, while the child was taken into custody.

Such a case provides a vivid sense of the process through which child protection powers began to be turned into practices and given meaning. Although socio-historical accounts have shown the importance in social policy formation of the institutional relationship between charity organization, social work and the ideologies and operations of the Poor Law, the relevance and consequences of these relationships to child protection have not been explored through the study of actual practices.[59] There may well have been nothing exceptional about the response of this mother to the demands placed on her by the state through the Poor Law.[60] But what was new was the way in which such traditional forms of welfare practice intersected with developments in childcare law, penology, medicine and social work to lead to new constructions of deviant parenting and child abuse in NSPCC cases.

Seen in the context of its historical novelty in Cleveland, the case thus exemplifies how child welfare professionals were led to a realization of the new disciplinary powers to protect children that were invested in them through the 1889 Act. This is clear from the fact that during the course of the court case the mayor (who was the chief magistrate) had to ask the clerk of the court when the PCC Act had come into force. Upon receiving the answer 'from and after 26th August', the Mayor commented that 'the Relieving Officer had spoken to him several times about this case, and he [the mayor] thought if he had the power under the Act to take children into the workhouse he ought to have exercised it'. Whereupon the relieving officer remarked that 'he did not think he [the relieving officer] had the power'. In bringing the case forward, the NSPCC can be seen to have influenced the way in which other penal-welfare agents came to perceive their new responsibilities. While the mother in this case was ultimately forced to accept the first incarnation of the new definition of 'child protection' – even if in her ambivalence she may have regarded it as a fate worse than the serious 'neglect' of one of her children and the death of another – penal-welfare expertise was realizing that in the face of that death they now had a power over life.[61]

The way in which this new power to protect children was exercised during the 1889–1914 period is difficult to represent in any straightforward fashion, for there was both continuity and change in its forms and effects. Nor is it possible to develop the analysis of it in an exhaustive fashion in the space available here. Central to the 'modern' notion of 'child protection', however, was the establishment of 'places of safety' in the form of the NSPCC children's shelters. By the early 1890s, each of the NSPCC branches in Cleveland was operating a shelter, the last of which to open was that at Middlesbrough in April 1893 after a ceremony presided over by the Marchioness of Zetland. (The ceremony was typical of the visibility given to the shelters; indeed, they could hardly have been more public since they sported large signs designating their whereabouts and function.)[62]

As symbolic as well as utilitarian institutions, the shelters were in many respects a cultural embodiment of the desire to restructure existing Victorian welfare practices in the name of the abused child and according to new conceptions of child protection. Stockton child protectors were emphatic about this when representing the need for the shelter that they opened in August 1891:

> It is so necessary to have some place to which ill-used and neglected children can, in serious cases, and by special warrant, be taken, pending the investigation of their wrongs. It is obviously not good that they should be taken to the Police Station; nor is it advisable that they should go to the workhouse. A little kind treatment in such a shelter will do much to open the minds of these little ones to tell the tale of their sufferings, and it is most desirable that the Officer should have access to them in preparation of his case for court.[63]

The shelters were in fact most often used by NSPCC inspectors who routinely took suspected abused children to them, as well as by the police, school board officers, the general public, and (albeit to a lesser degree) by parents who were struggling to cope. There is some evidence, too, that children presented themselves at the shelters when they felt in need of protection.[64] They operated, however, within a structure in which they were mainly adopted by the courts as 'places of safety' for children, often for many weeks and months during casework following NSPCC legal advice.[65]

The children admitted to the shelters ranged from those who had been seriously abused, to those simply found wandering on the streets.[66] On admission, they were examined by the shelter's elected honorary medical attendant, a function seen as particularly important and urgent with regard to young children, where keeping the child alive was the first priority. In fact, 15 per cent of the abused children in Cleveland over the period were infants, or those who, after 1908, were classified as 'babies under two years of age'.[67] Thus, in an important sense, the shelters were not just protecting against cruelty, but were life-protecting, a fact that was stressed in the child protectors' rhetoric. During the Stockton shelter's first year of operation (1892), for example, out of 455 children involved in cases, it was regretted that four had 'ended in the death of the little victims, the knowledge of whose sufferings came too late'.[68]

Of 11,819 children investigated by the Stockton and Thornaby committee between 1889 and 1914, 77 per cent were classified as cases of 'neglect'. A further 11 per cent were designated 'ill-treatment and assault', 4 per cent were to do with 'Begging and Improper Employment', and a further 6 per cent involved miscellaneous offences, ranging from 'abandonment' and 'exposure', to 'other wrongs'. A final 2 per cent were classified under 'Immorality', the category that included sexual offences, and which remained comparatively low even after the passage of the Punishment of Incest Act of 1908.[69] The figures require some qualifications, however. First, although the child protectors repeatedly claimed that one of the major roles of the shelters was to protect those children whose abuse at home might not otherwise come to light, there were limits to the forms of victimization deemed possible to speak about, or for adults to hear, inspect and disclose. Since so many of the serious cases brought to the shelters were pre-verbal infants, the idea of their disclosure was mostly irrelevant. More generally, however, sexual abuse was relatively easy to veil at a time when there was little apparent space for professionals to read signs of it and classify it in social practice. Second, it must be emphasized that although the sexual abuse of children was never allowed to gain the public visibility of 'neglect' or, to a lesser degree, physical child abuse, it *was* discovered, classified and worked with in practice. Despite the relatively low incidence in NSPCC casework – somewhat lower, it seems, than rates in incest found in the history of American family violence casework[70] – it was roundly condemned. What by 1914 were being identified as 'assaults on girls' were still statistically low, but their symbolic weight remained high in the Society's representations. There was, it was claimed, 'no more cowardly class of offence in the whole category of crime. Nor is there any offence in which the difficulty of proof is so great'.[71]

The Stockton shelter operated from 1891 to 1903. During this time almost 5,000 children were involved in the branch's casework, some 17 per cent of whom – over 800 – were taken into the shelter. This appears a surprisingly high proportion of child removals; however, 94 per cent of these children were quickly returned to their parents, either immediately, in the case of a court action not being pursued, or usually within 3 months, in the case of one or both parents being imprisoned. Only 6 per cent of the children who were admitted to the shelter did not return home, which means that just one per cent of the 5,000 children dealt with by the branch in the period 1891–1903 were permanently removed from parental custody. Thus while over 80 per cent of the cases dealt with in Stockton experienced no removal at all, for the overwhelming majority of those who were removed the experience was temporary, fully justifing the official regard of the shelters as 'Temporary Homes for Children'.[72]

Although institutional provision for children in need of protection became increasingly sophisticated after 1894, when the PCC Act obliged Poor Law guardians to accept all such children brought to them,[73] modern studies of childcare practice are mistaken in their assumption that abused children in this period were 'rescued' by being taken out of parental custody and then permanently institutionalized in one way or another.[74] In reality, the weight of child protection fell increasingly heavily *on parents*, the primary objective of the NSPCC being not to relieve them of the care of their children, but rather, to enforce their responsibilities as newly conceived for them by the child protectors and the state. The prosecution of parents was a key strategy towards this objective, occurring in 7 per cent of the Stockton and Thornaby cases over the period considered here. Prosecutions dropped, however, from 18 per cent of all cases investigated in 1891 to a steady 4 per cent after 1904. It is clear, therefore, that before the turn of the century the incarceration of parents in prisons was the main reformative resource – a disciplinary technique which corresponded with the protective function of the shelters where children were usually cared for during their parents' incarceration.

With the closure of the shelters, NSPCC casework strategy changed from that of punishment of parents to reformation through the supervision of parent–child relations in their own homes – a form of practice that was to extend on into our own time. The effects of this transformation in terms of childcare practices were subtle, yet profound. Although the PCC acts of 1889 and 1894, and the Poor Law acts of 1889 and 1899 gave new powers to local authorities to terminate the parental rights of abused and deserted children,[75] these changes were not accompanied by any increase in the number of children permanently removed. Up to 1914, permanent removals remained less than one per cent of all cases.[76] What had changed was the *form* the removals took. From 1904, social workers were formally obliged to remove suspected abused children to workhouses, hospitals, and the cottage homes that had come to supersede the shelters.[77] Coinciding with this was an apparent change in the *tempo* of practice, reflected most revealingly in the emergence of what became known as the 'emergency case'. In these cases, according to the NSPCC *Inspector's Directory* of 1904, the 'interests of a child are superior to rules'.[78] By 1914, in serious cases, a pattern had emerged in which children were systematically removed from their homes on the basis of professional collaborations begun *before* NSPCC workers consulted with their legal department.

Fundamental to this shift was the manner in which the 'interests' of abused children were redefined according to a new concept of risk necessitating immediate social intervention. This can be seen as paralleling new rationales for intervention in children's medicine generally around this time,[79] as well as with transformations in penal welfare practices. Emergency interventions were also facilitated by the realignment of the balance between national and local administrative powers. Legislation up to and including the 1908 Children's Act had progressively defined the power to punish the abusing parent and protect the abused child as a general and uniform function of the state. By 1912 the NSPCC was claiming as one of its 'greatest accomplishments' the 'setting up [of] something like a universal method of dealing with offenders'.[80] But one of the consequences of bringing this plan to fruition was the creation of a new kind of local autonomy in which the power to protect was now not in the hands of local NSPCC committees, but rather in those of the professional practitioners who had come to surround the suspected abused child. It was around these professionals that the power was invested to administer and supervise the reform of parents and the protection of children that prior to the early 1900s had been in the hands of local magistrates and NSPCC committees. In emergency cases, the courts now acted merely to rubber-stamp the disciplinary action already taken to protect children by the professionals. As opposed to the repressive, retributive, penal-welfare practice that characterized the pre-1904 years, this new practice of protecting children was tied to a new professional ideology which primarily extolled the moral reformation of both mothers and fathers. Practitioners thus gained new powers of discretion and autonomy to judge and carry out the newly conceived therapeutic tasks of child protection.[81] Although 'emergency cases' were to remain statistically untypical, the social intervention they legitimated became the defining characteristic of child protection work, and was to remain so through to the Cleveland affair of 1987.

CONCLUSION

One cannot overestimate the implications for the meaning of 'child abuse' that followed from the changes in the form of child protection powers, administration and practices over the 1880–1914 period. The changes amounted to far more than a transformation in the scale and meaning of child abuse; constructed was the modern form of the social problem and practice of child protection. The examination of this process through the case-study of Cleveland reveals the inadequacy of one-dimensional representations of the character of child protection. The latter leave the impression that consensus has always existed as to what was a socially just form of practice and response to childcare problems.[82] But in fact, as the Cleveland history bears out, such practices rested heavily on ambivalences mediated through local cultures. In this context, child protection could draw on a fund of goodwill and reciprocity: as the referral rates I examined indicate, some women and children who were victimized members of households were prepared to request help from child protection workers and draw the latter into their survival strategies. Many neighbours in working-class districts, too, took similar initiatives on behalf of children. Equally, however, there was a whole culture of resistance in working-class neighbourhoods which NSPCC inspectors, regardless of the severity of the case, often failed to overcome. Resistance pervaded many aspects of child protection work. Its meaning went well beyond the obvious fact that poor parents resented surveillance, and that mothers in particular feared the potential for loss of their children to protection agencies. An important source of resistance resided in what local people appeared to hate most about child protection practice in this period: its connections to other stigmatizing forms of welfare, particularly the Poor Law. While by the end of the period, households were acquiring at least some citizenship rights to health and welfare benefits which might help to ward off childcare problems, child protection became, if anything, more firmly tied in ideology and practice to these formative welfare state reforms. The 1908 Children's Act formalized the sanction for parents to be rendered culpable for child abuse and punished for not taking advantage of the state welfare provisions then available for the child.[83] Child protection had become established as the disciplinary end of the penal-welfare division of labour in the foundations of modern childcare policy and a practice more and more devoted to penetrating and differentiating households and individualizing parental responsibility. Especially after the closure of the shelters, this led to an increased use of Poor Law institutions to meet the objectives of child protection in emergency cases. By refusing the workhouse and, more generally, the conditional offers of help from the state, many parents, like the mother in the case-history cited above, continued to question and reframe the very meanings of social justice in the objectives of child protection. This response was usually defined negatively in the still ubiquitous rejection of the workhouse. These struggles intensified towards the end of the period surveyed here, as interventions into households increasingly came to be defined as 'emergency', and as the professionals in the employ of the state took on their autonomous roles in child protection. In the process child abuse came to be identified culturally as a 'shameful thing', especially when it occasioned uninvited surveillance.

As for the children who were caught between their parents' resistance and the efforts of child protectors to protect, their position was particularly ambiguous. For in practice the rights of abused children were now defined by the state not in absolute terms according to some authentic criterion of need or citizenship, but in the relative terms of the prescribed duties of parents to 'competently' rear children. A perverse outcome of this was that abused children were conceptualized within an ideology of innocence that barely constituted or empowered them as the active subjects of a practice ostensibly carried out in their name.

By the inter-war years, Cleveland child protectors were already locating their work firmly within a historical tradition. In 1936, for instance, the Middlesbrough NSPCC committee observed that during the forty-six years the branch had been in existence no fewer than 8,839 cases had been investigated involving 24,438 children.[84] A major problem in understanding child protection today, however, has been the lack of any sense of the process of historical and cultural formation of the power to protect abused children, and the forms of resistance, reciprocity, ambivalence and consensus that have been evident in the constitution and reception of its practices. Such gaps in our knowledge of cultural practices are perhaps most deeply felt at times of crisis, such as occurred in Cleveland in 1987. While the events and ambiguities that constituted the 'Cleveland affair' undoubtedly had unique characteristics – not least in helping to reconstitute child sexual abuse as a social problem – when viewed in terms of the historical perspective of this chapter, 'Cleveland' raised to an intense public level issues that have in most respects been at the centre of child protection since its modern beginnings. In 1987, so intense were the ambivalences and the struggles between parents, the wider community and state professionals as to what could be defined as 'child abuse' and a socially just child protection practice, that Lord Justice Butler-Sloss concluded her inquiry with the observation that suspected victims of child sexual abuse were in danger of being overlooked. She invoked the principle that differences must be resolved on the basis that 'the child is a person and not an object of concern'.[85] The problem is that the temper of the post-Cleveland debate has been such that it is far from clear what 'personhood' for abused children might mean in practice. More attention to Cleveland in history can, perhaps, not only enable us to understand the character and effects of child protection in the past; it might also help us to establish the crucial ground upon which the abused child of yesterday may be permitted to speak to us as a person today.

ACKNOWLEDGEMENTS

I am grateful to Roger Cooter, Judith Ennew, Jean La Fontaine, Martin Richards, Deborah Thom and Cathy Urwin for their comments on drafts of this chapter, and to Marietta Higgs and Sue Richardson for discussions which helped clarify my thinking. I would also like to thank the NSPCC for prolonged access to their archives, and the Durham County Record Office and the Cleveland County Archives for making available their files on children in care.

NOTES

1 Lord Justice Elizabeth Butler-Sloss, *Report of the Inquiry into Child Abuse in Cleveland in 1987*, London: HMSO, 1988; B. Campbell, *Unofficial Secrets: child sexual abuse, the Cleveland case*, London: Virago, 1988; J. La Fontaine, *Child Sexual Abuse*, Oxford: Polity, 1990: 1–19.

2 Although controversy has persisted about the actual Cleveland cases, high referral rates, a spate of government guidelines, and research evidence since the Cleveland affair have tended to support the efforts of Cleveland professionals in placing child sexual abuse on the public agenda. See the Violence Against Children Study Group (eds) *Taking Child Abuse Seriously: contemporary issues in child protection theory and practice*, London: Unwin Hyman, 1990: 1–6 and *passim*; and Carol-Ann Hooper, 'Rethinking the politics of child abuse', *Social History of Medicine*, 1989, 2: 356–64.

3 This perspective is to be found in the book by the local MP, S. Bell, *When Salem Came to the Boro': the true story of the Cleveland child abuse crisis*, London: Pan Books, 1988.

4 See, for example, 'Legal change needed to fight child abuse', *Manchester Metro News*, 20 May 1988.

5 See Bob Franklin, 'Wimps and bullies: press reporting of child abuse', in P. Carter, T. Jeffs and M. Smith (eds) *Social Work and Social Welfare Year Book 1*, Milton Keynes: Open University Press, 1989; Mica Nava, 'Cleveland and the press: outrage and anxiety in the reporting of child sexual abuse', *Feminist Review*, 1988, 28: 103–21.

6 G. K. Behlmer, *Child Abuse and Moral Reform in England 1870–1908*, Stanford: Stanford University Press, 1982: 224–5. Such an invalidation of history is not peculiar to the Cleveland affair; it pervades all aspects of contemporary discourse on child protection. For a corrective, see H. Ferguson, 'Rethinking child protection practices: a case for history', in the Violence Against Children Study Group (eds) *Taking Child Abuse Seriously*.

7 Geographically, what is today the county of Cleveland, then comprised parts of the counties of Durham and the North Riding of Yorkshire. However, the area covered by the work of the three branches of the National Society for the Prevention of Cruelty to Children in Middlesbrough, Stockton-on-Tees and Hartlepool, which constitute the focus of this chapter, closely corresponds to the existing county of Cleveland.

8 See, for example, J. S. Heywood, *Children in Care: the development of the service for the deprived child*, London: Routledge, 1959, 3rd edn 1978; I. Pinchbeck and M. Hewitt, *Children in English Society*, 2 vols, London: Routledge, 1969, 1973; J. Packman, *The Child's Generation*, London: Blackwell & Robertson, 1981; L. Pollock, *Forgotten Children*, Cambridge: Cambridge University Press, 1983; N. Parton, *The Politics of Child Abuse*, London: Macmillan, 1985; and Margaret May, 'Violence in the family: an historical perspective', in J. P. Martin (ed.) *Violence and the Family*, London: John Wiley, 1977. A notable example of a historical study going beyond these policy-oriented accounts is Linda Gordon, *Heroes of Their Own Lives: the politics and history of family violence, Boston 1880–1960*, London: Virago, 1989. See also, John Demos, 'Child abuse in context: an historian's perspective', in his *Past, Present and Personal*, Oxford: Oxford University Press, 1985.

9 Elizabeth Pleck, *Domestic Tyranny: the making of American social*

policy against family violence from colonial times to the present, Oxford: Oxford University Press, 1987: 69–87; and C. J. Ross, 'The lessons of the past: defining and controlling child abuse in the United States', in G. Gerbner, C. J. Ross and E. Zigler (eds) *Child Abuse: an agenda for action*, New York: Oxford University Press, 1980.

10 The Liverpool Society maintained a separate status until 1953, while the Republic of Ireland branches remained within the National Society until 1956. See A. Allen and A. Morton, *This is Your Child: the story of the National Society for the Prevention of Cruelty to Children*, London: Routledge, 1961: 26.

11 The NSPCC had its first taste of success as a moral reform movement with the introduction of the 1885 Criminal Law Amendment Act, though (unlike the PCC Acts) it played only a minor part in the events surrounding the passage of the Act. For a full account of these social and legislative developments, see Behlmer, *Child Abuse*.

12 The figures are from NSPCC *Annual Report*, 1914, NSPCC Archives.

13 NSPCC, *Child's Guardian*, 1888: 50.

14 Reported in the *North-Eastern Daily Gazette*, 14 June 1888. The importance of the Sunday School Union is discussed in Asa Briggs, 'Middlesbrough: the growth of a new community' in his *Victorian Cities*, Harmondsworth: Penguin, 1968: 255.

15 NSPCC, *Child's Guardian*, 1889: 136.

16 In 1899, for example, two 'working men', three JPs and two church ministers were among the fourteen members of the Stockton and Thornaby committee. *Stockton and Thornaby Branch NSPCC Annual Report*, 1899 (hereafter *STAR*).

17 *North-Eastern Daily Gazette*, 14 June 1888; *Middlesbrough and District Branch NSPCC Annual Report*, 1902.

18 *STAR*, 1892.

19 *STAR*, 1892: 6.

20 For parallels, see L. Davidoff and C. Hall, *Family Fortunes: men and women of the English middle class, 1780–1850*, London: Hutchinson, 1987: 313; and more generally, F. K. Prochaska, *Women and Philanthropy in 19th Century England*, Oxford: Clarendon Press, 1980.

21 Lady Bell's best-known work remains *At the Works: A study of a manufacturing town*, London, 1907, Virago reprint, 1985.

22 Notably Dr Barnardo, on whom see G. Wagner, *Children of the Empire*, London: Weidenfeld & Nicolson, 1982.

23 During the first two years of NSPCC practices, 15 per cent of the cases reported to the Stockton and Thornaby branch, for example, came from persons connected with it as subscribers, executive members or administrators: Stockton and Thornaby branch NSPCC *Register of Cases 1889–1891*, London, NSPCC Archives.

24 What I refer to as 'case-histories' have been reconstructed from newspaper accounts, local police court, and Poor Law records, as well as NSPCC sources, and apply most often to the earlier years for which fewer NSPCC case-files survive. In instances where the NSPCC case-file survives and is specifically cited, I refer to this source as a 'case-record'.

25 For example, *STAR*, 1899.
26 Quoted in *North-Eastern Weekly Gazette*, 25 May 1889, in an interview entitled: 'Society for the Prevention of Cruelty to Children: what the Middlesbrough branch is doing'.
27 Examples of reported cases are to be found in the *North-Eastern Daily Gazette*, 8 and 25 July 1879, 3 September 1888, 1 February and 1 July 1889, and *Middlesbrough News & Cleveland Advertiser*, 26 April 1879.
28 D. Garland, *Punishment and Welfare: a history of penal strategies*, Aldershot: Gower, 1985: ch. 2.
29 R. Dingwall, J. Eekelaar and T. Murray, 'Childhood as a social problem: a survey of the history of legal regulation', *Journal of Law and Society*, 1984, 11: 207–32.
30 By May 1889 the Middlesbrough Chief Constable had promised 'every help'. The police would now 'report any case desirable' for the Society to take up. Crane, 'What the Middlesbrough branch is doing'.
31 *North-Eastern Daily Gazette*, 28 June 1889, report of the meeting of the Middlesbrough Guardians; *STAR*, 1891: 5; and 1892: 7.
32 Report of the first AGM of the Middlesbrough and District branch NSPCC, cited in the *North-Eastern Daily Gazette*, 18 July 1889; and NSPCC, *Child's Guardian*, 1888: 50.
33 Crane, 'What the Middlesbrough branch is doing'.
34 *North-Eastern Daily Gazette*, 31 November 1889; see also 9 April 1889.
35 Crane, 'What the Middlesbrough branch is doing'; Middlesbrough and District branch NSPCC first AGM reported in the *North-Eastern Daily Gazette*, 18 July 1889.
36 By March 1892 there were fifty-seven branch aid committees submitting casework returns to the central office, twelve more than a year previous.
37 *STAR*, 1893: 9.
38 *Hartlepool and District Branch NSPCC Annual Report*, 1893.
39 *North-Eastern Daily Gazette*, 18 July 1889.
40 Report of the 1890 Middlesbrough branch AGM, cited in NSPCC, *Child's Guardian*, 1890: 151.
41 *STAR*, 1890.
42 These figures and those cited below are drawn from an analysis of the annual reports of the Stockton and Thornaby branch between 1890 and 1914.
43 Crane, 'What the Middlesbrough branch is doing'.
44 Briggs, 'Middlesbrough': 242, 247.
45 On the transformations in coexistence and trust relations that occurred with the development of an urbanized industrial society, see G. Simmel, 'The Stranger', in K. H. Wolff (ed.) *The Sociology of George Simmel*, New York: Free Press, 1950; R. Sennett, *The Fall of Public Man*, Cambridge: Cambridge University Press, 1974; A. Giddens, *The Consequences of Modernity*, Cambridge: Polity Press, 1990; on the neglected gender dimensions of these transformations, see Janet Wolff, 'The invisible Flaneuse: women and the literature of modernity', *Theory, Culture and Society*, 1985, 2: 37–46.

46 *STAR*, 1891. This rule has persisted to the present.

47 Stockton and Thornaby branch NSPCC, *Register of Cases 1889–1891*, London, NSPCC Archives.

48 NSPCC *Annual Report*, 1910: 17; on these general developments in medical surveillance, see D. Armstrong, *The Political Anatomy of the Body*, Cambridge: Cambridge University Press, 1983: 15.

49 H. Crane, 'What the Middlesbrough branch is doing'.

50 The controversy was such that in 1905 the Director of the NSPCC came to Cleveland to try to allay social anxieties by reassuring local citizens that the Society's inspectors 'were not, as some carping critics still described them, men of low motive who hung about streets and alleys in the hope of being able to trump up a case'. *STAR*, 1905: 10.

51 NSPCC, *Annual Report*, 1900: 53.

52 NSPCC, *Annual Report*, 1902. The Society made few concessions to the individuality of its inspectors in calculating regional rates and styles of casework. It sought to homogenize their practices by kitting them out in uniforms and demanding they follow agency rules prescribed in the *NSPCC Inspector's Directory* (1904, 1910). In work and life-style, high standards of personal and professional morality and efficiency were expected. Inspectors were always men, usually married and mature in age, who were recruited most often on the basis of proven experience in lower middle-class 'disciplinary' professions such as the police and the armed services.

53 *North-Eastern Daily Gazette*, 28 June 1889; *Child's Guardian*, 1889: 135.

54 Bell, *At the Works*: 6.

55 Briggs, 'Middlesbrough': 248.

56 On the national use of inebriate reformatories, see NSPCC *Annual Report* 1903, 'Inebriate mothers and their reform'; for a vivid case-work example from Cleveland, see Stockton and Thornaby NSPCC case-record 19134521.

57 See, for example, Stockton and Thornaby NSPCC case-history no. 190705.

58 Stockton and Thornaby branch NSPCC case-history no. 188910.

59 While the Charity Organization Society was relatively ineffective in Stockton and Middlesbrough, in Hartlepool it evolved into what was regarded as a model society, comparable to some London COS branches in scope, efficiency, and working relationship with the Poor Law. See Keith Gregson, 'Poor Law and organised charity: the relief of exceptional distress in north-east England, 1870–1910', in Michael E. Rose (ed.) *The Poor and the City: the English poor law in its urban context, 1834–1914*, Leicester: Leicester University Press, 1985.

60 On resentment towards the Poor Law and fear of the workhouse, see Pat Thane, 'Women and the Poor Law in Victorian and Edwardian England', *History Workshop Journal*, 1978, 6: 29–51; Jane Lewis, 'The working-class wife and mother and state intervention, 1870–1918', in Jane Lewis (ed.) *Labour and Love: women's experience of home and family, 1850–1940*, Oxford: Basil Blackwell, 1986; and M. A.

Crowther, *The Workhouse System, 1834–1929*, London: Batsford, 1981. But the relationships between Poor Law practices and child protection have remained unexplored.

61 On the relationship between the law, disciplinary practices and the modern state's 'power over life', see Michel Foucault, *The History of Sexuality*, London: Penguin, 1978, vol. 1; and J. Donzelot, *The Policing of Families*, London: Hutchinson, 1980. It is, however, a critical application of the latter approach which applies here. Feminist criticism in particular has been influential in shaping the following account: see N. Fraser, *Unruly Practices: power, discourse and gender in contemporary social theory*, Cambridge: Polity Press, 1989.

62 Reported in *North-Eastern Daily Gazette*, 19 April 1893. For further discussion of the Shelters, see H. Ferguson, 'Cleveland 1898: has anything changed in 90 years?', *Guardian*, 3 May 1989.

63 *STAR*, 1891: 8.

64 Stockton and Thornaby case-history no. 18956.

65 For example, Stockton and Thornaby case-history no. 18923.

66 See *North-Eastern Daily Gazette*, 1 October 1891.

67 While the Stockton committee provided details of the ages of abused children in their cases in the 1890s, from around 1908 each of the Cleveland branches initiated more sophisticated classifications.

68 *STAR*, 1893: 11.

69 These figures refer to agency classifications of cases. On their source, see note 42.

70 Linda Gordon in her study of family violence in Boston, 1880–1960, has found as many as 10 per cent of cases in some years involving incest: *Heroes of Their Own Lives*: ch. 7.

71 NSPCC *Annual Report*, 1913: 20. See also 1914: 32–3. Stockton and Thornaby case-record no. 190901 was the first to be considered by the branch for proceedings under the 1908 Punishment of Incest Act. On the Act itself, see V. Bailey and S. Blackburn, 'The Punishment of Incest Act 1908: a case-study of law creation', *Criminal Law Review*, 1979: 708–18. For analysis of the cultural meanings of child (sexual) abuse, childhood and professional ideologies in this period, see L. Wolff, *Postcards from the End of the World: an investigation into the mind of fin-de-siècle Vienna*, London: Collins, 1989, and A. S. Wohl, 'Sex and the single room: incest among the Victorian working classes' in A. S. Wohl (ed.) *The Victorian Family*, London: Croom Helm, 1978.

72 These figures have been compiled from information contained in Stockton and Thornaby NSPCC *Annual Reports*, NSPCC case-histories and case-records, and the records of Stockton Poor Law Union children's homes. These local practices typified national trends: see Behlmer, *Child Abuse*: 175.

73 The Stockton Union, for example, opened its Cottage Homes for Children in 1900 in which children were cared for separately from those in the workhouse. It was in response to such developments nationally that the NSPCC shelters were closed down in 1903: see *STAR*, 1903: 12.

74 Purveyors of this myth include Bob Holman, *Putting Families First: prevention and childcare*, London: Macmillan, 1988: 1–25; and Parton, *Politics of Child Abuse*: 20–47. For a more balanced appraisal, see Jane Lewis, 'Anxieties about the family and the relationships between parents, children and the state in twentieth-century England', in M. Richards and P. Light (eds) *Children of Social Worlds*, Cambridge: Polity Press, 1986.

75 T. Percival, *Poor Law Children*, London: Shaw & Sons, 1911: 151–65.

76 Sources cited in note 72 apply.

77 NSPCC *Inspector's Directory*, London, NSPCC Archives, 1904: 34–5; *STAR*, 1904.

78 NSPCC *Inspector's Directory*, 1904.

79 The importance of medical practice in shaping child protection interventions prior to the formative work of Henry Kempe in the 1960s has been almost wholly overlooked. An exception is M. A. Lynch, 'Child abuse before Kempe: an historical literature review', *Child Abuse and Neglect*, 1985, 9: 7–15. My research suggests that child protection work was greatly influenced by the developments in medical science during the Edwardian period discussed by Peter Wright in 'The social construction of babyhood: the definition of infant care as a medical problem', in A. Bryman, B. Blytheway, P. Allat and T. Keil (eds) *Rethinking the Life Cycle*, London: Macmillan, 1987.

80 NSPCC, *Annual Report*, 1912: 28–9.

81 The general background to this formulation derives from Michel Foucault, *Discipline and Punish: the birth of the prison*, London: Allen Lane, 1977: 231, 247 and *passim*. For extended discussions, see Ferguson, 'Rethinking child protection practices', and Garland, *Punishment and Welfare*.

82 An outlook that not only pervades most discourse on child abuse, but much of the discourse in the history of childhood itself. See Demos, 'Child abuse in context': 72.

83 Allen and Morton, *This is Your Child*: 179.

84 Middlesbrough and District branch NSPCC *Annual Report*, 1936: 5.

85 *Report of the Inquiry*: 245.

7

FROM BODIES TO MINDS IN CHILDCARE LITERATURE

Advice to parents in inter-war Britain

Cathy Urwin and Elaine Sharland

With hindsight, the knowledge produced by modern medicine and associated disciplines 'in the name of the child' has been as important for parents as for children themselves. The rapid growth of specialized knowledges on child health and development through the twentieth century has been closely linked to the emergence of social practices aimed specifically at the early detection or prevention of deviance. Michel Foucault's historical work on the implementation of preventive and interventionist philosophies in medicine, law and the practices of child-rearing have shown how targeting the deviant or abnormal has depended crucially on the production of particular conceptions of what is normal or healthy.[1] This has brought with it prescriptive notions of adequate parenting.

Although limits of intervention are pegged by legislation, prevention or surveillance depends on a network of social agencies with more or less access to the community as a whole. One of the most powerful aspects of Foucault's argument is the claim that, in targeting deviance, norms are established in a way which affects everyone.[2] Foucault's account regards this process as neither simply determined nor as achieved by coercion. But this raises questions about how such regulation comes about. To what extent, for example, does specialized knowledge become a reference point in the common sense of child-rearing? If parents are actively engaged rather than coerced, does the convincing presentation of this knowledge depend on identifying common priorities and preoccupations across different social groups and particular historical periods?

In this chapter we examine childcare literature as one source of information on how specialized knowledge was imparted to

174

parents in the first decades of the twentieth century. We have concentrated on advice available in Britain between the two World Wars and have deliberately selected literature which was sufficiently popular to justify several reprintings. 'The child' in this literature is generally, but not exclusively, of pre-school age, reflecting a focus which remains in most books sold under the generic category 'childcare literature'. However, it was not until the end of the period under discussion here that the infant emerged as having particular psychological as well as physical needs, dictating parental priorities.

Childcare literature of the inter-war years has been studied previously, notably by the developmental psychologists John and Elizabeth Newson, and in Christina Hardyment's and Daniel Beekman's popular social histories.[3] These accounts all delineate a shift from a hygienist emphasis on children's bodies and physical health to an emphasis on children's minds and emotions. Here we examine this emergence more closely and show how the presentation of new knowledge was linked both to the growth of child-centred intervention and to dominant social concerns.

Our account differs from previous accounts in that, rather than viewing psychology as replacing a hygienist emphasis, we describe a transformation in the understanding and regulation of the moral sphere. Our aim is to illustrate how, through this historical period, theories of what was right or wrong with the child not only brought prescriptive notions of maternal adequacy, but also carried dominant preoccupations of the nation with which parents were assumed to identify. Focusing on the uptake of three major theoretical or empirical traditions we describe how, towards the end of the 1930s, a space was produced for introducing various ideas from dynamic psychology and psychoanalysis.[4] In accounting for this uptake, we stress the importance of the Child Guidance Movement. But we also emphasize the role of international events and, in particular, the fear of social unrest which followed the First World War and the significance of widespread social and personal anxieties provoked by the anticipation of the Second World War. The congruence between parental preoccupations and the experts' themes produced an interest in children's aggression which was specific to this historical period. This illustrates the importance of including subjective processes within the account of social regulation put forward by Foucault.[5]

CHILD CARE ADVICE LITERATURE AND INFANT MORTALITY

Neither giving advice on how to bring up children nor writing about it is new.[6] Nevertheless, the inter-war years produced a transformation which has affected all childcare literature since. As Harry Hendrick has described in the context of the School Medical Service in his chapter in this volume, for the first time there was a mandate for writing a rubric which could, in principle, embrace every child in the nation. This was linked to the unequivocal authority given to experts who based their advice on scientific principles.

The potential contribution of a scientific approach to child-rearing had been evident as early as the 1750s. Hardyment,[7] for example, refers to experiments in management carried out by Enlightenment doctors upon infants deposited in the first foundling hospitals.[8] The focus on sick or deprived infants from poorer classes was equally evident at the turn of the twentieth century. As Hendrick has discussed, at that time the government's concern over the poor stamina of the British troops in the Boer War and a general demoralization over the state of the Empire contributed to promoting research on infant feeding and development.[9] Together with changes in welfare practice which linked child protection and infant needs to maternal responsibility, emerged the possibility of a scientifically justified body of knowledge on parenting.

From its inception the science of 'mothercraft' was inextricably linked to national priorities of increasing infant survival and maintaining an orderly population capable of adjusting to the demands of industry or the Army. Before the First World War education in mothercraft had become a focus for local government planning in some areas. These moves were actively supported by the Chief Medical Officer to the Board of Education, George Newman. He recommended training mothers as a way of improving the health of the nation's children and recognized the importance of beginning in the pre-school years. As early as 1914 Newman noted 'The environment of the infant is its mother'.[10] However, it was not until the reconstruction following the First World War that political imperatives facilitated establishing mothercraft as a matter of national policy.[11] This had direct effects on what was written for popular consumption.

In Britain the successful dissemination of mothercraft through childcare literature after the war is particularly associated with

Frederick Truby King, a New Zealand doctor whose system of infant feeding and management originated in experiments designed to cut the death rate in bucket-fed calves suffering from a disease akin to the gastroenteritis that was virulent amongst babies.[12] The possibility that infant mortality could be substantially reduced through following the Truby King method was taken up rapidly in New Zealand, where it was claimed that infant mortality had been halved by 1912. In Britain there was no comparable enthusiasm until Truby King made a visit in 1917. Shortly after this visit the Mothercraft School in Highgate, London, was opened to provide training courses for health visitors, nursery nurses and other professionals. The school also produced a child-rearing manual, *The Mothercraft Manual*,[13] which was to remain the major source of orthodoxy on infant care and management for the next 30 years.

The Mothercraft Manual was based on Truby King's *Feeding and Care of Baby*,[14] first published in 1913 and reprinted in Britain four times over the next 5 years. Early editions exploited press coverage of infant mortality and the declining birthrate, and appealed directly to mothers of all social classes to recognize child-rearing as a matter of national rather than personal concern. Indicative was the cover of the 1925 revised edition which bore a badge inscribed 'To help the mothers and save the babies' and advertized 'The Mothercraft Training Society (Babies of the Empire)'. In the text itself, copious illustrations of starving and subsequently healthy infants demonstrated the success of Truby King's methods of meeting infant needs, basic requirements including an abundance of cool air, clean water, absolute regularity and, above all, the baby's birthright, mother's milk, 'the only perfect food'.[15] To meet these needs required considerable foresight. Pregnancy demanded self-sacrifice and a determination to build a healthy lifestyle. Mothers were given recommendations on diet, temperance, the need for rest and for plenty of open-air exercise. Every woman should have 'sound boots and a light waterproof' for early morning walks – walks preferably followed by a cold douche.[16]

Thus, like war itself, at this time the scientific study of infant needs brought with it an explicit regimentation of mothering. In contrast to the emergent emphasis on the emotional importance of children described by Carolyn Steedman in this volume, references to parental love were conspicuously absent, though they were present in earlier literature and were, of course, to emerge again later.[17] In the mid-1920s, austerity was applied to the baby as well as to the mother. Toilet training was to begin from birth, using the methods of 'holding out' and/or the soapstick, which Truby King favoured over the use of the bulb enema.[18] Like the mother, the baby needed fresh air and cold baths. In feeding, the aim was to establish a strict three-hourly schedule. 'The mother who "can't be so cruel" as to wake her sleeping baby if he happens to be asleep at the appointed time fails to realise that a few such wakings would be all she would ever have to resort to.'[19]

Few of these instructions were actually new; what was novel was the claim that their effectiveness was backed by scientific evidence – a claim consistent with current theories of disease and the attempts to take medical practice into the community.[20] The emphasis on fresh air reflects contemporary methods of dealing with tuberculosis, as Linda Bryder's chapter in this volume makes clear, and many of the dietary recommendations were based on the newly discovered importance of vitamins.[21] Much of the invective against artificial feeding stressed the importance of hygiene. Poorly designed feeding bottles, according to Truby King, provided breeding grounds for infection, leading to often fatal diarrhoea.[22]

It is clear, however, that, in the goal of changing parental practice, more than infant survival was at issue. Intervention into the lifestyle of the so-called poorer classes was now also directed at equally pressing issues of national priority in the post-war era: civil disorder, unemployment, public morality, and the future of the race.[23] In linking these priorities to child-rearing, Truby King combined a psychology of morals inherited from the nineteenth century with early twentieth assumptions about the malleability and vulnerability of the infant nervous system. As Steedman has described in the context of Margaret McMillan's approach, emotional processes were thought of as impingements with concrete effects on the brain, often with lasting consequences. In Truby King's work lack of regularity in babyhood was held responsible, not only for hysteria, epilepsy and imbecility, but also for other forms of degeneracy or conduct disorder in adults. Parents were strictured never to lose sight of the delicacy of the infant's nervous organization and the dangers of an irreversible decline.

For the ordinary family ill health and instability mean unemployableness; unemployableness means morbid thought and feeling; and morbid thought and feeling means loafing, vice and crime.[24]

The importance of establishing regular habits in infancy, then, was not just to ensure infant survival. It was to secure a lifetime of good health and a firm moral character. The focus on deviance opened new possibilities for intervention into normal parenting. This could now be conceived as a process of promoting satisfactory habits, the terms of reference being essentially the same for the infant, the child and the adult.

THE PSYCHOLOGY OF HABITS

It was here that a psychological approach found a point of purchase through the initiatives taken by the American behaviourist John Watson. Behaviourism originated at the turn of the century in the conditioning experiments carried out with dogs by the Russian physiologist Ivan Pavlov. Applied to humans, behaviourism offered an account of learning which apparently by-passed such complex human mental phenomena as wishes, values or purposes.[25] By 1908, Watson – then a professor of psychology at Johns Hopkins University[26] – had begun observing and experimenting on numerous infants. Again the majority were orphans or abandoned children in city hospitals and institutions. Before moving on to give practical advice, however, Watson's academic career was punctuated by a highly successful, if brief, career in advertizing. A mastery of techniques for packaging and selling ideas is evident in his *Psychological Care of Infant and Child*, first published in 1928 and dedicated to 'The First Mother Who Brings Up a Happy Child'.[27]

As subsequent commentators have pointed out, Watson's child-rearing manual brought together a model child and the American way of life as the desirable goals of parenting.[28] Crucial to this was the idea that adults should be self-reliant and bulwarked against stress, strain and nervousness. To enable this, Watson, like Truby King, stressed absolute regularity. But he also took to extremes the taboo on tenderness implicit in Truby King's work. For Watson love was a mechanical matter, conditioned in the baby through 'stroking and touching its skin, lips, sex organs and the like'.[29] Parents were warned of the dangers of excess. Though it might tear the heartstrings a bit, it was necessary to learn to 'stifle a few pangs'.[30] Consequences of ignoring this advice included hypochondria, invalidism, the proliferation of nest habits and the 'mother's boy' syndrome. Thus mothers were encouraged to absent themselves from their children's company for a large part of each day. Here a great deal could be learned from institutions, and from various experiments being carried out in Russia and Eastern Europe. Indeed the institution could be taken as a model for Watson's 'own specified world', the ideal environment for rearing children.

> It is a serious question in my mind whether there should be individual homes for children – or even whether children should know their own parents. There are undoubtedly much more scientific ways of bringing up children which will probably mean finer and happier children . . . [But] the social pressures to have a child, to own a child, to be known in the community as a woman with a legitimate child [make this impossible].[31]

Ultimately, Watson's work was interpreted as promoting an open alliance between child-rearing and the state and it was because of this that it was eventually rejected by many childcare experts. But in the later 1920s and early 1930s, Watson's work was also popular in Britain, despite the American setting of its individualism. Here it was cited as a complement to Truby King's work or used to support an apparently ubiquitous emphasis on regularity and health as goals in themselves. This emphasis was even held by writers well known for their radical views. For example, the infant care manual *Radiant Motherhood*,[32] produced by the controversial proponent of birth control, Marie Stopes, is not the account of sensuous pleasure in mothering that the title suggests. It is primarily concerned with health and fitness, emphasizes the importance of routines and regimes and insists on scientific rationality as central to liberating women from the bondage of maternity. Similarly, Mrs Sydney Frankenberg's best-selling *Common Sense in the Nursery* (1922),[33] which ran to several editions up to 1954, is not a list of homilies or an invitation for the mother to do her own thing. As the preface to the first edition explains, 'No hearsay has been admitted; all the theories have been tested and proved'.[34] These theories are precisely those advocated by Truby King, Watson and other proponents of 'modern methods'. Indeed, the book follows the organization of the *Mothercraft Training Manual* extremely closely.

In discussing the generality of this austerity in the 1920s, John and Elizabeth Newson have pointed out that it was remarkably similar in tone to the exhortations against spoiling in the name of avoiding damnation which were characteristic of the nineteenth-century Evangelicals.[35] The Newsons argue that it was the power to speak on matters pertaining to life and death which lay behind the domination of the hygienist experts. They also suggest that being sure of survival is a precondition for the relative luxury of psychology. But the hygienist insistence on discipline differed significantly from previous childcare advice. Linked to the growth of communal medicine, social welfare and other practices focusing on the child, there was now an attempt to write a programme for child-rearing which in principle included everybody. Furthermore, concern over behaviour and mental healthiness, far from being absent, was highly visible in the hygienist accounts. Here the crucial questions are, how were the moral issues redefined, and in what sense did alternative psychologies topple the hegemony of regularity and the psychology of habit?

MATURATIONAL AND PSYCHOMETRIC ACCOUNTS OF THE NORMAL CHILD

By the early 1920s there were two possible contenders for behaviourism's position of dominance in childcare literature. One was the normative tradition which privileged a 'normal' course of development, conceived either as a sequence of developmental stages or as items of behaviour which can be predicted to emerge at particular ages. This tradition stemmed from the nineteenth-century Child Study movement which drew inspiration from Charles Darwin's theories of evolution and natural selection.[36] This movement has been described in the British context by Hendrick in this volume. The Movement was small and, on the whole, university-based until the 1920s and the early 1930s, when, in Britain, Europe and the USA, new alliances between medicine, education and welfare generated an explosion of research aimed at charting the growth of the normal child.

Investigators varied in priorities and methods. For example, one of the most important innovators, the American Arnold Gesell, believed that early child development was driven by processes of biological maturation. Beginning with newborn infants, and taking advantage of new developments in cinematography, he produced

181

detailed photographic records of infants, the idea being to capture with verisimilitude both the growth process and a natural basis to normality.[37]

Another significant figure, Charlotte Buhler, worked in Europe but also made extended visits to Britain.[38] Gesell had seen the potential for linking child study to practical problems in medicine. Buhler, in contrast, looked to educational priorities. These included the pressure to devise adequate instruments for assessment, selection and remedial treatment for slow learners. In the 1920s, however, educational priorities also included a mounting concern over delinquency and other manifestations of disturbance shown by impoverished children on the streets. Buhler began her studies with foundlings or orphans placed in institutions and focused on social adaptation, co-operation and conflict behaviour as well as on questions of physical growth and intellectual achievement. As an item included in developmental scales, by 1930 temper tantrums and 'troublesome twos' had been produced as objects of scientific interest.[39]

Despite differences in orientation and approach these child study enthusiasts were equally committed to the practical value of normative development scales. In 1930 Gesell presented his findings in a practical book for parents, available with illustrations in both Britain and America.[40]

It might be thought that the developmental progress of the standardized infant, who epitomized the inexorable march of biological growth and the limits of environmental intervention, would check some of the more extravagant claims of behaviourism. For example, according to Gesell's norms for 'Personal-Social Behaviour', it is not until 18 months that 'Bowel control is practically established'.[41] Surely such evidence would explode the mythology in texts advocating 'toilet training from birth'? In fact, normative evidence was taken up slowly and selectively. Infant testing did not become widespread until after the Second World War and, as we show later, other factors were to contribute to the significance of 'temper tantrums'. Further, not only was Gesell's book not immediately popular, but the departure from Watson was not as radical as first appears. Though apparently innovative, much of the new normative work relied on the familiar equation between mind and body and repeated the philosophy of the good habit. For Gesell, for example, 'wholesome habits of feeling' were to be obtained by respecting the organization of the nervous system, from which any escaping passion could, happily, be brought under control by proper training.[42] Growing up was, as for Watson, 'a steady process of detachment, first from the apron strings, later from the home itself'.[43]

Thus, neither Gesell's work nor Buhler's shook the behaviourist stranglehold. The production of developmental norms mapped neatly on to the prevailing morality which both endorsed self-sufficiency and yet also ensured considerable readiness to adapt to external demands. Indeed, in Gesell's scheme, accommodation was both normal and natural.

THE NEW PSYCHOLOGY, PSYCHOANALYSIS AND THE CHILD GUIDANCE MOVEMENT

Clearly, any challenge to the hegemony of the 'habit' would require both a contribution from theory and a reworking of the moral terrain. This came through the growth of child-centred intervention which incorporated particular ideas from psychoanalysis, and in particular from various versions of what was called the New Psychology,[44] discussed by Deborah Thom in her chapter in this volume.

This body of thought was forged in the aftermath of the First World War and drew proponents from medicine, experimental psychology, welfare, the legal profession and education. It encompassed views which differed sharply in emphasis, particularly over the centrality of Freud's psychoanalytic concepts and, indeed, over whether they were necessary at all. For example, the idea of 'unconscious' or 'deep' forces outside awareness was accepted more generally than was the concept of infantile sexuality, and individuals held differing views on what could be achieved through environmental modification. Nevertheless, as a whole, the New Psychology opened the possibility that the will, the emotions, the passions were not simply fuel driving behaviour which was then to be controlled by conditioning; they were part and parcel of an individual psychology. As a tradition it also gave cognizance to the idea that children could be in conflict with the environment in which they were growing up.

That such potentially subversive ideas eventually affected childcare advice literature had much to do with the generally critical climate provoked by the First World War and on a persistent despondency over its mass destruction and demoralization. Amongst liberals the

New Psychology was of particular interest because it recognized human proclivities to violence and aggression. To a wider population its relevance was linked to the irrefutable evidence brought by the war that otherwise ordinary and normal people could break down under conditions of extreme stress and fear.[45]

While the immediate effects of the war had been to promote child-rearing based on control and routine, the wartime experience also catalysed the emergence of movements which forefronted children's emotions, motivation and resistances and which eventually contributed to new kinds of intervention. The growth of these movements depended on the post-war legislation for enhancing and protecting the mental and physical health of children, as well as on the problems generated by the attempts of its implementation. For example, the 1918 Education Act brought with it the problems of managing difficult children within a system insisting on compulsory education for all, while legal measures to isolate young offenders focused attention on the problem of supplying appropriate treatment.[46] By 1922 juvenile crime had been discussed as symptomatic of a psychological problem with roots in the home.[47] The focus turned on to early intervention and prevention.

In Britain the emergence of the maladjusted child and the juvenile delinquent as objects for research and management was closely linked to the development of educational psychology and in particular to the work of Cyril Burt.[48] But as Deborah Thom shows in this volume, other initiatives were ultimately more influential in moving from diagnosis to psychological treatment. Particularly important was the importation of the principles of the Child Guidance Movement from the United States, leading to the establishment of the Child Guidance Council in Britain in 1927.[49] As Thom describes, this initiative followed that taken in 1920 by the wartime psychiatrist Hugh Crichton-Miller, who opened what was later known as the Tavistock Clinic.[50] By the end of 1927, the East London Child Guidance Clinic had been started by Drs Noel Burke and Emanuel Miller,[51] and by 1928 the paediatrician Margaret Lowenfeld had opened her 'Clinic for Nervous and Difficult Children'.[52] Practical and theoretical differences distinguished these clinics, as Thom has discussed. Nevertheless they shared a commitment to understanding children's problems, from acute anxiety, phobias and nightmares, to bed-wetting, truancy, stealing and aggressiveness – problems now to be understood in terms of deeper aspects of mentality and emotion.

In the late 1920s and early 1930s, these clinics expanded and further clinics were opened. Community links facilitated referrals from medical practitioners and hospitals, social workers, magistrates and schools. But, as Thom suggests, referrals also came from parents, and active steps were taken to extend the clinics' philosophy into the wider field of child-rearing. From the late 1920s short articles began to appear in British magazines for nursery nurses, teachers of young children and parents which presented the thinking of dynamic psychology in popular form. Lowenfeld, for example, focused on children's so-called antisocial behaviour, and indicated possible emotions or anxieties behind the behaviour and the value of allowing these to be expressed in a relatively free context.[53]

This recasting of children's apparently antisocial tendencies into emotional dilemmas was taken further by the educationalist and psychoanalyst Susan Isaacs, the most influential figure in promoting a psychodynamic approach to parenting in the inter-war period.[54] Her book for parents, *The Nursery Years*, first published in 1929,[55] did not supply a list of instructions. Although her tone was often didactic, her aim was to approach upbringing through an understanding of children's emotions and emotional difficulties. Using actual or hypothetical examples of problems facing parents, the focus was on enabling them to think about the child's point of view.[56] These problems included making sense of children's irrational fears, dealing with a child's lying, answering questions about where babies came from, and thinking about what to do if a child masturbates, hits a friend or bites a sibling.

Isaacs's book was reprinted four times before the outbreak of the Second World War, which suggests its popularity and the potential influence of an approach which contrasted markedly with what was still the dominant orthodoxy in the 1930s. Where Isaacs emphasized reason in children's emotions and disruptiveness, most experts still insisted on eradicating the undesirable through training and routine. Given this contrast, it is important to stress the considerable overlap in shared assumptions between the psychodynamic and behaviourist traditions. These included an insistence on children's mental health as a matter of national concern.[57] There was also a general acceptance of the need to place child-rearing on a scientific footing, as was acknowledged explicitly by Isaacs.[58] Furthermore, the behaviourist tradition had itself been motivated by many of the concerns now being addressed by the New Psychology and the Child Guidance Movement. For example, the Director of the Federal Children's

Bureau in the United States, Grace Abbott, drew attention to parental concern about children's anxiety and aggression in her introduction to *Everyday Problems of the Everyday Child* (1927), the major contribution of the American behaviourist psychiatrist, Douglas Thom.[59] Watson had begun with bulwarking the individual against strain and nervousness, and even he professed a great deal of interest in Freudian psychoanalysis. Nevertheless, Watson argued, the issues for child-rearing raised by Freudian theory could be circumvented or eradicated by appropriate conditioning or management.

But in Isaacs's approach, the voicing of parental anxieties shifted the preoccupations of parenting from problems of management to problems of meaning. Prompting parents to think from the child's point of view also brought to the forefront what was later known as the parent–child relationship. Again, however, the focus on 'problems' was potentially a source of prescriptions on parental adequacy. Here, the emphasis was less on how to control the child than on what to think and talk about within the family.

FROM HABITS TO EMOTIONS AND THE CHILD'S POINT OF VIEW

In an interesting parallel with what Deborah Thom describes as an increasing willingness to refer openly to psychodynamic concepts in presenting the work of the child guidance clinics to the public, many leading childcare books by the mid-1930s had registered some impact of the New Psychology. References to 'emotional stability' and 'social adjustment' were peppered throughout. A more specific and striking example indicates Isaacs's influence. This appeared in the 1934 edition of Frankenberg's *Common Sense in the Nursery*. Where previously she had recommended behaviourist principles, she now advocated distracting the child, and gave examples of how to think about possible underlying anxieties and infantile confusions. Her section on 'undesirable habits', such as thumbsucking, masturbation and aggressiveness, likewise underwent considerable revision.[60] Though generally avoiding naming particular experts here, she drew interested readers' attention to *The Nursery World*, a magazine in which Isaacs (under the pseudonym Ursula Wise) contributed a regular advice column from 1929 to 1936.[61]

This assumption of a change in public interest in psychodynamic approaches to child-rearing drew responses from the psychoanalytic community itself. Indicative is the collection *On the Upbringing of Children* (1935) which was based on a popular lecture series given by child analysts.[62] The original lecture series was entitled, 'Can upbringing be planned?' The psychoanalytic answer was, ultimately, a cautious 'yes'. The editor, John Rickman, argued that psychoanalysis had contributed to child study as a science and was now in a position to be more critical of other branches of psychology.

But if psychoanalysis was to have a practical face, it needed to address what the population as a whole might identify as dominant social concerns, and what individual parents could recognize as their preoccupations. A leading analyst, Ella Sharpe, set the scene in the Richman volume in the opening paper entitled 'Planning for stability'. Implicitly this assumed that social and personal stability were both desirable and necessary and that the problem was not just with producing a stable child but with producing a stable environment.[63] A contribution on 'Questions and answers' by Nina Searl took on board children's curiosity about sexual matters, a topic still infrequently covered in the mainstream manuals.[64] Otherwise the papers illustrated psychoanalytic approaches to topics already covered by other experts, including the issues of feeding and toilet training. Melanie Klein presented an ultimately very influential paper on 'Weaning',[65] which was more environmentalistic than was typical of her clinical and theoretical papers. One of its aims was to establish for a popular audience the idea that the infant–breast relationship met emotional rather than merely nutritional requirements. This theme was extended by her colleague Merrill Middlemore in 'The uses of sensuality'.[66] Finally Isaacs took the behaviourist approach by the horns in a magnificent diatribe against the mistaken excesses of soapsticks, holding-out and cold waterjets. Her paper was simply entitled 'Habits'.[67] By giving example after example of letters from anxious parents, she signalled something ridiculous, bizarre, and possibly barbarous in what was fast becoming the old tradition.

This was a popular lecture series and to some extent the speakers would have been addressing a converted audience. Nevertheless a more widespread and irrevocable change of sentiment was demonstrated in 1938 with the publication in the USA of one of the landmarks in childcare literature, Anderson and Mary Aldrich's *Babies are Human Beings*. This was published in 1939 in Britain, interestingly under the alternative title *Understand Your Baby*.[68] The volume did not seek to displace the necessity for mental hygiene and habit training, nor the medical expert. Rather, through a radical critique of instrumental approaches to baby care, it aimed to restructure the context in which habit training was applied. Challenging the idea that institutions and conveyor belts were desirable destinies for the young, it argued that if babies 'were all alike we could bring them up in huge infant incubators'.[69] Parents were now required to adjust to the rhythm of the individual baby who was no longer to be allowed to lie awake in the small hours, screaming.[70] Attitudes to toilet training, thumbsucking and sexual curiosity were more relaxed and the idea of a 'natural timetable' introduced. As for cuddling, the *bête noire* of Watson, it became not only acceptable but essential.[71]

Within a year of its publication, the Aldrichs' book became a bestseller in the USA. It affected the whole childcare book market, paving the way for what Martha Wolfenstein described as 'the fun morality' of the post-war era.[72] It was particularly influential on Dr Spock, whose first childcare book, published in 1946, marked a shift in the centrality of the expert. Instead of the instruction to 'follow the rules', Dr Spock offered a reassuring, 'you know more than you think you do'.[73]

Although this shift of emphasis displaced rather than removed the role of the expert,[74] the Aldrichs' work signalled crucial changes through the licence to feed on demand, the need to respect each baby's idiosyncrasies, and the permission, if not the imperative, to indulge in physical expressions of mother love. The priority given to emotionality clearly reflected the impact of psychodynamic ideas. It also indicated a broadening or redefinition of parental responsibility; the management of emotional relationships rather than the control of behaviour was now the key to social adjustment. How did this shift come about?

PSYCHODYNAMICS IN SOCIAL REGULATION AND WAR

That references to emotions and emotional stability should have emerged in childcare literature from the mid-1930s is consistent with what Nikolas Rose has described as the beginnings of a new form of social regulation within the family.[75] According to Rose's analysis, this depended both on the structure of welfare established after the First World War, and on the conditions leading to its decline in the 1930s.

In the 1920s the proliferation of child-centred practices provided a link between the state, which aimed to conserve and maintain the population at high levels of efficiency, and the family, conceived as a mechanism for promoting physical health and sober habits. But in the early 1930s, the impact of the economic depression made the old system of welfare virtually unworkable. It became increasingly difficult, for example, to maintain the old links between bad character and 'unemployableness'. Indeed, some of the economic measures taken to counteract the depression's effects, such as the 'socialist' insurance schemes, undercut the tie between relief and evidence of self-sufficiency or initiative insisted upon by the old welfare system. In the United States the economic depression prompted reaction against the individual enterprise philosophy and encouraged greater reliance on community support.[76] In Britain an interest in collective planning went considerably further. This is reflected in the mooting at this time of various proposals for the redistribution of wealth, public investment in distressed areas, the co-ordination of social services and even for financial allowances for mothers.[77]

As Rose points out, these developments contributed to separating the functions of personal casework from the problems of managing the financial entitlements of clients. This opened the possibility for a new kind of intervention into the family, now conceived of as a system embodying relationships between members rather than as a mechanism for inculcating morals and habits.[78] This transformation is usually associated with the burgeoning of psychoanalytically inspired family social work after the Second World War. But as Rose suggests, some of the conditions which made it possible were clearly operating before then. Sybil Clement Brown's comparisons of social work case-records made in 1924 and 1934 suggest that there were substantial changes in the practice of individual social workers over this period, with interest shifting away from such issues as honesty, cleanliness, sobriety and material conditions, towards personality and family relations.[79]

This shift in focus was tied to the priorities and practices supporting the development of the Child Guidance Movement. Despite, or perhaps because of, the effects of the depression, the 1930s saw an increase in the numbers of clinics opened and in the numbers of referrals in which a high proportion of working-class children continued to be represented.[80] More significant than numerical increase may have been the movement's contribution to expansion and redefinition within child psychiatry. This was acknowledged explicitly in the third edition of David Henderson and Robert Gillespie's leading *Textbook of Psychiatry* (1932). The authors observed that Child Guidance 'must now be considered an important part of the psychiatric domain'.[81] In the past child psychiatry had restricted itself to physicalist or hereditary explanations. But the Child Guidance Movement prompted an openness to the possibilities of improvement with age and treatment within the family, and the delineation of a 'specific' range of child disorders with roots extending into the earliest years.

These changes in definition and treatment of mental health were part of a general incorporation of psychology into medicine in the inter-war years and were accompanied by an increased emphasis on community care.[82] They were also paralleled in education, particularly in the nursery school movement to which both Lowenfeld and Isaacs contributed, a movement which by definition focused on the pre-school years.[83] Initially the movement focused on promoting the physical health and native intelligence of impoverished children. But it too came to stress the importance of promoting emotional stability. By the 1930s middle-class parents were also actively seeking nursery schooling. Although this partly reflected the shortage of cheap nannies and other domestic staff,[84] the active search suggests that nursery education had become both socially acceptable and desirable.

This shift in aspirations among middle-class parents was not a product of coercion; nor can it be explained simply as a result of familiarity with child guidance clinics, which were concerned after all with children for whom something had apparently gone 'wrong'. Nevertheless, it suggests that principles underlying the child guidance work had become accepted as defining aspects of enlightened parenting. Here, as Hardyment suggests,[85] was at least in part the appeal of an approach in which licensed emotionality and flexibility hinged on widespread antipathy to, or reaction against, both the hygienists' goal and Watson's dream of the child with 'good habits'. But this reaction must be situated historically. In the mid-1930s, the antipathy to the behaviourist tradition owed as much to international as to national events; movements within the New Psychology gained significance not only through emphasizing mother love, but also through giving meaning to the aggression and disruptiveness of little children.

As we have described, the normative testing movement established the scientific status of temper tantrums and aggressiveness in the late 1920s, as one response to social concern over social unrest and delinquency.[86] Although these concerns were of interest to exponents of psychoanalysis and the New Psychology, work in the latter traditions also continued to stress that it was imperative to understand the individual's contribution to war. Far from waning in the inter-war years, this concern persisted amongst liberal thinkers. Ella Freeman Sharpe, for example, in the paper mentioned previously, reflected a generally shared perspective. 'The problem of war will not be solved until individuals recognize their own aggressive impulses.'[87]

Planning for stability in this context, Ella Sharpe argued, would require changes in the social environment so that greater tolerance could be shown towards aggression in young children. But events on the wider international front cut across such developments. Within three years of the publication of Freud's *Civilisation and its Discontents* (1930),[88] Europe had seen the build-up of fascism, Hitler's accession to power and the beginning of the Nazi purges. In Britain fear of fascism was matched only by suspicion and fear over the ill-digested implications of the Russian Revolution.

Against this background what was at issue was not simply the nature of human aggression and human love but the social and political implications of how these emotions were handled in child-rearing practices.[89] By 1935 the compiler of *The Family Book* could synthesize the implications of the previous 15 years of child development research thus:

> It needed the impetus of the Great War to make the country realise the value and importance of infant life. The neglected toddler in everyone's way is the material which becomes the disgruntled agitator, while the happy contented child is the pillar of the State.[90]

Such is the wider context in which psychoanalysis and the New Psychology made their impact and behaviourism was displaced. The rigid inculcation of habits was identified with 'Prussianism' and the ideal of the institution equated with the totalitarian state.[91] The centrality of the family and a nurturant parent–child relationship was to be seen by contrast as allied to democracy.

THE IMPACT OF THE SECOND WORLD WAR

With the outbreak of the Second World War the theme of democracy was made explicit in American writings. Relentlessly these asserted that 'While we are making a world safe for democracy, we must preserve in children readiness for democracy – these are the people in whose hands the new world order will be moulded'.[92] Hitler and the German people were portrayed as soulless and authoritarian, and 'our' system of child-rearing as against 'theirs' was vehemently defended.[93] Democracy as an ideal was linked to a family shaped around a view of what the German family was not. Gesell and his colleagues, in particular, now took the normative approach into the study of the family.[94] According to this approach, 'a totalitarian "Kultur" subordinates the family completely to the state, fosters autocratic parent–child relationships, favours despotic discipline and relaxes the tradition of monogamy'. A democratic culture, on the other hand, 'exalts the status of the family as a social group, favours reciprocity in parent–child relationships and encourages human discipline of the child through guidance and understanding'.[95]

It was to facilitate this process that the American publications brought forward the imperative to enable children to express their fears and hostilities openly rather than to repress or deny them. 'Hostility well off the chest', it was argued, 'does not make children more war-like. It makes for peace'.[96] Although the idea that war arises out of frustration is not, strictly speaking, a psychoanalytic notion, in the USA during the Second World War a new urgency was given to the broad range of theories associated with emotional impulses and anxieties. A further consequence of the openness to hostility was, as Beekman suggests,[97] a moulding of the family into a closer emotional unit, often with clear pronatalist implications.

In Britain the pronatalist imperative was as great as in the USA, if not greater. In the 1930s the birthrate had declined considerably. But Britain had to respond to the actualities of bombing and the threat of invasion. By contrast to the outpourings of childcare literature in the USA during the War, in Britain there were relatively few new publications, and, apparently, little indication of change. It was not until after the War that the popularity of the Aldrichs' book soared, and links between the family and democracy were made explicit even later.

But against this apparent lack of development must be set the ultimately highly influential debates which were going on elsewhere. These set the stage for a further transformation in child-rearing orthodoxy which took place after the Second World War.

If many had recognized the inevitability of the Second World War, it was also true that effects on children were anticipated. In December 1939 a letter appeared in the *British Medical Journal* warning of the dangers of evacuation. It was signed by the paediatrician and psychoanalyst, Donald Winnicott, the child psychiatrist, Emanual Miller, and the newly qualified child psychiatrist and psychoanalyst, John Bowlby.[98] The letter referred to researches carried out in the London Child Guidance Clinic. These were John Bowlby's researches in which a causal connection was claimed between early child–parent separation and later delinquency.[99]

Bowlby's research was regarded as controversial by psychologists because it relied on retrospective data. Within psychoanalysis in 1939 the theoretical interest in separation was relatively marginal. However, in the Child Guidance Clinic separation was already an issue. An emerging family-based policy stressed working with the troublesome child within the family, only removing him or her as a last resort.

But if interest in the effects of separation was an innovation since the First World War, that experience had left a legacy which now dictated medical and psychiatric priorities. The First World War had produced the problem of enabling individuals to recoup from excessive fragmentation and despair. From the outbreak of the Second World War efforts by army psychiatrists and other medical personnel were directed towards minimizing such deleterious effects through maintaining high morale.[100]

It was against this background that Winnicott gave his well known series of wartime broadcasts to mothers at home with their infants and small children. Though Winnicott addressed children's understanding and experience of war, from the outset he was concerned with the morale of mothers whom he described as victims of deprivation.[101] Like Churchill, Winnicott spoke directly to the mothers of the nation. Now, however, a new meaning was being given to the observation made in 1914 by the Chief Medical Officer, George Newman, cited at the beginning of this chapter: 'The environment of the infant is its mother.'[102] For Winnicott, the mother provided the infant with an environment which was responsible not only for physical health but for emotional and psychological health as well.

In the decade after the Second World War, the mother as the primary source of emotional stability was established as a *sine qua non* in child-rearing literature. With this came an acceptance of infancy as a period in which particular emotional needs are paramount. As has been much documented, both the focus on the mother and on the special psychological needs of infancy owed much to the influence of Bowlby's insistence on the exclusive importance of the mother–infant relationship. As we have illustrated, the emphasis on infancy originated in the Kleinian tradition of psychoanalysis in the 1930s, and many of the crucial shifts necessary for the receptivity of Bowlby's later work were at least embryonic before the War. But as Riley has argued, the massive uptake of Bowlby's work depended crucially on post-war conditions. Included among these was the pronatalist drive to rejuvenate or reconstruct the family.[103] Furthermore, the relative success of this drive depended on its connection with widespread anxiety about re-establishing ties of belonging in the face of recent separations, losses and disruptions. This anxiety was born of the War itself.

By 1952 when Bowlby published his highly influential World Health Organization monograph on mental health in children,[104] he could assume that there would be considerable interest in the effects of separation, and in the claim that there was a fundamental need for security. These were among the facts which ensured that the popular version of the monograph, *Child Care and the Growth of Love* (1953), rapidly became a bestseller.[105] But in the transformation marked by the popularity of this work an emphasis that had been central in the psychodynamic work of the inter-war years was lost or occluded. Bowlby's insistence on one-to-one contact between mother and child was quite different from the pre-war emphasis on damaging effects of premature and prolonged separations. Furthermore, the post-war focus on separation and environmental provision displaced the inter-war concern with children's aggression, destructiveness and irrational fears.

Whether or not we assume that, after the Second World War, the latter concern became less pressing, or that it was voiced in a different way, this crucial omission had implications for redefining the locus of both child-rearing and social regulation which would affect the terrain charted by future experts. In so far as the focus moves from what is inherent in children to the need for satisfactory relationships between mothers and infants, the issues of child-rearing become less to do with raising satisfactory children than with managing the problems of being a mother.[106] By and large, becoming an adequate mother is given priority over the problems of managing difficult children in all childcare literature subsequently.

ACKNOWLEDGEMENTS

We are very grateful to the Margaret Lowenfeld Trust for financial support in producing this chapter, and to Roger Cooter, Shirley Prendergast, Deborah Thom and Valerie Walkerdine for comments on an earlier draft.

NOTES

1 See, in particular, M. Foucault, *The Birth of the Clinic*, London: Tavistock, 1973; *Discipline and Punish*, London: Allen Lane, 1977; *The History of Sexuality*, vol. 1, London: Allen Lane, 1979.

2 This argument is illustrated particularly clearly in Foucault, *Discipline and Punish*.

3 D. Beekman, *The Mechanical Baby: a popular history of the theory and practice of child raising*, London: Dobson, 1977; C. Hardyment, *Dream Babies: child care from Locke to Spock*, London: Cape, 1983; J. and E. Newson, 'Cultural aspects of child-rearing in the English speaking world', in M. P. M. Richards (ed.) *The Integration of a Child into a Social World*, Cambridge: Cambridge University Press, 1974.

4 For further discussion of the popularization of psychoanalytic theories and their impact within social regulation, see D. Riley, *War in the Nursery: theories of the child and mother*, London: Virago, 1983 and N. Rose, *The Psychological Complex: psychology, politics and society in England, 1869–1939*, London: Routledge & Kegan Paul, 1985.

5 For further discussion of the necessity of including such subjective processes into accounts of social regulation, see J. Henriques, W. Hollway, C. Urwin, V. Walkerdine and C. Venn, *Changing the Subject: psychology, social regulation and subjectivity*, London: Methuen, 1984: 203–4; also P. Adams, 'Family affairs', *M/F*, 1972, 7: 3–14.

6 The vast literature on child-rearing cannot be reviewed here. Hardyment, *Dream Babies*, gives a good indication of recurrent themes and a fuller source of references.

7 Hardyment, *Dream Babies*: 10–11.

8 See, for example, W. Cadogan, *Essay on the Nursing and Management of Children*, London: John Knapton, 1748.

9 See, for example, D. Dwork, *War is Good for Babies and Other Young Children: a history of the infant and child welfare movement in England 1898–1918*, London: Tavistock, 1987: 3–21; J. Lewis, *The Politics of Motherhood*, London: Croom Helm, 1980: 13–23.

10 *Annual Report of the Chief Medical Officer of the Board of Education for 1914*, London: HMSO, 1915: 25.

11 Dwork, *War is Good for Babies*: 210–13.

12 Hardyment, *Dream Babies*: 176–9.

13 M. Liddiard, *Mothercraft Manual*, London: Churchill, 1924, 6th edn, 1954.

14 T. King, *Feeding and Care of Baby*, London: Macmillan, 1913, revised edn, 1925.
15 Ibid: 3.
16 Ibid: 9.
17 Sigourney's *Letters to Mothers*, Hartford, Connecticut, 1838, is particularly striking for its model of maternal tenderness. See also E. Key, *Renaissance of Motherhood*, New York and London: Putnam, 1914. Some of T. King's own recommendations echo the controls insisted upon by the physician Luther E. Holt in his *Care and Feeding of Children*, New York: Appleton, 1894.
18 King, *Feeding*, 1925: 21
19 Ibid: 36.
20 D. Armstrong, *The Political Anatomy of the Body: medical knowledge in the twentieth century*, Cambridge: Cambridge University Press, 1983.
21 Hardyment, *Dream Babies*: 183.
22 King, *Feeding*: 86–7.
23 Rose, *Psychological Complex*: 145–7.
24 King, *Feeding*: 104.
25 For an account of Pavlov's impact on child study, see B. Sylvester-Bradley, *Images of Infancy*, Oxford: Polity, 1989: 32–3.
26 On Watson's life and work, see D. Cohen, *J. B. Watson, the Founder of Behaviourism*, London: Routledge & Kegan Paul, 1979, and Sylvester-Bradley, *Images of Infancy*: 32–3.
27 J. B. Watson, *Psychological Care of the Infant and Child*, London: Allen & Unwin, 1928.
28 Beekman, *Mechanical Baby*: 146.
29 Watson, *Psychological Care*: 43.
30 Ibid: 43.
31 Ibid: 5–6.
32 M. Stopes, *Radiant Motherhood*, London: Putnam, 1920.
33 C. Frankenburg, *Common Sense in the Nursery*, London: Cape, 1922. Revised 1934, 1946, 1954.
34 Ibid., 1934 edn: preface.
35 Newson and Newson, 'Cultural aspects': 53–82.
36 For an account of the impact of Darwin's work on child study, see Riley, *War in the Nursery*: 39–89.
37 A. Gesell, *The Mental Growth of the Pre-school Child: a psychological outline of normal development from birth to the sixth year, including a system of developmental diagnosis*, New York: Macmillan, 1925.
38 C. Buhler, *The First Year of Life*, New York: Day, 1930.
39 See C. Buhler, 'The social behavior of the child', in C. Murchison (ed.) *Handbook of Child Psychology*, Worcester, Mass: Clark University Press, 1931: 43–82.
40 A. Gesell, *The Guidance of Mental Growth in Infant and Child*, New York: Macmillan, 1930.
41 Gesell, *Pre-school Child*: 381.
42 Ibid: 381.
43 Ibid: 381.

44 For summaries of this tradition, see Rose, *Psychological Complex*: 182–90, and C. Urwin and J. Hood-Williams (eds) *Child Psychotherapy, War and the Normal Child: selected papers of Margaret Lowenfeld*, London: Free Association Books, 1987: 7–8. See also Thom's chapter in this volume.

45 Crucially important was the phenomenon of 'shellshock' which provided the occasion for small groups of British army psychiatrists to introduce various ideas from depth psychology into treatment and rehabilitation. See M. Stone, 'Shellshock and the psychologists', in W. F. Bynum, R. Porter and M. Shepherd (eds) *The Anatomy of Madness*, 2, London: Routledge, 1985: 91–110.

46 See Rose, *Psychological Complex*: 180.

47 Maurice Hamblin Smith, cited in W. C. Hall, *Children's Courts*, London: Allen & Unwin, 1926.

48 C. Burt, *The Young Delinquent*, London: University of London Press, 1925.

49 M. Horn, *Before It's Too Late: the child guidance movement in the United States, 1922–1945*, Philadelphia: Temple University Press, 1989.

50 H. V. Dicks, *Fifty Years of the Tavistock Clinic*, London: Routledge & Kegan Paul, 1970: 1–33.

51 N. Burke and E. Miller, 'Child mental hygiene – its history, methods and problems', *British Journal of Medical Psychology*, 1929, 9: 218–42.

52 Urwin and Hood-Willams, *Child Psychotherapy*: 44.

53 M. Lowenfeld, 'Behaviour problems in the nursery', *The New Era*, November 1930: 137–9; 'Understanding the child', *The New Era*, May 1933: 82–4; 'Destructiveness in children', *The New Era*, June 1933: 93–6; 'Irrational fears', *The Light of Reason*, London: Price's Candle Co., August 1933: 18–22.

54 See R. Gardner, *Susan Isaacs*, London: Methuen, 1969.

55 S. Isaacs, *The Nursery Years*, London: Routledge, 1929, revised edn 1932.

56 Isaacs, *Nursery Years*, 1932 edn: 63.

57 M. Lowenfeld, *The Children's Clinic for the Treatment and Study of Nervous and Delicate Children, Annual Report 1929–30*, London, printed 1930: 7.

58 Isaacs, *Nursery Years*: 1–7.

59 D. Thom, *Everyday Problems of the Everyday Child*, New York, Appleton, 1927.

60 Frankenburg, *Common Sense*, 1934 edn: preface.

61 Ibid.

62 J. Rickman (ed.) *On the Upbringing of Children*, London: Kegan Paul, Trench & Trubner, 1935.

63 E. Sharpe, 'Planning for stability', in Rickman, *Upbringing*: 1–31.

64 N. Searl, 'Questions and answers', in Rickman, *Upbringing*: 87–122.

65 M. Klein, 'Weaning', in Rickman, *Upbringing*: 31–56.

66 M. Middlemore, 'The uses of sensuality', in Rickman, *Upbringing*: 57–86.

67 S. Isaacs, 'Habits', in Rickman, *Upbringing*: 123–66.
68 A. and M. Aldrich, *Babies are Human Beings*, New York: Macmillan, 1938: idem, *Understanding Your Baby*, London: Black, 1939.
69 Aldrich, *Babies*: 53.
70 Ibid: 83.
71 Ibid: 14.
72 M. Wolfenstein, 'Fun morality: an analysis of recent American child-training literature', in M. Mead and M. Wolfenstein (eds) *Childhood in Contemporary Cultures*, Chicago: Chicago University Press, 1955.
73 B. Spock, *Common Sense Book of Baby and Child Care*, New York: Duell Sloan, 1946.
74 E. Sharland and C. Urwin, 'Doing it with style; changing conceptions of mother love since World War II', forthcoming.
75 Rose, *Psychological Complex*: 155–8.
76 Beekman, *Mechanical Baby*: 160–2.
77 See P. Addison, *The Road to 1945*, London: Quartet, 1977.
78 Rose, *Psychological Complex*: 176.
79 S. C. Brown, 'Family case work and mental health', *Charity Organization Quarterly*, 1939, 13: 40–50; 'The methods of social case-workers', in F. C. Bartlett, M. Ginsberg, E. J. Lingren and R. H. Thouless (eds) *The Study of Society*, London: Kegan Paul, Trench & Trubner, 1939: 34–62.
80 G. Keir, 'A history of child guidance', *British Journal of Educational Psychology*, 1952, 22: 5–29.
81 D. Henderson and R. Gillespie, *A Textbook of Psychiatry*, London: Oxford University Press, 1927, 3rd edn 1932: preface.
82 Armstrong, *Political Anatomy of the Body*: 32–53.
83 See M. Lowenfeld, *Play in Childhood*, London: Gollancz, 1935, and L. Smith, *To Understand and to Help: the life and works of Susan Isaacs (1885–1948)*, New York: Associated University Press, 1985. See also Adrian Wooldridge, 'Child study and educational psychology in England, c. 1850–1950,' D.Phil. thesis, Oxford University, 1985.
84 Hardyment, *Dream Babies*: 207.
85 Ibid: 220.
86 Buhler, 'Social behavior'. See also K. Banham Bridges, *The Social and Emotional Development of the Pre-School Child*, London: Kegan Paul, Trench & Trubner, 1931.
87 Sharpe, 'Planning for stability': 2.
88 S. Freud, *Civilization and its Discontents*, (1930), Standard Edition of the Complete Psychological Works of Sigmund Freud, London: Hogarth, 1963, 21: 57–145.
89 Some flavour of the debate is given in R. Muir, 'Liberty, authority, democracy', in J. Hadfield (ed.) *Psychology and Modern Problems*, London: University of London Press, 1935: 107–30.
90 G. St Aubyn, *The Family Book*, London: Bartier, 1935.
91 This shift had been heralded by A. N. Whitehead, *The Aims of Education*, London: Williams and Norgate, 1929. See V. Walkerdine, 'Developmental psychology and the child-centred pedagogy: the

insertion of Piaget into early education', in J. Henriques *et al.*, *Changing the Subject*: 153–202 for a related argument on education.

92 C. M. Dixon, *Keep Them Human*, New York: John Day, 1942.

93 Ibid.

94 A. Gesell and F. Ilg, *Infant and Child in the Culture of Today*, New York: Harper & Row, 1943.

95 Ibid: 9–10.

96 D. Baruch, *You, Your Children and War*, New York: Appleton, 1942.

97 Beekman, *Mechanical Baby*: 176.

98 Letter to the editor, *British Medical Journal*, 16 December 1939.

99 J. Bowlby, 'Forty-four juvenile thieves: their characters and home lives', *International Journal of Psychoanalysis*, 1944, 25: 19–53, 107–28.

100 See, for example, E. Miller (ed.) *The Neuroses in War*, London: Macmillan, 1940.

101 These broadcasts have recently been republished in C. Winnicott, R. Shepherd and M. Davis (eds) *D. W. Winnicott, Deprivation and Delinquency*, London: Tavistock, 1984: 25–49.

102 *Annual Report for the Chief Medical Officer of the Board of Education for 1914*: 25.

103 Riley, *War in the Nursery*: 150–96.

104 J. Bowlby, *Maternal Care and Mental Health*, Geneva: WHO Monograph, 1952.

105 J. Bowlby, *Childcare and the Growth of Love*, Harmondsworth: Penguin, 1953.

106 See Sharland and Urwin, 'Doing it with style', for a fuller discussion of these issues.

8

WISHES, ANXIETIES, PLAY, AND GESTURES

Child guidance in inter-war England

Deborah Thom

As [child guidance] clinics have grown in number a certain diversity of approach has shown itself, for clinical work is, in many ways, an art coloured by the personality of the director and the staff. While some variety of approach has been welcome not only to the clinics themselves but also to the [Child Guidance] Council, a too-great divergence of method is obviously unwise. Child Guidance is so young and so unfamiliar to the great mass of public opinion that confusion would be caused by the existence of a number of conflicting types of clinic.

(*Annual Report of the Child Guidance Council*, 1937: 6–7)

Between 1920 and 1939 a new institution developed in England: the child guidance clinic. While much has been written on the three major schools of thought that informed the clinics – the British child-study tradition, psychoanalysis from Vienna, and American psychological medicine – the clinics themselves and their incorporation of this thought have received little attention from historians. Those who have written on the clinics have either been the pioneers themselves, or (more recently) psychologists who have moved into history to explain the shift in professional discourse from 'dangerous children' to 'children in danger'.[1] The former commentators have tended to *assume* the importance of psychology for the development of the clinics and have stressed the role of professional practice and theory, while the latter have tended to treat the history of child guidance as if it were only to be found in texts.[2] Both, moreover, have sought to render the history of the clinics uniform.

This chapter argues for a more pluralist account – one that, besides recognizing the different theoretical bases of the clinics, sees choices in their organization emerging from a wide variety of political, economic, and administrative contingencies. In particular, this chapter elaborates how the shape that the clinics eventually approached in England was to be unlike that in America, even though it was from there that came much of the initiative, promotion and funding. It also offers some explanation for the success of the clinics among children and parents, and the route by which some local authorities came to provide them. In these latter respects, this account emphasizes the effects of consumers on a professional service – in particular, schoolchildren between the ages of 7 and 13.

THE STORY ACCORDING TO BURT

In the *British Journal of Psychology* in 1953 Cyril Burt argued that British child guidance practice was distinct and different from its American and European counterparts in that it relied heavily on the professional skill and expertise of psychologists.[3] According to him, child guidance clinics were the natural continuation of the nineteenth-century child-study tradition, which had shaped notions of children's emotional disorders.[4] Before psychology altered this theory, the 'malfunctions' of a child's psyche were seen primarily as inherited forms of developmental disorders.

Burt (1883–1971) has claims to be taken seriously since, in 1925, he was the first in England to publish a plan for a child guidance clinic.[5] Although mostly recalled today for his work on mental measurement and for his supposed use of false evidence to sustain claims for his hereditarian ideals, Burt was prominent in the 1920s among those who dealt with the emotional disorders of children and in marking out of this domain for psychologists.[6] He was also an early member of the British Psychoanalytical Society, underwent some analytical training, and was an advocate of certain areas of Freudian thought. His three major textbooks of the inter-war years – *Mental and Scholastic Tests* (1921), *The Young Delinquent* (1925), and *The Backward Child* (1937) – provided a groundplan for themes that were to be taken up in many studies in British child psychology. Moreover, his appointment to the London County Council in 1913 (a half-time post that has earned him the title of 'the first official psychologist in the world') enabled him to train many others.[7] By 1938 there were thirty-four local education authorities with psychologists in post, half of whom had undergone some training by Burt.[8] As a historian, however, Burt needs to be treated more cautiously: his 1953 article, besides being factually incorrect, was itself a part of a long-standing professional antagonism between doctors and psychologists. In truth, psychology was but one contribution among many to a service which was much less homogeneous than Burt suggested. Indeed, the course by which he himself became involved with child guidance clinics is itself illustrative of this diversity.

During the 1920s Burt developed both a method of assessing children and a model of a clinic in which to conduct such assessments. Together these constituted what he described in *The Young Delinquent* as the 'special method' of the child psychologist – a method which was to be deployed 'in searching for the cause of any particular misdeed'. The method, he explained, was 'nothing less than a taking of a complete case history . . . an intensive inquiry into the whole psychological situation, with a survey as detailed and as comprehensive as [the psychologist] could make it of the past, the present and the future [of the child]'.[9]

Burt confessed to a large number of troublesome children among his clients – street urchins, thieves, runaways, even murderers. The readjustment of such 'maladjusted' children, indeed, was the main argument he advanced in justification of child guidance clinics under the control of psychologists. In thus arguing, he was in some respects running against the current British orthodoxy of hereditarian notions of delinquency in children. Doctor A. F. Tredgold's *Mental Deficiency* (1908), for example, a book that was to become the standard textbook on the subject (a revised 6th edition appearing in 1937), described such children as innately and incurably bad.[10] Yet Burt also shared the hereditarian position as it developed from its Darwinian and Galtonian origins and, overall, he was more within that school of thought than outside it. His case-histories reveal that all forms of delinquency, from alcoholism to gambling, were regarded as contributing to deficiency in heredity, and he made little attempt at any alternative explanation.[11] Moreover, from his mentor Francis Galton he accepted that the observation of mental disorder and deficiency included both physiognomy and physiology, and he appears to have accepted the case for the visibility of degeneration. *The Young Delinquent* was copiously illustrated with such pictures, which may explain why it was probably the most popular of all his books. Several of the most striking of these pictures depict supposed innate defects through facial expression, demeanour, and even in the dress of the individual child. Burt was to argue, however, that only the psychologist had the specialized knowledge with which to 'discover' such defects and, hence, to deal properly with them. Thus was the treatment of juvenile delinquency to extend beyond the courts, possibly even supersede them.

Burt's methodology involved compiling individual case-histories on the medical model. Such histories included the assessment not only of a child's family (and therefore of its heredity), but also the child's environment and intelligence. Burt made no particular claims to psychological expertise in the assessment of such environments, except in so far as psychologists were assumed to be sociologically well informed. Intelligence testing, however, was an altogether different matter, both from the point of view of the specialized claims of psychologists and for the future of child clients. Whereas a child's 'past' was genetically engraved, according to Burt, his or her 'future' was partly based on the insights provided by the intelligence test. Burt developed tests of intelligence, and he also used some primitive tests of character or emotional adjustment. But primarily he based the claim of the psychologist to deal with children's 'maladaptation' on the grounds that psychologists could synthesize these different factors.

Burt also had an interest in unconscious motivations and he used children's drawings and handwritings to investigate them.[12] These were not meant to be quantified, however; rather, they were to enter into the intepretative art of the psychologist. Here Burt drew on the tradition of European psychoanalysis which at this time, in the early 1920s, was still largely the province of psychologists and was debated among them in the pages of journals such as the *Child* and *Child-Study*.[13] Although doctors such as David Eder and Ernest Jones, who first translated and interpreted Freud for English audiences, were among those who entered into these debates and discussions, they did so not for an audience of doctors, but for one of educationalists, psychologists and magistrates who were seeking better understandings of deviance. (Ironically, it was to be medical doctors who were to introduce psychodynamic thinking into the child guidance clinics in the 1930s at a time when psychologists like Burt were moving away from it in opposition to the attempts at medical monopoly.)

In the appendix to *The Young Delinquent* Burt outlined the needs of the specialized environment wherein could be conducted his 'specialized method' of study. This was the psychological clinic, staffed full-time by a minimum of two psychologists, one or more social workers and a shorthand typist. The idea for such a clinic was not new when Burt wrote of it, though the appropriation of it by a psychologist was novel. Like all readers of the specialist press, Burt was well informed about William Healy's clinic for 'child guidance' in Chicago, which was designed specifically for delinquents.[14] In the wake of Healy's work and the writings based on it, the Commonwealth Fund, a large philanthropic foundation, had begun to spread the practice of 'mental hygiene' throughout the USA by funding demonstration child guidance clinics, and by providing specialist training courses in psychiatric social work and child psychiatry. Most of the literature on delinquency available in England was based on the work done in America. Burt's clinic, however, though it drew on American example, was in many ways more like Galton's laboratory than Healy's clinic.[15] It was a research instrument as much as a substitute for corrective incarceration. This was why Burt was later to overstate the influence of Galton and to confuse his own work and experience with that of others involved in child guidance clinics.

Despite extensive searches, no records of Burt's clinic, nor case-notes, nor photographs have been found. Thus the personal account presented in the appendix to *The Young Delinquent* is all there is to go on. According to this, the clinic was wholly the fiefdom of the psychologist. All the activities in the clinic – assessment, diagnosis and therapeutic treatment – were carried out by the psychologist alone. The insights from tests, interviews, and history-taking were said to require the synthetic expertise of the psychologist, rather than the 'team-work' of the medical consultant's 'firm'. Yet despite Burt's description of the model clinic, and despite all the accounts of his work in the professional press, and his own dominant position on the editorial boards of journals and on the committees of psychology training programmes in England – all of which predated the first child guidance clinic proper – psychological clinics of Burt's sort did not become widespread. Nor was Burt's method practised by psychologists, though (for reasons we will come to) it was to be practised in modified form by psychiatric social workers. Burt remained an influential individual, but this cannot sustain his claim and that made by others that the work within the child guidance clinics was conducted primarily by psychologists. It was to be the exception not the rule for a clinic to be thus headed. And although Burt and other psychologists contested this, they were rebuffed. From the time the first child guidance clinic in England was established, in 1927, it was doctors who were in charge (most but not all with psychiatric qualifications), though, as it turned out, they were not to be the most significant group in the development of the clinics as a whole.

PSYCHIATRY AND SOCIAL WORK

A few psychiatrists read and wrote for the same child welfare journals as the psychologists. They also tended to have more practical experience with disturbed children, though this was often secondary to their other activities and functions. Increasingly, though, as children's problems came to be construed as developmental, and therefore different from those of adults, psychiatrists were called upon to organize special clinics for children. At the Tavistock Clinic a children's clinic was set up in 1920 after many bed-wetters, unhappy children and petty thieves came to be referred there. (In fact the Clinic's first client was a child.)[16] The Tavistock Clinic was the very first that could be called a child guidance clinic. But, in reality, it was more of a child psychiatric clinic: on the one hand, it was there that the psychodynamic work of Hugh Crichton Miller was carried out; on the other, the Clinic did not provide the extensive contribution from social workers which came to be characteristic of the English child guidance system. It did, however, reflect a major shift in *doctors'* attitudes to children and to psychotherapeutic explanations of children's behaviour, since it was they who referred the children to the Clinic. This shift in attitude is perhaps unsurprising given that the Tavistock Clinic was organized on the medical model for specialized consultation. But the Tavistock did not at this time provide a training programme and it remained independent of funding from government. Although influential in the field of child guidance as one of the main conduits for psychodynamics from Europe, it did not inspire the specifically English form of child guidance.[17]

Social work, the other profession integral to the emergence of child guidance, developed in England in association with education. Care committees of social workers were responsible primarily for children going to school, but many of them interpreted their brief more widely to include assessment of children's physical and social conditions, and the dissemination to hard-pressed city mothers of information on food and clothing, charitable relief, and state welfare services. The social workers who undertook this work were usually untrained and unpaid, but they often played a valuable part in local government discussions of child welfare. In London they were also to be active on the Central Association for the Care of the Mentally Defective (subsequently the Central Association for Mental Welfare), which dealt mainly with children.[18] After the London School of Economics organized the diploma-granting training programme for social workers, there was a substantial increase in the number of them dealing with orphans, runaways, delinquents, truants and other so-called problem children who lacked adequate parental support.

COMMONWEALTH FUND

As noted above, 'child guidance' in America owed much to the activities of the Commonwealth Fund. This had been established by the Harkness family primarily as a means to addressing the problem of juvenile delinquency, essentially by conducting clinic-based assessments of young offenders. But the initial efforts of the Fund were not hugely successful, partly because the clinics were too closely linked to the juvenile courts, and partly because few local philanthropists and/or state governments offered to take over the administration and funding of the clinics as had been originally anticipated. After operating for 5 years, there were only eight permanent clinics in America. In view of this a decision was taken to reorient the Fund from criminal deviance to more general preventive social functions. In 1927 the Fund's Committee on Juvenile Delinquency renamed itself the 'Program in Mental Hygiene and Child Guidance' and substituted the words 'child guidance' for 'delinquency' in all its publicity material. The change was justified on the grounds that 'if juvenile delinquency was to be prevented, early intervention was required; once the juvenile court was involved, it was too late'.[19] Five years later some 230 such child guidance clinics had been locally funded, although not all of them survived.

Extending the work of the Commonwealth Fund to England was largely a result of efforts by Mrs St Loe Strachey, a London magistrate who had come to similar conclusions about the futility of children appearing before the courts. Strachey had been inspired by Burt's account of the model clinic, but it was only after inspecting the work of the Fund in New York in 1925 that she became an evangelist for demonstration clinics in England to spread child guidance throughout the country and train doctors and social workers in good practice. Among those she enthused were Evelyn Fox of the Central Association for the Care of the Mentally Defective, as well as doctors, some psychologists (including Cyril Burt), and officials of the London County Council (LCC) and the Hospital Almoners' Association. By 1927 plans were afoot for the first demonstration clinic and for an English organization to propagandize for child guidance and child clinics.[20] Although the plan for the first clinic was actually drafted by Cyril Burt, it was much altered by the New York directors of the Fund. Consequently, the American model was adopted for the London Child Guidance Training Centre and Clinic, as it was entitled, which opened in Islington in 1928. The Clinic, under the direction of the psychiatrist, William Moodie, was run by a team which included a psychologist and one or more psychiatric social workers.[21]

It was not to this group, however, that fell the honour of establishing the first American-style child guidance clinic in England. While they were merely planning their clinic and sending personnel for training in America, a team of three Commonwealth Fund-connected workers were independently organizing a clinic at the Jewish Hospital, Whitechapel, in the depressed East End of London. There, under conditions which were not unlike those met at the Tavistock, the psychological problems of the slum child were discovered in a context of professional expansion in child psychiatric work. The first staff of this East London Child Guidance Clinic included the psychologist Meyer Fortes (later better known for his social anthropology) who was then conducting research on culture-independent intelligence tests for his doctoral thesis; the psychiatric social worker Sybil Clement Brown, who had been trained by the Commonwealth Fund on a six-month placement in New York and Chicago; and Dr Emanuel Miller, the director, who was one of the fifty psychiatrists who had visited the Commonwealth Fund's clinics and offices in America. All three were accustomed to working according to American procedures, with the psychiatrist leading the team.[22]

THE CHILD GUIDANCE COUNCIL

The year that the clinic at the Jewish Hospital was opened, 1927, also witnessed the formation of the Child Guidance Council out of the amalgamation of organizations concerned with child mental health. The Council was to be responsible for promoting child guidance procedures and for organizing and operating the demonstration clinic in Islington. However, there were differences within the Council, partly over the issue of medical control but more especially over whether mental deficiency should be a part of the clinic's interest. The Americans, and those like William Moodie and Miss Noel Hunnybun, who had been sent by Strachey's group to America for Commonwealth Fund training, were emphatic that it should not. Evelyn Fox, on the other hand, understandably wished that it should.[23] By 1931 the issue was decided by Fox being effectively removed from the Council. In the meantime, however, the old hereditarian concern with mental defect was replaced by controversy over the European influence of psychoanalysis on child guidance.

The Council stimulated and extended child guidance work in the same way as its American parent organization. England's child guidance clinics spread faster however, as a result of differences in geography and scale of operations. When the Council was training two psychiatrists and two social workers a year, it was creating a cadre which became a substantial element of the psychiatric and social work professions respectively. In the process, the Council rendered the procedures of child guidance open to professional scrutiny, and developed the basis for specialist scientific practices under the general heading of child guidance. Among other things, the Council adopted the American policy whereby the Fund supported a social worker in post where a hospital, school or clinic requested it.[24]

The Commonwealth Fund kept a close eye on the proceedings of its English offspring. Mildred Scoville, who ran the child guidance programme in New York, visited the Islington Clinic in 1935 and 1939, and Barry Smith, who was the director of the New York clinic also came twice. The records of the Commonwealth Fund indicate that the Americans experienced a vexed sense of difficulty with child guidance in England, reporting that it 'was more work than all the American [clinics put] together'.[25]

Yet, to the extent that the activities of the Council were successful, this was as much the result of demand from below as guidance from above on the part of the Commonwealth Fund. The clientele of the clinics at Islington and at the Jewish Hospital was not as deviant (in the criminological sense) as had perhaps been expected by analysts of society and advocates of a child guidance system. From the start the biggest single category of cases attending the clinics were those of enuresis (bed-wetting) mostly, initially, from working-class homes and mostly between the ages of 9 and 11.[26] Enuresis clearly presented a problem in poor households where beds were often shared, sheets could not be speedily replaced, and where washing had to be done by hand at home. It was also something for which child guidance experts did not have a ready answer. The important point here, however, is that from the outset parents were prepared to use the clinics to solve household problems.

Some fairly obvious explanations can be offered for the acceptance of the clinics. First, was that punitive officials, like the children's care officers, school truancy officers, or even the school authorities, were never connected with the clinics, and the clinics had no legal or coercive powers of their own. Unlike their American counterparts, they were not directly linked to the courts, except through the coincidence of personnel. Second, the publicity material of the clinics was careful to stress support for parenting, and to appeal specifically to mothers – mothers who were already being addressed by various other agencies as the most influential persons in a child's life. Mothers, of course, had already become used to health visitors and infant welfare clinics, generally regarding them as benign. A third and final reason was, relatedly, that in the wide range of pamphlets and booklets produced by the Child Guidance Council care was taken to dissociate the Council from psychoanalysis, which was almost as suspect for being 'foreign' as for focusing on sexuality and sexual liberation. Thus Moodie, the General Secretary of the Council during its first years, in a pamphlet published in 1931, went out of his way to stress that 'the psychoanalytic method is never employed in the Child Guidance Clinic'. The discussion with the psychiatrist, he reassured parents, would 'only follow the line of an ordinary commonsense conversation'. He also emphasized the team-work aspect of clinic practice, dissociating the clinic movement from the stigma of the treatment of mental deficiency.[27]

Not all of the Council's publicity material was aimed at the public, however. Following the practice of the Commonwealth Fund in America, much of its literature was directed to fellow professionals and was rewritten accordingly. Thus, in a pamphlet based on an address that Moodie gave to Justices of the London juvenile courts,[28] he expressed none of the reassurances in the above-mentioned pamphlet about the dissociation from psychoanalysis. On the contrary, psychiatric intervention was highlighted for this audience and the medical model of interview was described explicitly, while the professionally tricky question of psychological investigation was downplayed. The work of the clinician, he wrote, 'takes the form of a frank discussion of actual, conscious happenings and pointing out to the child how he might improve his outlook one way or another'.[29]

The Council always emphasized the medical nature of the work they supported in clinics. In their report for 1934, for instance, it was stated that it was

> the policy of the Council to consider Child Guidance Clinics as Medical Units and to advise that a psychiatrist be the director. This would seem to be logical, since a medical training compels consideration of life and its aberrations from many points of view and, followed by a study of psychiatry, probably forms a wider and more balanced view for the elucidation of human problems than can be developed in any other way.[30]

The passage is interesting for its suggestion that medical workers required no special training for the child guidance work, whereas, by implication, psychologists and social workers *did*, despite their familiarity with the home life and education of children. Such an emphasis might be seen as reflecting the altered membership of the Council by this date: of its 116 members, there were now only eight magistrates and five psychologists (of the largely academic sort), but there were thirty-seven persons with some sort of medical qualification.[31] The medical committee included Edward Mapother of the Maudsley Hospital and J. R. Rees of the Tavistock Clinic, as well as Emanuel Miller and R. Langdon Down. But none of the these medical men can be said to have held the same theoretical position or to have pursued the same therapeutic practice; thus there was no hegemony beyond that of the medical over other discourses on the child's psyche. But even the latter dominance was tempered, for there was also a separate psychological and educational committee of the Council which included psychologists, educationalists and social workers. Although this group, which was less London-based than the medical group, tended to be dominated by the psychologists, overall the make-up of the Council reflected a much wider variety of interests and orientations than that found within the American Commonwealth Fund. The American model can be seen as influential in the priority it gave to psychiatric social work, to medical dominance in administration, and in the clarity of aims demanded in the annual reports and policy documents of the English, but the Americans never laid down how diagnosis and therapy should be conducted.[32] The latter, they said, was an internal matter for the Council; their interest lay with spreading good practice, not penalizing bad. Thus when Moodie expressed irritation at the paediatrician Margaret Lowenfeld's use of the title 'Institute of Child Psychology' for her clinic 'for nervous and difficult children' at Paddington, the Fund sought only to calm Moodie by placing an American-trained social worker in the clinic. It speaks volumes both for Lowenfeld's clinic and for the history of the child guidance clinics in England as a whole, that the social worker could report back to Mildred Scoville that her experience was like 'Alice in Wonderland', but that the work of the clinic was quite good.[33]

PSYCHOANALYSIS

The report of the Child Guidance Council for 1937 wrote approvingly of the fact that increasing numbers of children were being catered for in the clinics, and that the turnover was becoming faster. In view of this it became possible to risk discussing the psychoanalytic treatments that went on in the clinics without risking public hostility. By this date those who worked with psychodynamic insights had strengthened their position within the child guidance clinics and the terminology and the techniques of psychoanalysis had become more stable. The adoption of the term 'New Psychology' was itself one of the ways in which psychoanalysis was rendered safe for the English audience. A crucial contribution to the growth of public understanding of psychodynamic thinking and clinical psychotherapy was made by Emanuel Miller, both through his work at the clinic at the Jewish Hospital and through his books. In *Modern Psychotherapy* (1930) he outlined the areas for which psychotherapy was a useful technique with children and gave a vivid account in non-technical language of its practical applications. The book's success suggests that empirical observation of the effectiveness of the psychodynamic method in diagnoses and therapy was a major factor in its eventual acceptance among doctors and social workers. Many were thus to subscribe to Miller's conclusion that 'in the interest of the future mental health of human beings . . . something should be done to diagnose and to treat the earliest manifestations of disordered behaviour', and that 'it is necessary to use some psychotherapeutic method to restore the [disordered or disturbed] child to normality'. Miller's book also served to familiarize the Viennese work of Hermione Hug-Hellmuth and Anna Freud in investigating the deep psychology of the child – in particular, the notion that 'children with neuroses and normal children too, reveal their attitude to the world outside them [through] . . . play and gestures'.[34]

Alfred L. Adler, the founder in Vienna in 1919 of the first child guidance clinic, was also responsible for spreading psychodynamic ideas. His widely read *Guiding the Child* (which was first published in English in 1930) discounted the Freudian imperative of sex and death, while raising the notion of confidence. He wrote of encouraging children to develop life-plans, to acquire the capacity for what David Copperfield called being 'a hero of my own life'. Notions such as self-assertion were emphasized in Adler's clinics and explicit analogies were drawn by him with the development of democracy or the self-empowerment of populations. Adler believed that his 'Individual Psychology' was the first to throw light upon 'the sources of backwardness, delinquency, criminality', to trace a 'direct line connecting delinquency and backwardness with neurosis', and thus to discover 'preventive methods in . . . [the] pedagogy and therapy of encouragement'.[35] His psychology was not therefore as psychometric as that practised in Burt's type of clinic; indeed, he claimed to 'set little store by intelligence tests' or in the use of life-plans for the feeble-minded. He did, however, place great store on counselling parents in the management of children, especially with regard to their exercise of power; for example, he argued that 'to beat a child is to lack an adequate means of defeating a child's will, thus showing the child that he is stronger'.[36] Adlerian child guidance was very much about power and focused heavily on the social as a means to channelling and organizing it. But while his work was relevant to assessing general ideas of child management, and influential on British psychology as a whole, it played only a minor role within the child guidance clinics.

The same can be said of the Viennese work with delinquents of August Aichhorn. He retained an allegiance to Freudian thought, which Freud in turn rewarded in 1925 by describing the result of the work depicted by Aichhorn in *Wayward Youth* (1925, English edition 1935) as showing that 'children have become the main subject of psychoanalytic research and have thus replaced in importance the neurotics on whom its studies began'.[37] So they had, but there is little evidence that the courses for child analysts that Aichhorn and

Anna Freud taught at the Vienna Psychoanalytic Institute (which had a dual focus on neurosis and delinquency as the essential components of childhood problems),[38] had any more impact on the clinics in England than any of the other psychotherapeutic perspectives emerging at this time. Aichhorn's was but one operating within an institutional system which as yet had little coherence or system to it. Thus, while Dr Kate Friedlander, in a clinic set up in West Sussex in the late 1930s, worked along the lines laid down by Anna Freud and the Vienna Institute,[39] in East Sussex, another clinic, newly established by the local authority, operated without psychoanalytic inputs of any kind.[40] Although by this date the connection of child guidance to delinquency had faded in theory and practice, and European exiles (mostly Jewish) were rapidly spreading psychoanalytic thinking in England, a number of other factors stood in the way of a psychoanalytical hegemony in the clinics, as indeed, of a hegemony by anyone else.

ECONOMICS AND DIVERSITY

Not least important among these other factors were the financial needs of the clinics. It was these that gave the American Commonwealth Fund such influence, not only through the direct funding of the clinics, but also through sponsoring the training of psychiatric social workers (usually for a year on half-time pay). Clinics were expensive to run, involving as they did often lengthy one-to-one interactions between professionals and children. In 1938 the Child Guidance Council recommended salaries of £400 per annum for psychiatrists and £250 for social workers working full-time.[41] This not only helps to explain why several of the early clinics in America failed once their funding was withdrawn, but also, why, in England as in America, it was mostly psychiatric social workers who kept many of the clinics going. To the degree that any systematization was obtained in England, it was in large part through them. Although the Commonwealth Fund continued to finance the training of social workers in England until 1947, it did *not* initiate its American policy for the in-hospital training of doctors in child psychiatry (as at the medical schools at Johns Hopkins and Yale). Only a few doctors were trained at the demonstration child guidance clinic in Islington, where they were granted a half-year bursary. Most doctors who gained expertise in this area, did so in an *ad hoc* manner. It should be noted in this connection, however, that several of the early clinics were closely tied to hospitals. The annual report of the Child Guidance Council in 1934 noted that in London, in addition to the clinic at the Jewish Hospital, there was one at Guy's Hospital, at the Maudsley, and at the West End Hospital for Nervous Diseases.[42]

Many more child guidance clinics were funded by progressive local education authorities (LEAs), among them those in Bath, Birmingham, Liverpool, Manchester, Leicester and Sheffield.[43] It was only the clinics in the last two towns that resembled Burt's psychological clinic, however. LEAs came to support the general idea of the clinics in the conviction that the benefits outweighed the costs, but they did not commit themselves to any particular practice (though they tended to favour clinics with a psychodynamic orientation). The Leicester clinic, under the direction of the Chief Education Officer, Elfed Thomas, who was also a psychologist, was unusual in its psychological orientation.[44] But LEA endorsement was not simply arrived at, nor was its funding total: in Birmingham, for example, the clinic was first established and funded by Geraldine Cadbury, who had been particularly impressed by the work of Healy in Chicago. In 1934 the Board of Education refused to take over the funding of the clinic. Only when the Chief Education Officer reported on an investigation into the local causes of juvenile delinquency was there a change of mind and a grant offered in partial support. Ultimately the clinic in Birmingham was to be highly influential in the training of social workers and child psychologists, but this was only after it became attached to the Department of Education at the University of Birmingham.[45] In other locations, it was only after 1937, when the brakes had been taken off local authority spending, that LEAs came to fund the clinics entirely. Of the nine new clinics that affiliated with the Child Guidance Council in that year, six were wholly LEA-funded, and only one partly so. Prior to this, state funding was scarce, despite the fact that psychologists surveyed schools for the Central Association of Mental Welfare and reported as many as 20 per cent of children educationally backward – 'ill in the sense that they are in conflict with themselves (the "nervous" or so-called emotional disorders) or with their environment (the anti-social disorders such as delinquency)'.[46]

In other locations the mix of first initiatives, funding and orientations was different again. In Bristol a clinic modelled on Healy's was set up by the magistrate, Lady Inskip, after initiatives taken by the local medical officer, Robert Freeland Barbour, who had trained in psychiatry both at the Maudsley Hospital and (under Leo Kanner) at the clinic at the Johns Hopkins. The Bristol clinic started out with Barbour, as its director, conducting half-time sessions, plus an educational psychologist doing two sessions a week, and a full-time psychiatric social worker on loan from the Islington clinic.[47] In Manchester the development and organization were similar, with a magistrate being the founder and a Commonwealth Fund-style team carrying out the day-to-day operations.[48]

CONCLUSION

Except possibly other than for London, where some twelve clinics of different sorts were in operation by the late 1930s,[49] it would be ludicrous to suggest that a culture of child guidance clinics arose during the inter-war period. At most, some 3,000–4,000 children a year were being seen by all the clinics put together in the mid-1930s, and the clientele of the clinics was limited to the localities in which they were based. As noted above, the majority of the children who attended the clinics were bed-wetters and, indeed, it was this problem that came to constitute the object of the first collective research carried out by the clinics. The clinics of course catered to others, among them children who suffered from 'night terrors' or who had 'bad habits', such as nail-biting. Yet rarely did they meet with those cases for which they were initially intended: the sexually precocious, the violent and the thieving. The latter continued to find their way into the courts and to by-pass the child guidance clinics.

But it has not been the purpose of this paper to attempt to measure the social or the therapeutic impact of the early child guidance clinics. Such a task would probably be impossible. Our purpose, rather, has been to indicate the diversity of forces behind the conception and initial implementation of the child guidance clinics in England. Much more evidence could be brought forward in support of this argument. For instance, no mention has been made here of the enormously important work in child development of Susan Isaacs at the London Institute of Education; nor of Melanie Klein, a leading figure in the theorization of child psychoanalysis and in the British Psychoanalytic Association; and we have referred to Margaret Lowenfeld only in passing. (The need to speculate on the significance of gender in all such work is still another matter.) Enough has been said, however, to substantiate that neither Burt's account of the rise of child guidance clinics in England, nor that of more recent authors holds much water. It would seem, rather, that Agatha Hilliam Bowley, the psychologist who became the director of the clinic in Leicester, came closer to the truth when she wrote in *The Natural Development of the Child* (1943), that:

> In the early days of child guidance clinics our knowledge of difficult or problem children was meagre. Confusion existed about what behaviour could legitimately be regarded as abnormal and even as to which children could be regarded as 'problem children'. Reading the early literature or case studies one can detect the unwarrantable but innocent pleasure which was taken in 'adjusting emotions' which would now be regarded as perfectly normal expressions of emotional development.[50]

The impression this gives of a group of interested people feeling their way among the discourses of psychoanalysis, psychiatry, psychology and criminology accurately reflects the complex network of theories and practices outlined in this chapter – theories and practices which by the end of the inter-war period were just beginning to gel into a unified system. The quotation suggests as well the problems faced by practitioners in reconciling occasionally competing claims to the 'proper' guidance of the children who came to the clinics.[51] Above all, however, it serves as a warning to those who would seek to write the history of the clinics without reference to the complex of historical, professional and intellectual interests projected in the name of the child in this area, and the myriad administrative, personal, local, political and economic contingencies through which those interests had to be negotiated.

ACKNOWLEDGEMENTS

I would like to thank the ESRC, who funded the initial work for this investigation, and the Warden and Fellows of Robinson College who continued it. I am indebted to Drs Cathy Urwin, Gillian Sutherland and Roger Cooter for much help. Any remaining errors are all my own.

NOTES

1 Cyril Burt, 'Symposium on psychologists and psychiatrists in the child guidance service', *Britsh Journal of Educational Psychology*, 1953, 23: 8–28; G. Keir, 'A history of child guidance', *British Journal of Educational Psychology*, 1952: 22: 5–29; Olive Sampson, *Child Guidance, its history, provenance and future*, London: British Psychological Society, 1980; J. Donzelot, *The Policing of Families*, London: Hutchinson, 1980.

2 N. Rose, *The Psychological Complex*, London: Routledge, 1985.

3 Burt, 'Symposium'; and Keir, 'History'.

4 B. Bradley, *Visions of Infancy*, London: Polity Press, 1988.

5 In the appendix to his *The Young Delinquent*, London: University of London Press, 1925.

6 G. Sutherland and S. Sharp, '"The fust official psychologist in the wurrld"; aspects of the professionalization of psychology in early twentieth century Britain', *History of Science*, 1980, 18: 181–208; G. Sutherland, *Ability, Merit and Measurement*, Oxford: Clarendon Press, 1984.

7 L. S. Hearnshaw, *Cyril Burt, Psychologist*, London: Hodder & Stoughton, 1979. R. B. Joynson in *The Burt Affair* (London: Routledge, 1989) does not in fact deal with Burt's contribution to the field. Although Burt misrepresented the history of child guidance, he claimed less for himself in its development, than for the profession of psychology.

8 Sutherland, *Merit and Measurement*: 93–5. Only fifteen of these psychologists were employed full-time.

9 Burt, *Young Delinquent*: 5.

10 A 10th edition appeared in 1963, edited by R. F. Soddy.

11 Burt, *Young Delinquent*. He argued clearly, however, for the interaction of heredity and environment, and in some places in the text emphasized the role of environment. His effort to seek graphic exposition, as in genealogy, led to inconsistency, as for example on p. 57 where he writes of 'the degeneracy of the family thus operating indirectly through the resulting environment, instead of directly by its influence on the germ-cells'.

12 Ibid, Appendix 1; Burt, *The Subnormal Mind*, London: University of London Press, 1935: Appendix 3: Questionnaire on neurotic symptoms.

13 Both journals reflect a mixed readership, but contributions and correspondence reflect greater involvement by psychologists than by doctors.

14 Healy's *The Individual Delinquent: a text-book of diagnosis and prognosis for all concerned in understanding offenders*, Boston: Little, Brown, 1915, was approvingly referred to by Burt, and was cited four times more than any other author. See, especially, the 1938 edition of *The Young Delinquent*.

15 A. McGehee Harvey and S. Abrams, *'For the Welfare of Mankind': the Commonwealth Fund and American medicine*, Baltimore: Johns

Hopkins University Press, 1986: 40–56. I am grateful to Dr Martin
Bulmer for drawing this book to my attention. For Galton's clinic,
see Sutherland, *Merit and Measurement*: 114.

16 See H. V. Dicks, *Fifty Years of the Tavistock Clinic*, London:
Routledge & Kegan Paul, 1970: 2; and H. Crichton Miller, *The New
Psychology and the Teacher*, London: Jarrolds, 1921.

17 Training at the Tavistock got seriously under way in the mid-1930s.
See the appendixes to Dicks, *Tavistock*.

18 Two 'social workers' were to be found on any organization for mental
health in the 1920s. Evelyn Fox, the honorary secretary of the Central
Association, negotiated with both health and education authorities
over the welfare of the 'mentally defective'. Miss Vernon organized
social workers for the London County Council.

19 Harvey and Abrams, *Commonwealth Fund*: 45–7. Unfortunately,
Margo Horn's excellent history of the Commonwealth Fund, *Before
It's Too Late: the child guidance movement in the United States,
1922–1945*, Philadelphia: Temple University Press, 1989, reached me
too late for full and proper consideration here.

20 See the records of the Commonwealth Fund, Rockefeller Archives,
New York (hereafter CF): English Mental Hygiene Program: memorandum, from Mildred Scoville to Barry Smith, 27 July 1926, report
of a trip to England; and correspondence of Mrs St Loe Strachey.

21 CF, Box 10, folder 107: memorandum by Cyril Burt; letter 27
June 1926.

22 Interview with Sybil Clement Brown. She had been sent to America
for training by Alexander Carr-Saunders. After 2 years of operation,
the Clinic was sponsored by the Commonwealth Fund. See also
G. Renton, 'The East London Child Guidance Clinic', *Journal of
Child Psychology and Psychiatry*, 1978, 19: 309–12.

23 See CF, Box 2, folder 17 for correspondence on this between Fox,
William Moodie, Mildred Scoville and Barry Smith.

24 The annual reports of the Child Guidance Council for 1935–40
indicate that the most frequent call on this service was from hospitals,
rather than from child guidance clinics which preferred a full team.

25 Mildred Scoville, after her 1939 visit, in CF, Box 3, folder 32.

26 See Renton, 'East London Clinic': 311, who refers to 'behavioural
disturbance' for what Brown recorded as enuresis. Cathy Urwin
records enuresis as characteristic of the early referrals to Margaret
Lowenfeld's Institute of Child Psychology in Paddington, although
overall, more were referred for 'nervousness': Urwin, *Child Psychotherapy, War and the Normal Child*, London: Free Association
Books, 1987: 58.

27 *Child Guidance by Team Work*, London: Child Guidance Council,
1931: 4, 6.

28 *An Address on Child Guidance to the Presidents and Justices of the
Metropolitan Juvenile Courts*, London, printed 1930.

29 Moodie, *Child Guidance and the Schools*, reprinted from *Educational
Research* supplement of the *Head Teachers Review*, St Albans,
1931: 7.

30 W. Moodie, *Report of the Child Guidance Council for 1934*: 3.
31 Ibid: 1–2 lists members as of February 1935. The occupations of the other sixty-six members are not readily determined.
32 In this respect the directors behaved in the same way as in the USA; see Horn, *Child Guidance in the USA*: chapter on 'the Philadelphia experiment'.
33 Letter from D. Lilley to M. Scoville, 21 March 1931: CF, Box 1, folder 8.
34 Emanuel Miller, 'Early treatment and prevention', in his *Modern Psychotherapy*, London: Jonathan Cape, 1930: 110.
35 Adler and associates, *Guiding the Child*, trans. B. Ginzburg, London: Allen & Unwin, 1930: 10, 105–6.
36 Ibid: 111.
37 Quoted in E. Young Bruehl, *Anna Freud*, London: Macmillan, 1988: 101.
38 Ibid: 158.
39 Ibid: 254–5, 331.
40 East Sussex County Record Office, R/E2/45/1–160, records of the Brighton Child Guidance Clinic, for access to and help with which, I am grateful to the Chief Education Officer and the Record Office archivists.
41 *Annual Report of the Child Guidance Council for 1938*: 4.
42 *Annual Report for 1934*: 11.
43 See Deborah Thom, unpublished report to the ESRC on project 'Maladjustment and child guidance clinics in England and Wales, 1920–1972', deposited 1989.
44 Leicester Education Committee, *A History of the School Psychological Service*, Leicester, 1952; Sampson, *Child Guidance*: 8, 17, 38. Sampson herself worked in Leicester between 1949 and 1961.
45 City of Birmingham Education Committee, 1935, in Home Office files, quoted in Victor Bailey, *Delinquency and Citizenship*, Oxford: Clarendon Press, 1987: 102. Birmingham magistrates had first queried the incidence of delinquency among juveniles in 1920; see Sampson, *Child Guidance*: 17.
46 *Annual Report of the Child Guidance Council for 1938*: 4.
47 The annual report of the School Medical Officer for Bristol for 1959 provides a history of the service. See also Sampson, *Child Guidance*: 8.
48 British Psychological Society, *Bulletin*, May 1955: 29; Sampson, *Child Guidance*: 8, 21.
49 The annual reports of the Child Guidance Council lists the member clinics; there were twelve in London by 1938.
50 *The Natural Development of the Child*, 2nd edn, Edinburgh, E. & S. Livingstone, 1943: ix.
51 Burt, for example, argued strongly that psychoanalysis was dangerous if the practitioner – including physicians – was not professionally trained: *Subnormal Mind*: 319.

9

DARKLY THROUGH A LENS

Changing perceptions of the African child
in sickness and health, 1900–1945

Jennifer Beinart

INTRODUCTION

At a time when infant welfare in Britain was associated with the
imperialist desire to produce a healthy race for war and colonial
expansion, how were the children of the colonized peoples seen?
Colonial apologists have argued that Western medicine rescued
Africans from a heritage of tropical diseases, while recent Africanist
scholarship has illuminated the complex, often deleterious effects of
economic dislocation on health and nutrition.[1] All accounts agree
on the tardiness and paucity of provision for child health by the
colonial authorities, but there is little suggestion for Africa – as
for the white dominions – of deliberate or accidental genocide.[2]
Explanations for the initially desultory approach to child health
also need to account for exceptions to the rule, and for the later
expansion of services. Where there was a demand for labour, as
in plantation economies, children's health could come on to the
agenda as part of the process of reproduction of the labour force. An
alternative (though not exclusive) hypothesis characterizes the child
as present and future consumer of goods manufactured in Europe,
increasingly important in the search for expanding world markets. A
third variant arises from the analysis of imperial hegemony, in which
health services, Western medicine, and health education are seen as
entrenching colonial control through means which are acceptable
to local populations.[3]

This paper approaches such issues obliquely, while examining
directly the question of perceptions of 'the African child'. An
empirical exploration has been undertaken, in which the main
data are photographic images with their accompanying captions or
other contextualizing clues. Reference to alternative documentary

sources has been cut to a minimum to strengthen the impact of the visual sources.[4] The pictures are, obviously, an interface between the photographer and the child. Though revealing more about the former than the latter in terms of perceptions, they allow the child a certain presence in the historical record, an individuality lacking in the written sources. They also represent an interface between two intangibles – social forces and the colonial collective mind – in an excitingly concrete form.

Debates on the benefits and pitfalls of photographs as sources in African history echo those surrounding oral evidence.[5] Many of the interpretations of the evidence offered here are necessarily tentative. A particular problem in the present instance has been a restriction on the number of prints that could be reproduced in a volume of this kind. Many of the images are referred to without being shown, rather in the way documents are used; the few photographs that are reproduced can be regarded as the equivalent of direct quotes. The six prints selected for reproduction have partly been chosen to represent different occupational categories of photographer, partly also different points of view and points in time. Perhaps the most illuminating discovery in the photographic collections has been one that cannot be illustrated at all: that is, the virtual absence of children from the bulk of photographic records. If photographic images can help to support or refute theoretical interpretations, the scarcity of this category of subject – a large proportion of the population – bears witness to the relative unimportance of African children and their health in colonial preoccupations.

THE AFRICAN CHILD AT THE MARGINS c.1900–20

Harry Martin arrived in the Gold Coast from England in 1902, to work for the trading firm of Swanzy. At an up-country trading station, he learned to select 'boys' for employment, preferring Kru from Sierra Leone to local men who were less accustomed to wage labour.[6] The ubiquitous usage of the term 'boy' by white colonials referring to servants, implying a racist view of adult Africans as childlike, deserves a discussion in itself.[7] Among the photographs taken in Martin's early years at the station, several show children incidentally. They appear among a group who have brought in headloads of rubber, cocoa and oilpalm kernels, or among people seated beneath the trees, waiting to hear what price the white trader will offer for their goods.[8] As with other amateur photographs of this period, the impression is that of children participating freely in the economic activities of their elders, at least as observers.

When Martin deliberately pointed his camera at children – which he rarely did – they appear far more passive. One picture shows a long row of naked children. Undated and uncaptioned, it would be a puzzle but for its similarity to several others taken by contemporary European photographers in West Africa.[9] It was a favourite group pose of the period, in some ways resembling the way slum children were photographed in contemporary Britain or America. By contrast, the family group in Europe would be a carefully composed setting, with father and older children ranked around a mother holding the youngest child. The way that Europeans photographed lines of children in Africa suggests a lack of understanding of family structure, and a desire to show them as physical specimens rather than members of inter-related groups. Perhaps a more charitable interpretation, in the case of a naïve and genial person like Martin, might be the European's wonder at the large number of children fathered by one polygamous man. Another picture in Martin's album shows a small African child dressed in a post office worker's uniform, with the large cap at an angle on the child's head.[10] The trader probably thought the subject entertaining. Now, it carries a disquieting message of social Darwinism; the child echoes a dressed-up monkey. Yet Martin was, by his own account, sympathetic to the culture of the Africans he worked amongst. He attributed his good health and longevity, despite years in 'the white man's grave', to following the advice of a chief to eat local food, in contrast to many expatriates who ate imported, tinned European food.[11]

The photograph can be seen as one type of description, or report.[12] In a wide range of written as well as visual reports, published and unpublished, for this period, the pattern illustrated by Martin's photographs is repeated many times over. Children can be seen, if one searches diligently, but often at the peripheries of an account which concentrates on the activities of adults, European and African. In the reports of the Medical and Sanitary Departments of the Gold Coast before the First World War, there is more attention to the health of Europeans than of Africans, and scarcely any mention of children's health.[13] In some photographs, the children are literally at the edge of the picture, out of focus. In Martin's picture of the first steam car in the Gold Coast, with a gaping crowd behind, children can just be seen at the margins (illustration 9.1).[14]

9.1 Major Nathan, Governer, with his colonial secretary in a white
steamcar, Gold Coast, *c.* 1904 (photographed by H. Martin, trader)
Source: Martin collection (by kind permission of Mrs Fanny Wright and
Rhodes House Library).

Elsewhere, they may be clinging to a mother who is the subject,
perhaps selected because she was wearing some item of ornament
considered exotic, such as lip-plugs.[15] More often, babies appear
tied to their mothers' backs with cloths, in photographs of market
scenes or of women carrying water, fuel or produce on their heads.
In all of these pictures, the child is an adjunct of its mother, hardly
registered by the European photographer.

Just occasionally a photographer, usually a woman, portrayed a
mother and child or a child alone, with evident interest in the child.
Olive Macleod, travelling in the Lake Chad region in 1910–11,
included children among the subjects of hundreds of photographs,
many of which she used in a book about her journey.[16] Although
the pictures are captioned, both in the albums of originals and in
the book – often with different wording – they are rarely linked to
the text, making interpretation often conjectural. For example, 'A
Banana piccan' appears to be a moving study of a naked child against
a background of severe material deprivation, with a woman hard at
work trying to prepare some food.[17] It is a stark scene in which the
child seems possibly sick, certainly downcast, but we cannot be sure

223

9.2 Children at play, Kamerun, 1910–11 (photographed by O. Macleod, lady traveller)
Source: Macleod/Temple collection (by kind permission of Rhodes House Library).

this was Macleod's perception. In 'Guria Buduma Mother with her Children', the photographer's own shadow stretches across the sand to the mother's feet; is this a gesture of cross-cultural contact, or a classic mistake of the amateur photographer?[18] Elsewhere, Macleod shows what very few observers chose to record: children at play, in a delightful picture which conveys with astonishing freshness the children's absorption in their game (illustration 9.2).[19] There is a description of the game in the text – but nothing about the children. A blurred photograph of 'Mud toys, moulded by native boys' is replaced in the book by a sketch of the same artefacts; it would seem that some effort went into recording children's creativity and playfulness.[20] Photographs in this sort of traveller's account contain a high level of observation, with the air of recording a way of life about to disappear – the 'vanishing Africa' syndrome. The children exist only in the photographic present, their future uncertain.

For a medical view we can turn to the collection of J. W. S. Macfie, who served in the West African Medical Service between 1910 and 1922, in Nigeria and the Gold Coast. He recorded children at play in only one among several hundred photos – an image of some boys sliding down a polished surface of rock.[21] Many of Macfie's photographs have a consciously scientific intent, more immediately revealed in the meticulous captions than in the images themselves. His interest in the transmission of sleeping sickness led him to take several pictures of small children carrying water, since this chore took them to fly-infested locations where their lack of clothing, he thought, put them at greater risk than adults of being bitten by flies infected with the trypanosome.[22] Children appear, too, among the inmates of a sleeping sickness camp at Kotobo in Nigeria in 1913. Macfie interpreted the extreme emaciation of some of these latter children as a result of the disease, rather than exogenous malnutrition, a point highlighted by the healthy appearance of other children in the same camp.[23]

The view of what constituted a 'normal' or 'healthy' child clearly varied according to the observer, as we can see from attitudes to swollen bellies. Macfie labelled as 'malaria and oedema' two children with grossly enlarged abdomens, whom he photographed in the Gold Coast in 1916.[24] For a surveyor-photographer, a child with a huge pot belly, following women with vessels on their heads, was an object of humour: 'Going for water, boy bringing up rear apparently just dined'![25] In one of Macleod's pictures, 'The Lamido of Léré with some of his twenty children', the younger of the fourteen children appear very pot-bellied; but there is no comment from the observer.[26] In contrast, in Lady Clifford's 1919 fund-raising book for the Gold Coast Red Cross, a plump toddler of about 2 years old, naked except for a string of beads, gazes from the middle of a wide dusty city street, above the caption: 'What we love best on the Coast'.[27] This is 'the African child' as an appealing and healthy child of nature, albeit in an urban setting.

Photographic and documentary evidence suggests that many Europeans regarded children as a less interesting species of local fauna. The photographic record in general bears out the obsession with animals; photographs of pets and dead 'game' greatly outnumber those of children.[28] In the case of women diarists, there tend to be more frequent references to brushes with strange, potentially dangerous animals, or to the amusing antics of pet animals, than to children – though children can be analogous to either category, alien or domestic.[29] Men often recorded their encounters with animals in terms of what they shot, although they were not above recording their fear, or even their sentimental attachment to animals on occasion.[30] Servants ('boys'), pets and children were attributed common characteristics of playfulness and malleability, with outbursts of wilfulness; but the photographs show that they entered the European consciousness to very different degrees, with animals in the lead and the African child trailing far behind.

TRANSFORMING THE AFRICAN CHILD 1920–40

The processes described in this and the next section follow conceptually from the vision of the 'child of nature' seen in the period before the First World War, though the chronology was not as neat as this periodization implies. It should be remembered that the pace of change varied in different parts of the continent so that, for instance, in southern Africa, there was a greater black membership of Christian churches already in the nineteenth century than in West Africa, while in many regions the impact of mission Christianity came later.[31] In West Africa, particularly in the coastal cities, élite families could count conversion to Christianity and higher education for several generations by 1920.[32] Still, the photographic record gives a sharp focus to changing perceptions of 'the African child' in the inter-war period, as the examples given here will illustrate.

The prizewinner at an Accra baby show of the 1920s appears in a photograph remarkably like the portrait of 'What we love best on the Coast' referred to above, except that this child is wearing rosettes and a medallion round its neck, and holding a silver cup (presented by Queen Mary).[33] In another picture, the same child is shown with a white woman and an African woman, presumably its mother (illustration 9.3).[34] Neither the mother nor the child conforms to European styles of dress. The activity they are engaged in, however, is the distinctly European one of competing to see whose baby is best, on the theory that such competitions encourage all mothers to strive harder in babycare.[35] By comparison with the 'child of nature', this infant has been domesticated; its position is somewhere between a fatted calf at a livestock show, and a star pupil at a school prizegiving.

The prize baby represents the beginning of a process of anglicization, mainly carried out through education. The notion that African children could be transformed by education into something akin to the child as the colonials knew it at home, broke across the boundaries between missionaries, government officials, and medical personnel; even across colonial national frontiers. Though

226

9.3 Prizewinner at Accra baby show with mother and patroness,
Gold Coast, 1920s (photographed by Miss G. Smyly)
Source: Smyly collection (by kind permission of the Royal
Commonwealth Society Library).

the British never subscribed to the French ideal of 'assimilation' they certainly displayed as great a zeal in some quarters for transforming African children into a new citizenry.[36] This was partly to create Africans whom the colonials could understand; more importantly, perhaps, it was to create a group who would fully understand the colonials. Indeed, not only understand, but crave the colonists' culture and material goods.

The transformation had begun with the missionaries prior to colonization. Following the First World War, it is typified by a comment from Eileen Fraser, a missionary who worked with her doctor husband in the southern Sudan. She records in an illuminating remark that soon after their arrival, she and her husband felt they must 'get some boys' and educate them in the Christian faith, which also meant teaching them to read and write.[37] As elsewhere, adult converts were made through medical and surgical treatment, but children inducted into the foreign religion were seen as particular prizes, and probably more reliable converts.[38]

Elise Lincé, who worked as a missionary teacher in the Gold Coast in the 1930s, took many snapshots of children at school at Mbofraturo, Kumasi, and at the Wesleyan Girls' High School in Accra. She recorded the girls' names – in many cases, Europeanized names like Eleanor and Rosaline – in captions to pictures of girl guide and school activities. One series of Lincé's photographs shows kindergarten infants at play, learning through 'number games', or involved with washing.[39] The teacher herself makes an appearance in local dress; and she recorded in the Ga language a comment on one infant, held in her arms – as though she were especially close to that child.[40] But children in mission schools became altogether more fluent in the language and mores of the colonial rulers than vice versa.

Government schools followed the mission schools, with demand for European education growing among the urban population. The European passion for drill and regimentation is illustrated in a postcard of pupils in the playground of the government school, Accra: about 600 children form neat rows and perform identical exercises.[41] A verbal picture of Accra schoolchildren in the 1920s is provided by Dr Magill, a school medical officer, who felt that African children were 'very similar in physique and incidence of disease, to the English child'. According to him, there was a greater incidence of malnutrition in Accra than in the UK, but the cases he recorded as malnourished were not as bad as some in England: 'The majority of the young Africans are chubby little fellows and therefore the defectives stand out all the more markedly by contrast. None of those I examined in any way approached the extreme degrees of malnutrition met with in the poorer districts of London.'[42] The schoolchildren of Accra represented only a small section of the population, however – mainly the more prosperous.

Perhaps the greatest effort to remake the black child in the image of the English child, educated according to progressive ideas, was instituted at Achimota school and college near Accra. Photographs taken in 1930, by F. G. Guggisberg, the 'father of Achimota' (governor of the Gold Coast from 1919 to 1927), show not only conventional classrooms, but also craft rooms with children making clay models and learning woodwork, younger children drawing on the floor with chalks, and a school orchestra. In the modelling class, the children are producing animals, rather as Macleod had recorded, but in a formal anglicized setting. When the picture is examined closely, the completed models appear to include horses, which could not be kept in this region because of tsetse, and an English medieval castle.[43] Achimota staff were black and white, male and female; many barriers were reckoned to be broken down. The head of the college, Revd A. G. Fraser, displayed enlightened views on the need to work 'shoulder to shoulder with African colleagues' who better understood their people's customs.[44] In spite of this respect for Africans' abilities, Fraser headed an institution that largely replaced African values with European ones, in religious beliefs, language, codes of behaviour, and clothing.

School pupils became suitable candidates for European-style medical treatment, which could also be offered to non-school village children on occasion. Among the photographs taken by Jessie Griffith, the wife of one of the medical officers at Achimota (and herself a nurse), are some of children suffering from yaws. The remark that one child had started a course of treatment may indicate an intention to show 'before' and 'after' cases.[45] We do not know whether these children were photographed naked – with backs to the camera, heads turned – in order to show their sores, or because that was their usual condition. In another of Griffith's pictures, two children dance to their reflections beside a car, naked except for a string of beads.[46] The Achimota pupils, by contrast, wear simple shifts and shorts, as in photographs of a master, under a pawpaw tree outside a classroom, with 'some of his boys and girls, preparing lufas with which to wash and scrub their little shiny bodies'.[47] Though it is not spelled out here, improved personal hygiene and clean clothing were believed to inhibit transmission of yaws.

The guide and scout movement also visibly transformed the child, encouraged drill, and emphasized health and hygiene. Promoted both by voluntary effort, and semi-officially by government employees, the movement acquired a large following, at least in urban areas, and could produce impressive crowds for parades.[48] Mary Johnson, who joined her brother in Lagos in 1930, after he had been appointed Director of Medical and Sanitary Services, recorded guide activities in a series of photographs. The African girls in their uniforms, grinning broadly beside their tents or solemnly holding out bandaged arms in first aid demonstrations, appear identical – apart from their colour – to girl guides at a similar period in England. Johnson's guides really appear as her own property or creation. They contrast strongly with other African children, wearing few clothes or weeping dreadfully, who appear in the same collection.[49] In another group of guides, from the Lincé collection, the white uniform of one girl appears to radiate light from the centre of the photograph – a visually striking expression of colonial 'enlightenment' (illustration 9.4).[50]

SAVING THE CHILD 1920–45

Alongside the transformation of some African children into honorary whites, the photographic record reveals a growing view of the African child as sick or hungry, needing physical salvation. There was some transfer of infant welfare concerns from the metropolis; moves to counter the waste of infant life included the appointment of women medical officers, and the encouragement of volunteer support.[51] It was widely recognized in this period that the main causes of infant and child death were the same as in Britain – gastroenteritis and respiratory diseases. Yet European observers saw three areas of special vulnerability related to the child's Africanness: tropical diseases, various forms of malnutrition, and 'bad practices' of the child's carers and/or traditional healers. Disease, nutrition, childcare – all areas of concern in Britain – were seen as transformed by the tropical climate and African culture, so that the European vision entailed threats to the child from dark forces.[52]

Attitudes to traditional practices, reflected in the photographs, clearly depended on the role of the photographer. Anthropologists like E. E. Evans-Pritchard and R. S. Rattray, recording the rituals

9.4 Girl guides picnic group at Achimota, Gold Coast, 1932
(photographed by E. M. Lincé)
Source: Lincé collection (by kind permission of Miss Elise Lincé and
Rhodes House Library).

associated with the first 'coming-out' of a newborn infant in
different parts of Africa, convey solemnity and the robustness of
the child.[53] The practices they record, however, were interpreted by
other observers as 'primitive' and dangerous, or simply comical.[54]
T. H. Dalrymple, a doctor and amateur anthropologist in British
Cameroon, turned the divination of a child's illness through a
spider oracle into a sort of pantomime; in the final scene the
mother, beaten by her husband as the suspected instigator, appears
to be smiling. There is more than a hint that the whole thing was

staged at the visitor's request.[55] In a near-contemporary picture by the anthropologist Max Gluckman, a Zambian boy is cupped for a tooth abscess, with gourds attached to his temples; here the anthropologist's intervention is evidenced by a white bandage around the boy's recently circumcized penis.[56] The occasional bandage intrudes a curious note in a series of Gluckman's photographs of the circumcision ceremony, which otherwise constitutes a form of note-taking, a careful record rather than a statement.

A photograph of 'A Hausa Doctor' treating a small girl in Accra in the 1930s is harder to read – it is reproduced as a postcard, photographer unknown. The two figures make a sympathetic doctor–patient dyad, the choice of caption indicates respect, but a row of horns and a snakeskin which figure prominently in the foreground may be intended to draw attention to the exoticism of indigenous *materia medica*.[57] Muslim practitioners were probably better regarded by Europeans than animist healers, often portrayed as 'witch-doctors'; so the child in this picture could be perceived either as under threat from magical remedies, or in receipt of culturally appropriate care.[58]

For the Western doctor's view, we can examine the printed photograph in a variety of sources. Children scarcely form a separate category in much of this work; when they do appear, as in Gelfand's *The Sick African*, only part of the child's body is shown, with some shocking deformity caused by disease – in line with the rest of the illustrations.[59] This genre exemplifies the fascination and horror of tropical diseases, with the heroic doctor, metaphorically at the centre of the picture, performing miracle cures. Attitudes to traditional healers tended to be skewed by the high proportion of patients who sought Western medical aid after indigenous treatment failed, and in the case of mission doctors, by hostility to African cosmologies.[60]

When special attention was given to sick children, by medical officers appointed for that task, less spectacular conditions moved into the picture – especially, in the inter-war period, malnutrition. Reflecting research into nutrition in Europe, there was interest in special diets in the 'colonial laboratory': diets given in institutions, and those of delineated social groups described as 'tribes'.[61] Childhood malnutrition was then analysed in terms of deficiencies of certain factors. Cicely Williams, a doctor in the Gold Coast, used photographs in three ways in her accounts of a nutritional disease of childhood, for which she used the local name 'kwashiorkor'; first, to show kwashiorkor symptoms, in a long-running battle with specialists who quarrelled over the nature of the disease; second, to show causation, by juxtaposing the healthy baby and the malnourished older sibling – this was the 'disease of the deposed child' – implicating maternal ignorance; third, to demonstrate prevention, by showing malnourished village children with healthier, larger children of the same age who had regularly attended a child welfare clinic.[62] The main solution, as in Britain, was to educate the mothers.

Williams was using the photograph in a deliberately didactic way; Dr F. M. Purcell, another doctor in the Gold Coast medical service, became embroiled in the politics of nutrition through his use of photographs. He succeeded in publishing a copiously illustrated monograph on dietary diseases of children in the southern region of the Gold Coast, focusing on specific dietary deficiencies.[63] However, his official report on a broader nutritional survey was refused publication by the Gold Coast government, with the collusion of the Colonial Office, on the grounds that it painted too stark a picture of the state of health of the population. Purcell resigned in protest.[64] He maintained that the report had been suppressed because it might cause official embarrassment, since 'no one may starve in the British Empire'.[65] When photographs from the report were published in the *West African Review*, they revealed drought conditions in the Northern Territories, with emaciated children, and a blind man.[66] The rival magazine, *West Africa*, responded by publishing an article under the heading 'Recall Dr Purcell: facts from photographic record' in which it praised the use of the photos by *West African Review*, and interpreted the comment on starvation in the Empire as: 'nobody must be allowed to *know* that anybody starves'.[67] People would think the Purcell photographs came from a poor area of India, the article remarked.

Official photographs of development work in British West Africa, produced during the Second World War, showed scenes from the Northern Territories very similar to Purcell's. Soil exhaustion, however, was identified as the cause of children's and adults' starving appearance, and the solution – agricultural extension work – was illustrated alongside the problem.[68] Periodic famine, unacceptable in Purcell's report, was translated into a technical issue related to the war effort; young men were away fighting 'by the side of the United Nations', but improved agricultural techniques would make good the shortfall in labour.

9.5 Mandingo women after listening to a talk on child welfare, The Gambia, 1935 (photographed by Mrs T. F. G. Hopkins, wife of administrative officer).
Source: Hopkins collection (by kind permission of Rhodes House Library).

Infant welfare innovations were less controversial, and more visible, than debates over imaging malnutrition or famine. From the baby shows of the 1920s, and clinics with voluntary helpers, to the more comprehensive services of the post-War period, the message of reaching the babies through the mothers remained reminiscent of the metropolitan programme.[69] In general, the demand for curative services prevented the clinics operating as advice centres, but there were exceptions. For example, a snap-shot taken in The Gambia in 1935 shows 'Mandingo women after listening to talk on Child Welfare'. The three women are half-turned from the camera, as though to show the thriving babies tied to their backs, already benefiting from the welfare advice received by the mothers (illustration 9.5).[70] A series on rural welfare work in post-War northern Nigeria shows the white nurse and her black staff engaged in examining children, deliver-ing medicine, and giving open-air classes for mothers. Here, the curative side of the service predominates. Malnutrition makes an appearance, to be treated with medicine, as a black nurse holds out a bottle of medicine to a father holding a sick child in his arms.[71]

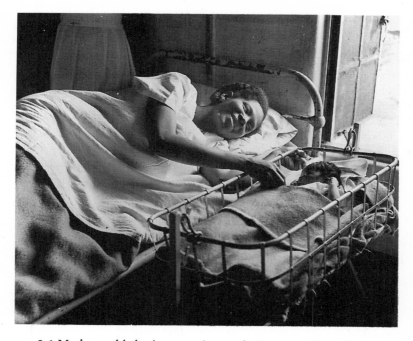

9.6 Mother and baby in maternity ward, Freetown, Sierra Leone
Source: British Official Photographs (by kind permission of the Royal
Commonwealth Society Library).

Maternity and infant welfare work in the setting of an urban
hospital are displayed in official wartime photos from Freetown,
Sierra Leone. One of these pictures, of a baby being bathed by a
white-robed young woman, was cribbed by *West African Review*,
which incorrectly implied that the figure was a novice mother –
yet another instance of the perception of the mother as ignorant
and in need of instruction.[72] She was actually a pupil midwife,
which explains the array of modern scientific aids beside the
bath, such as a sterilizing box full of cotton wool.[73] Modern
science is less in evidence in a charming picture of a mother
with a newborn baby beside her in the ward, from the same
hospital (illustration 9.6).[74] Nevertheless, the hospital bedstead,
the separate cot for the baby, the white sheet turned back, a nurse's
apron in the background, and the open casement window all tell of
the role of Western medicine in providing a hopeful prospect for
the African child.

CONCLUSION

Oxfam was founded to relieve starvation in war-torn Europe, not in Africa. The African child of 1945 was going to thrive, because it was the child of the United Nations, and with the countdown to independence beginning for many African countries, optimism was the keynote. The breakdown of entire ecological systems, the awful inadequacy of the hospital-based medical services for developing countries, the continuing vulnerability of children's health at the mercy of international market forces, were all present in 1945, but their image was yet to be seen. The official line was to contain the dark message of the photograph of sick or starving children within the framework of progress under Western auspices.

In the early period, while adults were dismissed as childlike, children were often ignored altogether, or regarded as mere appendages of their mothers, as objects of amusement, or as a form of wildlife. Children's widespread participation in adult social and economic life meant they appeared in the photographic record, but rather by accident than intention. Activities specific to childhood were cultural curios, if they were perceived at all. The ideal type of the African child, for many Europeans, was the 'child of nature' detached from a social context.

Transforming African children into black versions of English children, mainly through education, virtually created the child anew. With a European language, religion, clothing and culture, the 'whitened' child became a consumer of Western medicine and Western products in general. There was some evidence from the photographic record of a hygienic evangelism shared by missionaries and secular workers, voluntary and official. African children were 'saved' by contact with Western ideas, while non-school children remained surrounded by, and vulnerable to, disease and dirt. The schooled children, joining a core of middle-class urbanites, would in turn become 'missionaries' of Western culture and hygiene.

The notion of the vulnerability of the African child was further explored through contrasting perceptions of anthropologists, doctors and others, who looked at children's disease and nutrition, and at medicine and healing. By the end of the Second World War a 'development' model was emerging; child health was amenable to Western scientific medicine, but also to overall social and economic development. The heartiness of the official photographs contrasts with the suppressed pictures of Dr Purcell, while the official pictures could themselves be used to propagate the evergreen view that educating the mothers was a mainstay of progress in child survival.

Above all, the pictorial sources at this later period illuminate a purposefulness in the European perception of the African child and a series of didactic messages or programmes for reform. While anthropologists saw children as part of a society under threat, potential victims of dislocation caused by culture contact, others sought to accelerate intervention. Wives of colonial officials, without employment in their own right, saw appealing but sickly children in unhygienic surroundings, to be improved by their own voluntary work. Missionaries saw a dreadful array of damaging customs and propagated a drastic restructuring of the people's whole cosmology, with children the vanguard. Clinicians saw terrible tropical diseases or dietary deficiency, together with common childhood complaints. Compared with colleagues in the United Kingdom, they were less ready to blame the mothers, more inclined to call for help, medical and developmental. Meanwhile, the majority of Europeans continued to ignore the African child.

What, then, does the photographic record reveal that is absent from the documentary record, and how does this relate to the questions we began with? Overall, the image of 'the African child' shifted from a marginal position to one that was more purposeful. The photographs suggest a primacy for educational rather than health restructuring, with the schoolchild a potential missionary of Western values, fitting in with both hegemonic and consumerist interpretations of the value of the African child to the colonial project. The notion of saving the sick African child through health interventions appears as an extension of educational programmes of transformation. Acceptance of Western medicine for the child, according to this reading of the images, places on the child's kin an obligation to acknowledge the dominance of Western scientific thought. Thanks to recent Africanist studies, we can now be fairly certain this was not the clients' perception.[75] These photographs cannot answer questions about the precise timing of developments in the provision of services, but they show children as 'go-betweens', whose image grew in importance in the colonial lens as the need to establish a dialogue increased in the face of the growing movement for self-determination in the colonies.

NOTES

The following abbreviations have been used:
RH Rhodes House Library, Oxford.
RCS Royal Commonwealth Society Library, London.

1 For the former, see for example L. H. Gann and P. Duignan, *Burden of Empire: An Appraisal of Western Colonialism in Africa South of the Sahara*. London: Pall Mall Press, 1967: 282–92; some contributions to E. E. Sabben-Clare, D. J. Bradley and K. Kirkwood (eds) *Health in Tropical Africa during the Colonial Period*, Oxford: Clarendon Press, 1980. For the latter, see L. Doyal, *The Political Economy of Health*, London: Pluto Press, 1979: chs 3, 7; M. Turshen, *The Political Ecology of Disease in Tanzania*, New Brunswick: Rutgers University Press, 1984.

2 See A. W. Crosby, *Ecological Imperialism: the biological expansion of Europe, 900–1900*, Cambridge: Cambridge University Press, 1986; M. Nicholson, 'Medicine and racial politics: changing images of the New Zealand Maori in the nineteenth century', in D. Arnold (ed.) *Imperial Medicine and Indigenous Societies*, Manchester: Manchester University Press, 1988: 66–104; for a collection of extracts from documents, see H. Reynolds, *Aborigines and Settlers: the Australian experience 1788–1939*, Melbourne: Cassell, 1972.

3 For the first, see N. R. Hunt, '"Le bébé en brousse": European women, African birth spacing and colonial intervention in breast feeding in the Belgian Congo', *International Journal of African Historical Studies,* 1988, 21: 401–32; for the last, see D. Engels, 'Conference report. Foundations of Imperial Hegemony: western education, public health and police in India and Africa, 1859 to independence', *Germ. Hist. Inst. Lond. Bull.*, 1989, 11: 29–35. The 'consumerism' explanation has received less attention but will be explored in a forthcoming thesis by T. Burke of Johns Hopkins University, 'The social history of soap in Zimbabwe 1895–1975'.

4 For a discussion dealing with verbal rather than visual images, see J. Beinart, 'Imaging a nutritional disease of African children: the kwashiorkor story revisited', unpublished seminar paper, Wellcome Unit for the History of Medicine, Oxford, 1989.

5 A. Roberts, 'Photographs and African history', *Journal of African History*, 1989, 29: 301–11.

6 RH MSS Afr. s. 610, H. Martin, Reminiscences as a member of the trading firm of Swanzy in the Gold Coast, typescript, with letter dated 19 October 1965.

7 The subject is touched on in P. D. Curtin, *The Image of Africa: British ideas and action, 1780–1850*, Madison: University of Wisconsin Press, 1964; see also M. Banton, *Racial Theories*, Cambridge: Cambridge University Press, 1987.

8 RH MSS Afr. s. 611, H. Martin collection, (1) fo. 10: 'Small chief

bringing in cocoa, palm oil and rubber for sale'; ibid., fo. 17: 'Cocoa sellers waiting to go in to have their loads weighed' (both date between 1902 and 1906).

9 Ibid. (3), last page, group of twenty-six children; RH MSS Afr. s. 1665(2), T. F. G. Hopkins, 'Children at Ogodu 1933'; RCS Y304311, Johnson collection, 69, shows line-up reflected in water.

10 Martin collection, (2), child in government telegraph suit (leaves of album not numbered).

11 Martin, 'Reminiscences', accompanying letter.

12 D. M. Fox and C. Lawrence, *Photographing Medicine: images and power in Britain and America since 1840*, New York, Westport CT, London: Greenwood Press, 1988; S. Sontag, *On Photography*, New York: Farrar, Straus & Giroux, 1977.

13 E.g. Gold Coast government, *Medical and Sanitary Report for 1902*, Gold Coast: government printers, 1903, gives detailed analysis of climatic variation in relation to health of European personnel, but sparse information on health of Africans.

14 Martin collection, (1) fo. 8: 'Major Nathan, the Govenor (*sic*) afterwards Sir Mathew Nathan, with his Colonial Secretary in a White Steamcar, at Kpong somewhere about 1905'.

15 RH MSS Afr. s. 2000, O. Macleod, in Temple collection, (2) ff. 47–8: 'Banana women at Musgum'.

16 O. Macleod, *Chiefs and Cities of Central Africa*, Edinburgh and London: Blackwoods, 1912.

17 Ibid., facing p. 110; original in Macleod/Temple collection, (2) fo. 32: 'In a Banana compound'.

18 Macleod, *Chiefs and Cities*, facing p. 228; original in Macleod/Temple collection, (3) fo. 41 verso: 'Mother with piccans'.

19 Ibid., facing p. 126, 'Children Playing with Nuts', with description of game in text; original in Macleod/Temple collection, (2) fo. 54.

20 Ibid., p. 270.

21 RCS Y3043C, J. W. S. Macfie West African collection, 1910–22, 111: Boys sliding down a polished surface of rock, Shao, 17 March 1912.

22 Ibid., 324–5: children carrying water, Ikotobo, Nigeria, 15 and 23 December 1913.

23 Ibid., 305–8, 312–21: children in sleeping sickness camp, Ikotobo, 1913.

24 Ibid., 432–5: Akoo, aged 4 and Kah, aged 3, malaria and oedema, Accra, 6 October and 7 November 1916.

25 RH MSS Afr. r. 61, E. S. Shrimpton, photo book, Gold Coast c. 1923.

26 Macleod, *Chiefs and Cities*, facing p. 48; original in Macleod collection, (2) fo. 11: 'The Lamido of Léré, with some of his twenty children'.

27 Lady Clifford, *Our Days on the Gold Coast*, London: John Murray, 1919 (originally produced in aid of the Red Cross, 1918), facing p. 304.

28 Many of the photographic collections searched for this study featured photographs of animals; for a full discussion of the relationship of colonialists to the natural environment, see John M. Mackenzie, *The*

Empire of Nature: hunting, conservation and British imperialism, Manchester: Manchester University Press, 1988.

29 For example: RH MSS Afr. s. 572, Diary of Mrs Scott, fo. 27, 16 February 1930, 'in bush'; RH MSS Afr. s. 1044, E. Wilkinson papers, fo. 82: account of Christmas at Wiawso, written up at Dunkwa, 5 January 1933; both describe throwing chocolates on the ground for children 'to scramble for'. Both documents refer to snakes, and Wilkinson is eloquent about a pet mongoose.

30 RH MSS Afr. s. 593: Papers of A. C. Duncan-Johnstone, vol. 4/2, diary of overland journey, Gold Coast to Dakar, 1919, fo. 21; death of pet dalmatian.

31 This is a vast generalization, of course. See A. Hastings, *African Christianity*, London and Dublin: Geoffrey Chapman, 1976. For a specific study relating Christianity to medicine, see T. O. Ranger, 'Godly medicine: the ambiguities of medical mission in southeast Tanzania, 1900–1945', *Social Science and Medicine*, 1981, 15B3: 261–77.

32 Medicine and the law were favourite professions for the sons of such families; see M. J. Sampson, *Gold Coast Men of Affairs*, London: Dawsons, 1969; R. W. Cole, *Kossoh Town Boy*, Cambridge: Cambridge University Press, 1960 – the childhood story of a surgeon from Sierra Leone; A. Adeloye, 'Some early Nigerian doctors and their contribution to modern medicine in West Africa', *Medical History*, 1974, 18: 275–93.

33 RCS Y30443L, collection of Miss G. Smyly (daughter of Chief Justice of Gold Coast Colony, 1911–29, Sir Philip Crampton Smyly), 43: first-prize winner, Accra baby show, 1920s.

34 Ibid., 42: 'The English lady in this photograph is Mrs Armstrong, wife of an engineer. . . . During the 1st World War . . . she came to know Her Majesty Queen Mary . . . the Queen entrusted Mrs Armstrong to bring to Accra, as a prize for a Baby Show the silver bowl which the child is holding. I have no record of the names of Mother and child, it would be in the 1920s' (donor's note).

35 Mass participation in these events in Accra is evidenced in Gold Coast government, *Report on the Medical and Sanitary Department for the year 1929–1930*, Accra: government printers, 1930, photographs facing p. 46: 'Kumasi Health Week, 1929–30. Babies in Judging Pens' and 'Group of Prize-winning Babies'.

36 For a comparative overview, see M. Crowder, *West Africa under Colonial Rule*, London: Hutchinson, 1968; for a more recent study of the French sphere of influence, which points to contrasts and parallels with the anglophone territories, see P. Manning, *Francophone Sub-Saharan Africa 1880–1985*, Cambridge: Cambridge University Press, 1988.

37 E. Fraser, *The Doctor Comes to Lui*, London: Church Missionary Society, 1938: 28.

38 Cf B. Carmody, 'Conversion and school at Chikuni, 1905–39', *Africa*, 1988, 58: 193–209, esp. 194, quote from Zambesi Mission Report 1898, on importance of school in conversion process: 'It cannot be too often repeated that the only chance of converting the natives is to *get the children*' (my italics).

39 RH MSS Afr. s. 1530, E. M. Lincé, Missionary life in the Gold Coast and Rhodesia, 1931–8, fos. 4, 18: 'Kindergarten Number Games' and 'Kindergarten washing'.

40 Ibid., fo. 33: 'Efua kese ne ketewa'.

41 Ibid., fo. 48: 'Assembly, Government School, Accra' (postcard).

42 E. M. Magill, *Report on medical inspection of schoolchildren in Accra during 1923*, sessional paper no. 11 of 1924–5, Accra: government printers, 1924: 5. Magill examined 3,095 of a school population of 4,665 (66.6 per cent).

43 RH MSS Afr. s. 1563, R. E. Wraith, Material collected for biography of Guggisberg, File 5, photographs of Achimota, c. 1930; see also R. E. Wraith, *Guggisberg*, London: Oxford University Press, 1967.

44 A. G. Fraser, 'The effect on established social customs of modern knowledge and economic conditions', *Health and Empire*, 1933, vol 8: 264.

45 Three photographs of children with yaws, kindly supplied by Mrs J. M. Griffith, one captioned 'Two patients suffering from yaws. The smaller has had one injection of Italarsol'. These and the photographs referred to in the two following notes date from the 1930s.

46 RH MSS Afr. s. 1858, 'The Gold Coast – the wives' experience', collected by Heather Dalton – no. 15, J. M. Griffith, memoir accompanied by three fos. of snapshots, 13: 'Dancing to their reflections'.

47 Photographs of Achimota pupils kindly supplied by Mrs J. M. Griffith.

48 RCS Y3043 DD, Prince of Wales visit to Nigeria, April 1925, 15: parade of 14,000 schoolchildren on Lagos racecourse, 21 April 1925 – mainly scouts and guides.

49 RCS Y3043 II, M. Johnson collection, girl guide activities in Nigeria 1930–1937, esp. 24: First Aid demonstration; 50: four girl guides in white uniforms in garden with bowl and large white doll, learning to bath baby; 51: Sunbeams holding hands with toddler, at Miss Johnson's residence; 68 and 69: groups of unclothed people including children; 70: crying baby.

50 Lincé collection, fo. 27: 'Picnic at Achimota – Nov 30th 1932, Lieutenants and Patrol leaders: Eliz. Laryea, Victoria Grant, Hester Otoo, Vida Dsane, Thelma Buckle [in white], Sarah Okai'.

51 For the Gold Coast, see K. D. Patterson, *Health in Colonial Ghana: disease, medicine and socio-economic change 1900–1955*, Waltham, Mass: Crossroads Press, 1981: 23–4, 92–3; for comparative examples, see A. Beck, *A History of the British Medical Administration of East Africa*, Cambridge, Mass: Harvard University Press, 1970; R. Schram, *A History of the Nigerian Health Services*, Ibadan: Ibadan University Press, 1971.

52 In addition, the African child could represent a 'dark force' whose proximity threatened the European with disease.

53 Pitt-Rivers photographic collections: EP.A., E. E. Evans-Pritchard, Azande, 205; ceremony of bringing out newborn baby; RY.A., R. S. Rattray, Ashanti, 448–50: Ashanti mother and child at *Ntetea* rite when infant is eight days old, including first feeding with metal spoon.

54 Disparaging remarks about 'native customs' abound, but for a particularly interesting attempt to balance respect for the 'good' (psychological) and condemnation of the 'bad' (physical) aspects of traditional childcare, see S. D. Onabamiro, *Why Our Children Die*, London: Methuen, 1949. The author was a Nigerian science graduate, a true product of the hegemonic process.

55 RCS Y3043BB, T. H. Dalrymple, British Cameroons, 84–92: consultation of *Ngam*, the tarantula, in case of sick child, Banso, 9 June 1939.

56 Royal Anthropological Institute photographic collection, KYW Zambia, M. Gluckman, June 1940, 29365: boy being cupped for abcess on tooth, at Mbambo's Lubale homestead.

57 Lincé collection, fo. 47: 'A Hausa Doctor'.

58 The Hausa literary tradition and link with Arabic medicine interested some Europeans, though it was transmitted in a largely oral culture; see R. S. Rattray, *Hausa Folk-Lore*, Oxford: Oxford University Press, 1913. Traditional spirit healing came under anthropological scrutiny earlier than Islamic medicine in southern Ghana; see M. J. Field, *Religion and Medicine of the Ga People*, Oxford: Oxford University Press, 1937.

59 M. Gelfand, *The Sick African*, Cape Town: Stewart, 1944: figs 60, 61, 106, 107, 116.

60 Fraser, *Doctor Comes to Lui* (n. 37 above); A. Schweitzer, *On the Edge of the Primeval Forest & More from the Primeval Forest*, London: Adam & Charles Black, 1948 (*Zwischen Wasser und Urwald*, first published 1922; *Mitteilungen aus Lambarene*, first published 1931); P. White, *Doctor of Tanganyika*, Sydney: George M. Dash, 1942.

61 M. Worboys, 'The discovery of colonial malnutrition between the wars', in Arnold, *Imperial Medicine and Indigenous Societies*: 208–25; *Africa*, 1936, special issue on nutrition; A. Richards, *Land, Labour and Diet in Northern Rhodesia*, Oxford: Oxford University Press, 1939.

62 C. D. Williams, 'A nutritional disease of childhood associated with a maize diet', *Archives of Disease in Childhood*, 1933, 8: 423–33; Williams, 'Child health in the Gold Coast', *Lancet*, 8 January 1938: 97–102; latter based on Williams, 'The mortality and morbidity of the children of the Gold Coast', MD thesis, University of Oxford, 1936, which contains original photographs.

63 F. M. Purcell, *Diet and Ill-Health in the Forest Country of the Gold Coast*, London: H. K. Lewis, 1939.

64 Public Record Office, CO 859 68/1, 1941–3, Nutrition Research Survey Gold Coast, 12603/C/1. There is a note of Purcell's photos being given to Platt's secretary for copying, to be returned to Purcell's report; but I have not yet located them.

65 *West Africa*, 4 December 1943: 1095, second of two letters from Dr Purcell.

66 *West African Review*, September 1946: 618.

67 *West Africa*, 8 June 1946: 512.

68 RCS Y304E, Brit. Off. Photos, 139–59, 'The fight against soil exhaustion in the Northern Territories of the Gold Coast'.

69 The classics on the policy of 'educating the mothers' in Britain are A. Davin, 'Imperialism and motherhood', *Hist. Workshop Jl*, 1978, 5: 9–65; J. Lewis, *The Politics of Motherhood*, London: Croom Helm, 1980; conditions were very different, of course, in Britain's African colonies.

70 RH MSS Afr. s. 1665 (3), (Mrs) T. F. G. Hopkins, The Gambia 1935: 'Mandingo women after listening to talk on Child Welfare'.

71 Museum of Mankind [British Museum] MM034102, Waterfield collection, 1–12, esp. 9: nurse proffers medicine to father holding marasmic child.

72 *West African Review*, June 1946: 634.

73 RCS Y304E, Brit. Off. Photos, 127–38, 'Maternity and child welfare in Freetown, Sierra Leone', 134: pupil midwife bathing a baby.

74 Ibid., 133: mother and baby in maternity ward.

75 See J. M. Janzen and S. Feierman (eds), *The Social History of Disease and Medicine in Africa*, special issue of *Social Science and Medicine*, 1979, 13B4; S. Feierman, 'Struggles for control: the social roots of health and healing in modern Africa', *African Studies Review*, 1985, 28: 73–147.

10

WELFARE, WAGES AND THE FAMILY

Child endowment in comparative perspective, 1900–50

John Macnicol

INTRODUCTION

'It is a curious fact about the movement we are studying', wrote Eleanor Rathbone in 1927, 'that it seems to have begun, spiritually if not in material results, almost simultaneously and quite independently in several countries, and in several minds in each country'.[1]

With characteristic modesty, the leader of the family allowances campaign in Britain was pointing to a salient feature of twentieth-century welfare development – that remarkably similar social, economic and political forces were at work in all advanced industrial societies such as to produce comparable policy innovations. However, crucial differences between such societies produced marked variations in the scope, coverage and material levels of welfare protection; most of all, these differences affected the timing of policy introduction, and, indeed, whether policies were introduced at all.

Since examination of the complex interaction of these factors across several countries over time demands enormous breadth and depth of knowledge and analysis, it is not surprising that comparative welfare development remains the most challenging and undeveloped aspect of social policy analysis. A comprehensive theory of cross-national welfare development would need to consider all the principal social forces that have brought welfare states into being, creating a particular 'welfare mix', and rank them in some order of importance: the relative strength of organized labour and trade union membership; the extent to which citizens enjoyed a democratic franchise; the existence of state bureaucracies and the administrative mechanisms for policy implementation;

demographic pressures; ideological, religious and cultural factors dictating attitudes to women, the family and the care of old people; the degree of industrialization and urbanization, and its precise timing; the formulation of a particular class structure. It would also need to examine the inter-relationships between the various media through which welfare may be provided – notably, state, employers, trade unions, family and kin, voluntary bodies and commercial organizations.[2] It is not the purpose of this essay to discuss these broad causal factors in depth; space does not permit it. Instead, this essay seeks to show how, in a number of advanced industrial societies in the first half of the twentieth century, family allowance systems were introduced in response to social, economic and political pressures common to several countries, and that there was also a consistent pattern in the stages of this development.[3] The available literature on the subject is very extensive, and this essay can only explore the broad contours of development.

A very important element in twentieth-century welfare states were those policies that were introduced in the name of the child; and, of these, some of the most controversial were the forms of cash assistance directed at children and at the family as a unit. There was also a movement for 'family endowment in kind', through health and welfare services targeted at children, and the question of in-cash versus in-kind endowment was one that frequently troubled reformers. For example, in Britain it split the Trades Union Congress and Labour Party Joint Committee on the Living Wage: though the majority produced a recommendation in favour of cash assistance, a minority report argued that there was more urgent need for policies such as the extension of health insurance to wives and dependants, better maternity services, a raising of the school leaving age with the provision of maintenance allowances, an improvement in the supply of pure milk, the provision of nursery schools and the elimination of tuberculosis.

However, family endowment in cash was much more controversial, since it raised crucial questions about state encroachment into the private domain of parental control and the family, the reinforcement of gendered divisions of labour in the home, the rights of women and children, the rewarding of motherhood and investment in children as social capital. Yet often these questions – explicitly discussed by feminist and reformist campaigners at the time, and so important to historians in retrospect – were of

245

secondary importance in the actual process of policy formulation. Frequently they were obscured by more immediate considerations of economic management, class conflict, industrial efficiency and political strategy – as, for example, in the way that the introduction of the school health service in Britain in 1907 (a measure with enormous potential for monitoring and improving child health) took place primarily for stark 'economic efficiency' reasons, on the grounds that it would be a waste of the state's educational resources if children were too ill to benefit from their schooling. Much in the same way, this essay will seek to show that, whilst family allowance systems brought real economic benefit to the families and children that they targeted, arguments about child poverty, pronatalism, and the role of women were usually secondary to the prime causal factors that had little to do with improving the quality of family life, raising the living standards of children nor, indeed, with perpetuating the economic dependency of women and 'traditional' gendered divisions of labour, since these were taken as axiomatic.

The main stages in the family allowances campaign in Britain can be quickly summarized. By the early 1920s, there had developed a debate on whether the concept of the 'living wage' should contain some monetary acknowledgement of varying family needs – to which feminists (notably, Eleanor Rathbone and the Family Endowment Society) added the complementary argument that a state system of family endowment would both recognize the rights of women as mothers *and* pave the way to equal pay for women workers. Discussion in the 1920s thus centred on the wages question, with the British trade union movement generally suspicious on the grounds that family allowances would act as a wage-depressant. In the 1930s, however, the debate shifted to arguments on child poverty and pronatalism, with mass unemployment and recession creating an economic climate inimical to policy innovation. Finally, in the third stage – during the Second World War – family allowances enjoyed renewed support as a means of assisting the anti-inflationary wage control policies essential to the stabilization of the war economy; back on the political agenda and benefiting from the wartime tide of reformism, they were eventually introduced in 1945 as part of the Beveridge-inspired reorganization of Britain's social security system.[4]

THE 'FAMILY WAGE' CONTROVERSY IN EUROPE IN THE 1920S

If we make cross-national comparisons, we can see that these stages of development were broadly replicated in most advanced industrial societies. In several countries, family endowment campaigns had developed strongly by the early years of the century, for remarkably similar reasons. Indeed, by the 1920s there existed quite an extensive literature on cross-national family allowance systems.[5] The leading country was undoubtedly France, which had a long history of pronatalist policies dating back at least to Napoleonic times. The first modern instance of a family allowance system appears to have been that introduced by the industrialist Leon Harmel at his factory at Val-des-Bois in 1840, and over the next half-century several other systems appeared.[6] In 1862, for example, the French Ministry of Marine granted 10 centimes per day for each child below the age of 10 to families of seamen up to the rank of quarter-master having more than 5 years' service.[7] Further industrial schemes were launched in the late nineteenth century, usually concentrated in heavy industry where labour unionization was strongest (such as the schemes in the iron and steel works at Lille, Roubaix and Turcoing in 1891), and some railway companies and coal mines began supplementing the wages of their married workers by various methods: 'in kind' payments, such as free coal, were frequently made to married men. By 1914, various forms of family allowances were being paid to workers in over thirty firms, and schemes also covered schoolteachers, certain ranks in the Army, and civil servants in the Treasury, Post Office and Colonial Office.[8]

The motives behind these early developments were clearly related to the increasingly confrontational relations between employers and labour that were a feature of a number of late-industrial societies at this time as growing trade union membership, technological innovation and changed working practices led to a greater polarization of capital and labour. The development of a trend of thought favourable to a 'family wage' (voiced, for example, in the 1891 papal encyclical *De Rerum Novarum*) reflected the growing concern on the part of employers to solidify industrial loyalty, especially among married men with family responsibilities who would be least likely to go on strike.

In all European countries, the period during and after the First World War created massive economic dislocation, marked by food shortages, inflation, industrial unrest and falling real wages. Significantly, the year that witnessed the fastest rise in the cost of living in Europe – 1917 – also marked the beginning of a rapid development of industrial family allowance systems.[9] In response to growing hardship and a wave of strikes, employers began to pay cost-of-living bonuses, which soon became adjusted to family needs. The best illustration of this is the case of the Joya metal works, where in 1916 the manager, Emile Romanet, persuaded the firm to introduce graded allowances for dependent children under 13 years of age; other firms in the Grenoble area quickly followed suit, and in 1918 an 'equalization fund' was created. This was to be the form in which most private industrial schemes in Europe developed thereafter: a group of employers would agree to pay into such a fund sums of money proportional to the number of their employees, and from this fund the family allowances would be paid. It was hoped that this method would allay trade union fears of a wedge being driven between single and married men – somewhat contradictory fears that in hiring a workforce employers would either favour the former (whose wages would be lower) or the latter (who could be bribed into industrial docility by a relatively small family allowance).[10]

Rapid developments took place in 1918–25, so that by mid-1925 fully 180 equalization funds were in existence in France.[11] In 1918, equalization fund schemes covered only 598 employees and paid out a total of 113,352 francs per annum in family allowances; by 1925, this had risen to 1,210,000 employees and 160,000,000 francs. In 1924 the average amounts paid out by equalization funds were 19 francs per month for the first child, 27 francs for the second, 35 francs for the third and 43 francs for the fourth; this, on average, constituted additions to a married man's wages of 4 per cent for one child, 9 per cent for two, 16 per cent for three and nearly 25 per cent for four.[12]

By the mid-1920s, roughly 20 per cent of all those working for wages and salaries in France were covered by some form of family allowance system, and the practice had spread into many areas of employment. By the autumn of 1920, eighty French regional Departments (out of a total of ninety), three Algerian Departments and 206 towns with more than 10,000 inhabitants were paying family allowances to their public servants, and from 1922 a succession of laws stipulated that firms tendering for government contracts had to affiliate to an equalization fund. In addition, many equalization funds had developed supplementary family services: about two-thirds of them granted maternity benefits, about one-fifth gave nursing allowances, and some even employed social workers to visit mothers in their homes.[13]

This rapid growth of family allowance systems in France in the 1920s was quite remarkable. It is clear that it was an employer-led movement aimed at wider economic and industrial-relations goals, and that employers were very reluctant to let the initiative pass from their hands. In 1920, for example, a bill was introduced into the Chamber of Deputies by Maurice Bokanowski with the aim of making membership of an equalization fund compulsory, but it had to be dropped in the face of employer opposition. Later in that year the employers formed their *Comité Centrale des Caisses de Compensation* to consolidate their control over the funds. Only in 1932 – after a decade of struggle between employers and trade unionists over the issue of control – could an Act be introduced giving legal recognition to existing family allowance systems and providing for the gradual extension of compulsory equalization fund membership to almost all employers in France.[14]

Some employers, such as Emile Romanet, were at pains to stress that they took a genuinely sympathetic interest in their workers' welfare and introduced family allowance schemes after witnessing the severe hardship endured by married men in times of rapidly rising prices.[15] These liberal employers pointed with pride to the maternity and child welfare services provided by their funds, which often included health and hygiene education, crèches for infants, the employment of nurses and health visitors and sometimes even sickness benefits: in Nancy, for example, the fund maintained several hospital beds for sick children of employees, and a doctor and nurse visited mothers at home. Anxious to demonstrate the power of their philanthropy, French employers made somewhat exaggerated claims for these family policies: at Lyons, for example, an equalization fund maternity service was credited with having cut the infant mortality rate among children of employees from 123 to 44 per 1,000 live births, and it was claimed that the introduction of nursing allowances in the Auxerre district fund had increased the incidence of breast-feeding among infants of employees from 50 per cent to 93 per cent in 2 years.[16]

Not surprisingly, French trade unions viewed these claims with some scepticism. They could recall that similar services in kind had been introduced during the First World War with the crudely explicit aim of solidifying the loyalties of the female workforce. They argued that family allowance systems were attractive to employers primarily because they were a cheaper alternative to across-the-board wage rises. The distribution of children made such schemes an effective way of buying off the loyalty of married men and mitigating the worst hardship of rapid inflation whilst adding relatively little to the total wages bill. In 1922, only 160,000 out of 700,000 employees covered by French equalization funds were fathers (of 270,000 children) – a proportion of only 23 per cent.[17] The payment of family allowances added only about 2 per cent to the total payroll. The efficiency of this targeting can be illustrated by the scheme set up by the Union of Metallurgical Manufacturers in 1931: for a cost of only 1.2 per cent of the wages bill, this provided an allowance of 8 francs per month per child; yet the same total amount of money, if distributed equally to all workers in the form of wage rises, would only have provided 36 francs per annum per worker – hardly covering the cost of a daily cigarette.[18]

Thus in the 1920s in France there took place a bitter struggle between employers and trade unions over whether family allowances should be regarded as an acceptable alternative to wage rises. Each side wanted their own interpretation institutionalized in the running of the funds, and each tended to take up a rather paradoxical position. Employers insisted on using the term '*allocation familiale*' (family allowance) and regarded the payment as a philanthropic addition to wages which could be withdrawn at their discretion; hence one of them proudly commented that the establishment of equalization funds was evidence of the 'creative and generous spirit of French employers'.[19] No doubt reflecting their more pronatalist, Roman Catholic cultures, in France and Belgium the allowance was seen as directed at the *family*, the monetary payment usually going to the mother and kept physically separate from the worker's pay packet. By contrast, in Germany the few family allowance schemes that existed in the 1920s made payments as part of the worker's wage. French employers also insisted that the value of the family allowance should be excluded from consideration when industrial accident pensions were granted on the basis of the basic wage, arguing that eligibility for the allowance only existed for the period of parenthood rather than for the duration of employment. The matter repeatedly went before the French courts in industrial accident cases, with the Court of Appeal eventually ruling that allowances were a consequence of the employment contract, and hence *were* part of wages.

Workers, on the other hand, tended to use the term *'sursalaire'* (family wage), and regarded the allowances as a right, legally to be paid for as long as wages were paid but quite separate from them.[20] They complained that they had found innumerable instances where employers had obviously used allowances to cut real wage levels, and they thus retained a lingering suspicion towards family allowance systems throughout the 1920s. In his meticulous examination of foreign family allowance systems in the mid-1920s, Hugh Vibart constructed a detailed analysis demonstrating their effect on wage levels, and the American economist Paul Douglas found numerous telling examples of their use in industrial relations. In 1920, for instance, the Roubaix-Turcoing equalization fund was paying allowances of one franc per day per child; after a strike in March of that year a local agreement was established by the Ministry of Labour providing for the periodic adjustment of wages according to the fluctuations in the cost-of-living index. Between March and October the cost of living rose by 13 per cent, but basic wages were increased by only 7.5 per cent; however, family allowances were raised to 3 francs per day, thus putting workers with families in a better position than if they had been awarded a full wage increase with no raising of the allowance. In the following year, the Roubaix employers ignored the Ministry of Labour agreement and cut wages more rapidly than the fall in the cost of living, such that now wages were 17.5 per cent below their March 1920 level but the cost of living only 8.5 per cent below. Yet family allowances remained at 3 francs.[21] Some employers were quite candid about this. For example, at the Second Congress of Compensation Funds, M. Bonvoisin, Director of the Central Committee of Compensation Funds, said: 'we could cite examples where the family allowances have made it possible to carry out, without damage, reductions in wages which had become essential'.[22] Even the philanthropic Emile Romanet stressed that one advantage of a family allowance system was that it tended to reduce production costs.[23]

Granting of allowances would usually be conditional upon the worker's 'good conduct', and payment could be stopped in cases of strikes, absenteeism or lateness. Even if an industry had to work short time through scarcity of materials or a breakdown of machinery, the allowance would be reduced in proportion to the time lost. Some funds, like the one in Strasbourg and the Lower

251

Rhine, had regulations stipulating that the family allowance 'may be withdrawn from any one who puts it to bad uses, or if those assisted are naturally careless. The clearing fund may take any necessary measures to ensure the proper expenditure of these amounts when it is shown that they are being employed for a purpose other than that for which they are intended'.[24] Thus at the large Roubaix-Turcoing fund, a representative declared that these conditions attached to payment caused the workers 'to think before listening to agitation, to talk matters over with the employer, and to quit the shop only in exceptional circumstances'; again, at the 1923 Nantes Congress of Compensation Funds, the Secretary of the Textile Consortium of Roubaix asserted that 'the withdrawal of family allowances for the current month in the case of a strike has proved a most efficacious means of preventing strikes'.[25]

Nevertheless, it was obvious that such family allowance payments benefited workers' children, and French trade unionists were not quite so myopic as to see them purely in terms of industrial conflict: for example, the administrative secretary of one large 'Confédération Générale du Travail' declared in the mid-1920s that 'the Family Wage makes possible a fairer distribution of the product of labour, and increases the well-being of children . . . . It cannot be maintained that the trade union movement has been injured by the institution of the Family Wage . . . [which] is purely and simply a redistribution on sounder and more humane lines of the wage-bill'.[26] They thus directed their energies at the question of control of the funds, seeking governmental protection in the matter. This they largely attained with the Act of 1932 that made membership of an equalization fund compulsory (by stages) for employers, and established minimum rates for allowances. In addition, it was specifically made illegal to use allowances to avoid paying across-the-board wage rises.[27]

Similar conflicts between employers and trade unions took place in Belgium in the 1920s. As in France, early developments had been rather sporadic – for example, from 1910 civil servants in the Post Office received allowances of 36 francs per annum for each third and subsequent child under the age of 14 – but in 1915 the first private industrial scheme was established in the coal mining company at Tamines, and after the war other coal mines followed suit. The first equalization fund was founded in 1921, at Verviers, and other funds followed rapidly.[28] An interesting feature of Belgian developments was the formation in 1920 of a family policy pressure group whose aims are often cited as an example of the explicitly pronatalist family policy ideology that exists in Roman Catholic countries, the *Ligue des Familles Nombreuses de Belgique*.

As in France, the motives of employers were at first deeply distrusted by Belgian trade unions, but by the mid-1920s this suspicion was lessening, and the British Family Endowment Society – searching around for evidence with which to assuage the equivalent suspicions of British trade unionists – could cite the Secretary of the Belgian Miners' Federation, who declared in 1924 that 'the allowances have had no effect on the basic wage. Neither have they in any way affected trade union solidarity. On the contrary, they have to some extent furthered trade union influence. When a workman thinks himself injured by the suppression or diminution of the allowance due to him, he appeals to his trade union delegate to secure the fulfilment by the employer of the rules regulating the allowances'.[29] In 1924, all Belgian coal mines adopted schemes and in 1928 an Act made membership of an equalization fund compulsory for all employers who obtained contracts from the state or other public bodies. In 1930 an Act introduced, by stages, compulsory coverage over all employees in industry, commerce and agriculture, and established minimum rates of employers' contributions and child allowances; in addition, as in France, it was illegal for an employer to use allowances as a wage-depressant or as a means of enforcing industrial discipline.[30]

By contrast with France and Belgium, Germany's development of family allowances in the 1920s was unspectacular. Private schemes, such as the one at the Zeiss optical works, were fairly common before the First World War, and some developments had taken place in local government, where employee fringe benefits tended to be more common: by 1912, 31 German cities were paying to their municipal employees allowances which added percentages of the basic wage in respect of each child. As in France, many German industries in wartime paid family-related cost-of-living bonuses that reflected the artificial prosperity of a war economy and the need to keep pace with inflation. Rapid price rises in 1920 led to a further expansion as an alternative to across-the-board wage increases, and in that year the first equalization funds were established, initially in the metal industries of Berlin, and then in the Cologne chemical industries. The controversies aroused by these schemes were identical to those in France and Belgium, employers viewing allowances as a way of buying off the loyalty of married men at a time of political turmoil and shop-floor militancy. But German trade unions seem to have been able to mount a much stronger opposition at an early stage and post-war inflation created economic chaos; thus German equalization funds never exceeded eleven in number throughout the 1920s.[31]

France, Belgium and Germany enjoyed the most extensive developments of family allowances in Europe in the 1920s, but schemes were also to be found in Austria, Czechoslovakia, the Netherlands, Switzerland, Poland, Sweden, Norway, Denmark, Finland, Yugoslavia, Italy, Spain and the Irish Republic. In many cases, pioneer developments took place in public service employment. Subsequent equalization fund systems in private industry were usually connected with cost-of-living bonus schemes based on family size that were introduced on employer initiative during and after the First World War, as a consequence of price inflation; indeed, some schemes continued in the 1920s as little more than that. Initial opposition from trade unions was common, and often dictated the extent of growth thereafter. In all countries, developments centred on the mining industry, which possessed the most sensitive links between changing wage levels and fluctuations in industrial profitability.[32]

AUSTRALIA AND NEW ZEALAND IN THE 1920S

In the 1920s, the development of family allowances was also taking place in two countries outside Europe that led the world in social welfare provision – Australia and New Zealand. Whereas in Britain in the 1920s the question of wages and family needs never went beyond the confines of theoretical discussion, in the 'social laboratories' of Australia and New Zealand interesting practical solutions were emerging.

Australia's position as a pioneer in welfare development was caused by the convergence of several interesting factors. Because of their history as convict settlements, judicial social controls were overt and powerful in the Australian colonies. Thus they had a long tradition of state intervention in many aspects of economic life, especially in developmental work (such as the railway boom of the 1870s and 1880s). Vital component parts of the economic infrastructure (for example, transport, power supply and drainage) were government-sponsored, with a workforce able to exert their wishes more effectively than they would have been able to do with a private employer. Indeed, by 1900 the state was the largest single employer in Australia, utilizing some 10 per cent of the workforce (twice the proportion in Britain at the time). Australian industry was relatively labour-intensive and high-wage – two essential pre-conditions for a strong trade union movement. Another crucial impetus was the fact that, in the late nineteenth century, there occurred a rapid transformation in the social structure to a modern capitalist/labour relationship with formation of large companies that took over economic activity from small producers (most notably, in gold mining); urbanization developed rapidly, as did trade union membership and socialist activity. By the early 1890s, the New South Wales Labour Party had won a third of seats in the local parliament, and the Australian Workers' Union made steady progress in that decade.[33]

By the early 1900s, however, there was increasing concern in Australian society over the slowing down of economic growth, compared with the boom years of the 1860s, 70s and 80s. Hence there emerged a politico-economic strategy analagous to the 'national efficiency' movement in Britain: this was the policy of New Protection, which comprised import tariffs, compulsory state arbitration in industrial disputes, state welfare and the controversial 'White Australia' policy. A highly protected industrial structure, it was believed, would be prosperous enough to pay wages at a level that would placate the emerging labour unions. The corporatist state would mediate class conflict through liberal-interventionist policies, and the trade unions would be won over by being allowed greater participation in economic policy decision-making. Indeed, by the 1900s, both sides of industry found the notion of the minimum wage highly attractive: for employers, it was a method of buying industrial peace and imposing legal regulation on unions; for organized labour, it established the notion of the union minimum, in the setting of which they would be required to play a major role.

This was the context in which there was passed the 1904 Commonwealth Conciliation and Arbitration Act, which established an official arbitration court to mediate in industrial disputes. In 1907, this Court heard an application by the Sunshine Harvester Company for exemption of excise duties under an Excise Tariff Act: to qualify, it had to show that its wage rates were 'fair and reasonable'. The President of the Court, Justice H. B. Higgins, declared that, having examined all the evidence relating to minimum poverty standards, his view was that the subsistence level for a family of five was 7s. 0d. per day (with margins for skill on top).

The 'Harvester Judgement', as it became known, has passed into the history of industrial relations as a remarkably early precedent in minimum wage-fixing, all the more startling because in public rhetoric it appeared that the basic wage was set by a radical disregard of whether industry could afford it. It is clear, however, that Higgins's calculations were based on a deference to prevailing wage-levels – yet another historical illustration of the fact that minimum subsistence poverty lines are usually influenced by political considerations. He did examine a sample of nine working-class family budgets which showed an average weekly expenditure on food, fuel and rent of £1 12s. 5d. for a family of five. The Harvester Company was paying only 6s. 0d. per day, or £1 16s. 0d. per week – which left only 3s. 7d. for all other expenditure in a family with three young children. Higgins thus declared that the Harvester wage was not 'fair and reasonable'.

But his suggested minimum wage level of 7s. 0d. per day for such a family was hardly a radical improvement: it still left a pitifully small margin for expenditure above bare subsistence. Higgins arrived at this figure merely by looking at what 'reputable' employers (defined as 'public bodies which do not aim at profit, but which are responsible to electors or others for economy') were already paying. This tended to be about 7s. 0d. per day.[34]

Essentially, Higgins was attempting to introduce a family needs element into wage-fixing that would not substantially threaten the profitability of capital, but would grant some measure of social justice to the worker and hence mitigate class conflict. Judicial intervention into the wage-structure was thus an attempt to nurture political stability by establishing a correct balance between the increasingly confrontational powers of capital and labour. Such was the tenor of several similar arbitration rulings at the time – for example, the 1909 Broken Hill Mine agreement or the 1907 judgement in New Zealand (which, not surprisingly, had similar arbitration procedures) by Justice Sim.[35] Although, ironically, the Harvester Judgement was never formally implemented (since in the following year the High Court of Australia declared the Excise Tariff Act illegal), it nevertheless became the basis for subsequent wage-fixing; within each Australian state there existed legal machinery for minimum-wage regulation, and where an industrial dispute occurred the solution tended to follow the Harvester precedent.

Price rises during and after the First World War and a newly confident labour movement produced a massive wave of strikes in 1919 and in consequence there arose the same kind of 'living wage' demands that were being voiced in Europe at the time. In response to these events the federal government appointed a Royal Commission on the Basic Wage in October 1919, with the lawyer A. B. Piddington as chairman, to investigate the question of how a minimum wage might be calculated according to human needs. Essentially this was an attempt by the government to head off demands by labour that the Harvester principle should be extended far more widely, but the move was to have consequences for the development of family allowances, for it raised again the question of how an adequate 'family wage' should be calculated.

Like the post-Harvester arbitration awards, this minimum wage was conceived of as an *adult male* wage: as Beilharz comments, it 'embodied the interventionist but masculinist principles of the new liberalism'.[36] Women had theirs set considerably lower – at just over half of the adult male rate up to the Second World War. Minimum-wage enforcement in Australia thus undoubtedly consolidated those gendered inequalities in the labour market and in the domestic division of labour that already existed, as Bettina Cass argues,[37] but this was widely accepted at the time on the justification (accurate or not) that by and large women workers were not primary breadwinners and that the share-out of the total wages bill should reflect this. The concept of the 'family wage' was deeply embedded in the Australian working-class consciousness, both male and female.

Thus the question of economic assistance to children crept into Australian social politics on the coat-tails of the much broader issue of industrial harmony: in announcing the appointment of this royal commission, the Australian prime minister, W. M. Hughes, said:

> If we are to have industrial peace we must be prepared to pay the price, and that price is justice to the worker . . . the cause of so much industrial unrest, which is like fuel to the fires of Bolshevism and direct action, arises with the real wage of the worker . . . once it is admitted that it is in the interests of the community that such a wage should be paid as will enable a man to marry and bring up children in decent, wholesome conditions . . . it seems obvious that we must devise better machinery for insuring the payment of such a wage than at present exists.[38]

These political concerns forced the commission to investigate the problem in meticulous detail: indeed, its proceedings stand as one of the most important but least-known inquiries into the measurement of minimum subsistence. An enormous volume of evidence was taken – from no less than 796 witnesses – on clothing needs, food requirements, rent levels, transport costs, and so on – even down to the amount of floor polish a housewife might need.[39] There was an element of absurdity in the exercise, and after reading through the earnest and rather ponderous attempts to define the minimum needs of the 'average' Australian family, Eleanor Rathbone poked fun at the spectacle of the seven commissioners – all men – 'considering whether the supposititious wife of the typical Australian workman should be allowed six blouses a year (two silk, two voile and two cambric or winceyette) as claimed by the Federated Unions; or only three . . . as suggested by the Employers'.[40]

In the commissioners' report of 1920, they established the basic minimum needs for a family of man, wife and three children as £5 16s. 0d. per week for Melbourne, with slight variations for other states (roughly 36 per cent higher than existing basic wage rates). This, it was calculated, would cost industry in the region of £93,000,000 – equivalent to one-third of total industrial production in 1918. Not surprisingly, the Australian government regarded this as economically impossible and asked Piddington to present an alternative scaled-down scheme. This he did, recommending a minimum weekly wage of £4 plus family allowances of 12s. 0d. per child per week. Piddington stressed the 'statistical fallacy' argument later used to devastating effect by Eleanor Rathbone in *The Disinherited Family* – that the three-child minimum wage was forcing Australian industry to pay for 450,000 non-existent wives and 2,100,000 non-existent children. (The actual number of children in Australia was 900,000.) Retreating rapidly, the federal government agreed in principle to the minimum wage, but reduced the proposed level of the family allowance to 5s. 0d.[41] Some trade unionists suspected that this tactical retreat had been long planned, and that by notionally aiming to establish a 'reasonable standard of comfort' rather than one of minimum needs, the commission was trying to produce a recommendation that would be so costly as to prove impossible for industry to implement, hence discrediting the whole idea of the minimum wage.[42]

In fact, nothing practical was done to implement even this limited promise, except that in 1920 the Australian government introduced a means-tested family allowances scheme for its own officials, designed to buy off a large wage claim by them. Apart from an unsuccessful bill in 1921, the only other development at federal level was the appointment in 1927 of a Royal Commission on Family Endowment, following a discussion of the subject at the Conference of Commonwealth and State Ministers in June that year. The majority report of the commission opposed family allowances on the grounds that basic wage schemes then in operation already contained an element of family needs adjustment, 'sufficient, if directly applied, to provide for all existing children', that the cost would be prohibitive and that parental responsibility would be weakened. The minority recommended family allowances for each child after the second. But it was the majority report that, not surprisingly, found favour with the government; strong opposition also came from trade unionists, who feared the effect of such a scheme on the wage levels of childless men.[43] While they were not unfavourable to the concept of family needs being incorporated into minimum-wage fixing calculations (since it would boost the monetary level), they were, like British trade unionists at the time, deeply suspicious of any attempt to meet family needs outside wages, by a separate system of allowances.

However, in the Australian states in the 1920s the question of family allowances remained a live issue, reappearing every time a state's industrial tribunal fixed the basic wage in relation to 'average' family needs. In 1925, for example, both Queensland and South Australia unsuccessfully tried to introduce family endowment bills.[44]

The most noteworthy achievement was in New South Wales, where in 1916 there had been presented to the state legislative assembly a motion proposing family endowment in very general terms from Dr Richard Arthur, who was to publish his plan for a tax-funded highly redistributive scheme three years later.[45] As in the other states, however, it was to be industrial unrest that precipitated governmental action: in 1919, the state industrial arbitration court fixed the basic wage for males at £3 17s. 0d., calculated on the three-child family, but in response to vociferous protests from employers over the amount this would cost, the New South Wales government introduced a Maintenance of Children Bill.[46] (Employers had argued that capital would flow into other states where wage costs were not so high.) Under this legislation, the New South Wales Board of Trade would have been obliged to calculate annually the cost of maintaining a child and, on this basis, operate a family allowance system on top of a man-and-wife minimum wage.

Opposition from both trade unions and employers was very strong, however: the former objected to the fact that no payments would be made during strikes or unemployment (since the allowances were to be financed wholly by employers as part of wages) and because the scheme appeared to them as a device for avoiding the enforcement of the minimum wage (which would have cost about double the family allowances scheme – £11,930,000 as against £6,520,000); on the other hand, employers feared that, once introduced, the scheme would be greatly expanded in the future.[47]

This combined opposition prevented the bill becoming law in 1919, and a similar fate befell a Motherhood Endowment Bill of 1921. However, New South Wales did establish a 'Ministry for Motherhood' (with a man in charge, the crudely pronatalist Greg McGirr) and investigated alternative methods of raising the necessary money (such as by a state lottery). Finally, in 1927 the Labour government introduced a family allowances scheme that provided 5s. 0d. per week for each child under 14 years of age where the total family income was less than the basic wage plus £13 per annum. Until 1933, the scheme was financed by a payroll tax on employers, and thereafter out of general taxation.[48]

Thus Australian developments in direct economic assistance to children in the 1920s were brought about primarily by economic and industrial conflicts. A crucial factor was the existence of a strong trade union movement, capable of industrial militancy and able to present high wage demands: faced with a far more intense level of industrial conflict than existed even in Britain in the early 1920s, federal and state governments were forced to intervene, first in the matter of minimum-wage fixing, and then – when by the early 1920s this was proving something of an economic hornet's nest – through family allowance schemes that promised to be cheaper and better-targeted alternatives to general wage rises. However, trade union strength effectively prevented a federal family allowances scheme being introduced until 1941.

By contrast, the New Zealand Family Allowances Act of 1926 was quite separate from minimum-wage discussion. Since it took no regard of the employment status of parents and was financed out of general taxation, it stands as the first true state family allowance system in the world. In New Zealand, the family endowment principle had been acknowledged in several ways before 1914 – for example, through income tax child allowances, and the payment of allowances to married schoolteachers – and during the First World War further extensions were added in the form of service pay separation allowances and dependants' benefits for the unemployed.[49] Some discussion of the minimum wage took place thereafter and as early as 1894 Conciliation Boards had been set up on Australian lines to pronounce judgement in intractable wage disputes.[50] In many respects, New Zealand was socially more advanced than Australia, having passed universal male suffrage in 1879, votes for women in 1893 and the world's first Old-Age Pensions Act in 1898. But with a much more rural social structure and agricultural economic base, it never developed quite the same ferocity of industrial conflict as did its immediate neighbour. The question of the 'family wage', and how best to establish it, received relatively little discussion in New Zealand, and private members' family endowment bills introduced into parliament in 1922, 1924 and 1925 (by the Labour member M. J. Savage) failed to pass. By the mid-1920s, New Zealand still had no industrial family allowance schemes.

Yet in 1925–6 family endowment suddenly became a live political issue. The stimulus was the 1926 general election campaign, during which the Australian family wage experiments were discussed and, to forestall the Labour opposition, the government promised to introduce a bill. (The growing strength of Labour can be seen by the fact that only nine years later, in 1935, they swept in to office with 47.4 per cent of the total vote and 69 per cent of parliamentary seats.)[51] This promise was kept, and the 1926 Act passed with most controversy in the New Zealand parliament merely being over the level of payments, rather than the general principle.[52] This New Zealand scheme paid only 2s. 0d. per week to third and subsequent children where the family income did not exceed £4 per week plus the monetary equivalent of the allowances. It was also hedged in with very strict nationality and racial criteria – for example, no payments were to be made to 'Asiatics', even if they were British subjects – and allowances could be withheld if an applicant was deemed to be of bad character or if a child was illegitimate. In 1939, the system was expanded in scope, and renamed 'family benefit'.[53]

PRONATALISM AND ECONOMIC RECESSION IN THE 1930S

Whereas in the 1920s family allowance developments in Europe and Australasia were closely connected with the question of minimum wages, in the 1930s the main impetus changed to that of raising birthrates. In this decade, Germany and Italy replaced France, Belgium, Australia and New Zealand as the main pioneers of family allowances, and in both countries pronatalist policies were deeply imbued with fascist ideology.

By the early 1930s the comparatively minor developments in private industrial family allowance schemes in Germany had been all but wiped out by the effects of inflation, and there remained only a few systems for public employees. In 1933, however, Hitler came to power and almost immediately there was launched a wide-ranging pronatalist and eugenic policy.

In common with other European nations, Germany had been experiencing a falling birthrate since the 1880s – from 39.2 births per 1,000 total population in 1876–80 to 14.7 in 1933 – and since the beginning of the century there had appeared a continuous spate of books and pamphlets expressing concern over this.[54] But only after 1933 was there a concerted attempt to raise the German birthrate by both positive and negative eugenic policies. The most important of these was the 1933 Marriage Loans Act, under which interest-free loans of up to 1,000 marks were made available to newly married couples, to be repaid at a rate of only one per cent per month. The aim was to encourage couples to purchase furniture, kitchen utensils, bedlinen, and so on, and thus payments were made in the form of coupons which could be exchanged for such items. One-quarter of the initial loan was cancelled on the birth of each child, and, in addition, a birth entitled parents to postpone further repayments for up to one year. Loans were, of course, only made to 'pure Aryans' who suffered from no inherited disease.[55]

On the one hand, the Marriage Loans Act was aimed at encouraging women to leave the labour market, thus lowering unemployment, and was a legislative expression of the fascist conception of motherhood: loans were only made if the wife had been gainfully employed for at least 9 months in the previous 2 years, and on marriage she had to stay out of work unless her husband had an income of less than 125 marks per month. On the other hand, of course, the Act was a blatantly pronatalist measure. In this latter aim, much was claimed for it: the marriage rate per 1,000 total population rose from 9.7 to 11.1 in the first year of its operation, and the crude birthrate rose from 14.7 births per 1,000 total population to 18.0 over the same period – an apparently striking tribute to the success of the loans, and claimed as such by the Nazi regime. But in fact commentators pointed out – then and subsequently – that the real cause of the fertility and marriage-rate upturn was the general economic recovery which occurred after 1933.[56] In any case, the contribution of the marriage loan system to Germany's total births was always meagre: between August 1933 and February 1937, 694,367 marriage loans were granted and 485,258 children were born under them; the total number of births in Germany for the three years 1934, 1935 and 1936 was roughly 3,716,000.[57]

Many other pronatalist measures were introduced. From 1935, special grants were given to families with four or more children under 16 years of age: up to June 1936, these were being paid to about 190,000 families out of an estimated 750,000 with four or more children. Child tax rebates (rising steeply with each successive child), reduced railway fares, rent allowances, housing assistance, preferential treatment in employment selection – all of these were available to parents of large families.[58]

Such schemes can be considered family endowment in a general sense, but in addition there were more specific family allowance payments. Equalization funds were sponsored by the government, covering various occupational groups like panel doctors, dentists and apothecaries. Several local family allowance schemes were set up, such as the one run by the Berlin municipality: a number of carefully selected families were awarded 'baby sponsorship' grants for each third or fourth planned child of 30 marks per month for the first year and 20 marks per month for the subsequent 13 years. All such schemes were only available to parents deemed to be of eugenically sound stock. The Berlin 'baby sponsorship' scheme, for example, was strictly limited to parents who passed the most rigorous examinations into their social, educational, medical and genetic background: hence out of over 2,000 applicants in 1934, only 311 babies received sponsorship.[59]

Much the same motivation lay behind the Italian pronatalist policies. In 1927 Mussolini had expressed alarm over Italy's ability to be an expansionist, imperial nation without a rapidly increasing population. 'What are forty million Italians', he asked, 'as opposed to forty million French plus the ninety million in their colonies, or as opposed to the forty six million English, plus the four hundred million in their colonies?'[60] Thereafter, a number of pronatalist measures were introduced: encouragement of migration from towns to areas of reclaimed land in the country, suppression of contraceptive information and severe restrictions on abortion, a tax on bachelors, generous tax concessions for large families, preferential employment selection for married men, cheap honeymoon journeys to Rome, and so on. Family allowance systems before 1934 were mainly confined to some state employees, but in that year an industrial scheme was set up (partly for pronatalist reasons, but also in the wake of wage reductions) which in 1935 covered 650,750 workers with dependent children. In 1936 and 1937, further extensions were made to provide family allowances for workers in industry, commerce, agriculture, banking and insurance. As in the case of Germany, these measures appear to have had little effect on birth or marriage rates.[61]

In France and Belgium, by contrast, the 1930s saw no rapid advances; instead there was a gradual consolidation of the situation established by the Acts of 1932 and 1930 respectively. As the provisions of these Acts were enforced by stages, so an increasing number of employers joined (though evasion continued to be a problem), and more and more workers were covered. Pronatalism in France increased in intensity in the 1930s, though, and culminated in the 'Code de la Famille' of July 1939, which greatly extended family allowance coverage to all occupied persons and introduced a number of fertility inducements (including loans to assist young couples to set up home in rural districts).[62]

In the Protestant democracies of Australia and New Zealand, however, pronatalist sentiments were less in evidence and progress in the 1930s was unspectacular; as in Britain, the economic depression of the 1930s effectively removed family allowances from the realm of political possibility.

However, in a few other European countries population concerns produced improved economic assistance to children. In the Soviet Union after 1934 there was a reaction against the sexual freedom of the 1920s (when, for example, abortions had been very readily available) and a number of pronatalist measures were introduced, culminating in the 1936 'All-Union Code of Family Law' that made divorce more difficult, prohibited abortion and introduced family allowances for each child after the seventh.[63] By the end of the 1930s, Spain, Hungary and Chile had introduced schemes, and the subject was under discussion in several South American states.[64]

264

WAGE CONTROL IN THE SECOND WORLD WAR: CANADA AND AUSTRALIA

The final phase in the cross-national development of family allowance systems took place during the Second World War, for reasons relating primarily to wage control and anti-inflationary policy in the peculiar circumstances of war economies. Not surprisingly, those countries in the eye of the military hurricane – France, Belgium and Germany – experienced no innovation. But in the more tranquil societies of Australia and Canada, distanced from the conflict, there took place developments that exactly mirrored the British experience.

Despite its cultural affinities with Britain, Canada's social and economic structure was not immediately favourable to welfare innovation. In 1901, fully 40 per cent of the Canadian workforce were employed in agriculture, and only 16 per cent in manufacturing; even by 1950, these proportions were 21 per cent and 26 per cent. By contrast, in 1901 agriculture employed only 9 per cent of British workers, and manufacturing 33 per cent; the equivalent proportions for 1950 were 4 per cent and 41 per cent.[65] Thus with a high proportion of its workers in agriculture, a relatively low level of labour unionization and little state involvement in its few large industrial concentrations, Canada lacked the institutional pressures that would have created a wide public debate on wages and the family. Wage settlement tended to be by free collective bargaining, and there was no equivalent of the arbitration procedures that existed in Australia and New Zealand.

After the First World War, family policy pressure groups had directed their energies towards a successful campaign for mothers' pensions, which had produced legislation in Manitoba, Saskatchewan, Alberta, British Columbia and Ontario between 1916 and 1920. Allowances were paid to mothers who were widowed or who could not be supported by an insane or disabled husband, in respect of themselves and their children. The aims of this movement were fairly traditionalist, pensions being a way of helping a single-headed family to remain intact and thus keeping its children in a normal domestic environment; also, fewer children would have to enter institutions, with the cost to the state being thereby lessened.[66]

A small family endowment movement had existed in Canada, however: in 1929 a proposal had been considered by the House of Commons Select Standing Committee on Industrial and International Relations; the Catholic priest Father Leon Lebel had been an advocate in the 1920s and 1930s; the League for Social Reconstruction (which included Leonard Marsh) suggested family allowances on top of a statutory basic wage, along with a comprehensive social insurance system, in their democratic-socialist report on *Social Planning in Canada* (1935);[67] and, significantly, the Liberal politician William Lyon Mackenzie King had referred to them in his 1918 text, *Industry and Humanity*.[68] However, in Canada there was a strong conservative movement against all such interference in the family, led by the highly influential *doyenne* of social work, Charlotte Whitton, and their view dominated discussion in the recession-hit 1930s, which was in any case a decade unfavourable to policy innovation; incredibly, Whitton seems to have feared the effect such allowances might have on the Quebec birthrate. Thus by the late 1930s little progress had been made: not even in the Roman Catholic-dominated provinces was there a strong family endowment movement.

However, on the outbreak of the Second World War the Canadian government was faced with identical problems to those encountered in Britain. In order to construct an effective economic policy against wartime inflation, strict wage control would have to be enforced for the duration of the War; but this could only attain legitimacy if the lowest-paid with large families were protected. In Britain, the problem was considered within the Treasury by the 'Stamp Survey' of 1939–40 and publicized by the economist J. M. Keynes in *How to Pay for the War* (1940); in Canada, wage- and price-control policy was initially formulated by an economic advisory committee, set up in September 1939, and, once implemented, was successful in keeping the rise in the cost of living for the first 4 years of the War to a mere 18 per cent. But Mackenzie King's government were continually apprehensive on the question of wartime inflation.

Renewed impetus was provided by the publication of the Marsh Report on social security in March 1943. This was produced with remarkable speed by a committee set up immediately after the publication of the Beveridge Report in Britain in December 1942, and justly deserves the title of 'Canada's Beveridge Plan' since it contained very similar proposals and justifications. Like Beveridge, Marsh argued that child allowances should be part of a policy of a national minimum, given that wages could not provide for the needs of all children; and he made the familiar 'less eligibility' argument that unless they were paid to all families 'dependency income' would be higher than wages, thus creating a disincentive to work.[69]

The Marsh Report gave rise to some discussion, but little practical action. The crucial event that triggered off policy innovation came in August 1943 – the submission to the Cabinet of a report from the National War Labour Board, written largely by Justice C. P. McTague, a judge of the Ontario Supreme Court, in which family allowances were urgently advocated as a means of protecting the lowest-paid in an anti-inflationary wage control policy.[70] McTague's report appeared in an atmosphere of increasing governmental concern over labour protests against the wage-freeze. Canadian trade unionists were vehemently opposed to this proposal, though they were not completely against family allowances as a general item of social security. Gradually, Mackenzie King came round to the view that family allowances could only be accepted in the context of post-war social security reorganization. After some discussion within Cabinet, he won his colleagues over, and the Canadian Family Allowances Bill was voted through in Parliament in July 1944 by the overwhelming majority of 139 votes to nil. In his speech in Parliament, it was the anti-poverty argument that Mackenzie King stressed, in order to convert his colleagues: he pointed out that fully 84 per cent of Canadian children under 16 were dependent on only 9 per cent of the gainfully employed.[71]

In Australia, identical economic pressures led to the passage of the federal government's Child Endowment Act of 1941. In August 1940, the Full Commonwealth Court of Conciliation and Arbitration had declined to consider an application by the trade unions for an increase in the basic wage, arguing that the incipient danger of wartime inflation made this economically unwise. Within government, discussions were taking place on wage control and other policies to reduce levels of aggregate consumption. Thus although the Labour leader John Curtin had made child endowment an element in his 1940 general election campaign, political considerations took a firm second place to economic ones. The primacy of economic motives can be seen in the fact that the Department charged with piloting the bill into legislation was the Ministry of Labour and National Service; the Minister, H. E. Holt, openly acknowledged his debt to Keynes's *How to Pay for the War*, and emphasized the wage-restraint case.[72]

New Zealand, incidentally, experienced no comparable developments for obvious reasons. A family allowances scheme had existed since 1926, and the long-standing compulsory arbitration procedures had been made even tougher by the new Labour government via the 1936 Finance Act. All that was needed in wartime was mild reinforcement by the 1940 Rates of Wages Emergency Regulations and strict government control of the cost of living. A substantial 'welfare revolution' had already taken place in 1936–8 under Labour.[73] After the War, in 1946, the income limit eligibility criterion for family benefit was removed and the scheme became universal.

We can see, therefore, that events of the 1940s in both Canada and Australia replicated the British experience, with family allowances enjoying sudden popularity within government as part of an urgent economic strategy to hold down wages and control potentially disastrous wartime inflation; by the middle of the War, they were being viewed as essential components of the reorganized social security schemes that these liberal democracies fashioned in the context of their post-war economic restructuring – an exercise that was partly directed at solidifying public support behind the war effort, but was also a vital ingredient of Keynesian planning for the stability and growth of their capitalist economies.

Indeed, it is striking how often Keynesian 'demand management' arguments were used to justify Canada's family allowances scheme, both before and after its introduction. For example, in introducing the bill in the Canadian House of Commons, Prime Minister Mackenzie King said:

> The expenditure of money paid out for family allowances will create a demand for goods and, thereby, a demand for labour for the production of those things that are in daily use in all parts of the country ... this instrument will help prevent anything like the depressions that have followed in previous periods in the wake of wars.

And the Canadian government's statement of post-war economic aims presented social security payments as 'a powerful weapon with which to ward off general economic depression'.[74] (In his report, Beveridge had justified the payment of unemployment benefit for unlimited duration on similar grounds.)[75] Family allowance advocates in the 1950s and 1960s frequently mixed together such macro-economic arguments with evidence of the beneficial effect that payments had on the material status of children. Thus Joseph Willard observed that they would direct federal funds to low-income areas in Canada such as to improve living standards. In addition, they would place purchasing power in the hands of those who would exercise it immediately and had a high marginal propensity to consume, thus stimulating the economy. Similarly, Daniel Moynihan pointed out that, in the first year after the introduction of family allowances, the number of pairs of children's shoes sold in Canada rose from 762,000 to 1,180,000 per month.[76]

CONCLUSION

By 1950, most advanced industrial societies had introduced family allowance systems. The most notable exception was, of course, the United States of America, which only possessed Aid to Dependent Children – a benefit that, as Aid to Families With Dependent Children, was to become increasingly controversial in the 1960s, 70s and 80s, since it overwhelmingly targeted single-parent families and was thus accused of creating them. (Longitudinal data on welfare mothers showed this allegation to be largely unfounded.) By the 1980s and 1990s, the American family allowances movement was experiencing something of a revival as a means of targeting *all* families, and thus avoiding the allegedly harmful (and much exaggerated) effect of AFDC receipt on welfare mothers. Liberal reformers belatedly realized that the working poor needed cash assistance. Intriguingly, there was also emerging in the USA a concern that stagnant male industrial real wages plus the increasing labour-force participation of married women was breaking down the old concept of the family wage that, as this paper has shown, was crucial to the emergence of family allowance systems in several countries. Indeed, among working-class black Americans economic prospects were worsening for men (through de-industrialization) and improving for women (through the expansion of feminized, service jobs), thus leading to a decline in marriage rates as men became less attractive economic propositions.

By the 1960s France – the pioneer of developments – was also the most generous provider, its family allowances being part of a broad package of explicit family policies. The 'explicit/implicit' categorizing of family policies in Europe noted by some observers did broadly follow a Roman Catholic/Protestant division: for example, family allowance payments as a proportion of national income in 1961 amounted to 4.78 per cent in France, 3.12 per cent in Belgium and 2.57 per cent in Italy, but only 0.64 per cent in Great Britain and

269

0.39 per cent in West Germany.[77] Religious and cultural factors thus dictated to some extent the popularity enjoyed by family allowance systems within countries; but overall their fortunes tended to vary inversely with economic prosperity. Hence in the full-employment 1950s, governments took little interest in them; but in the 1960s, 70s and 80s, with recession and high unemployment again raising questions of child poverty and the relationship between benefits and wages, they returned to the political agenda.

From this necessarily brief account, it can be seen that the development of family allowance systems in several countries in the period 1900–50 followed a remarkably similar pattern. The historical forces at work were complex, and there were subtle variations according to each nation's peculiar social, economic, political and cultural mix. These forces produced a confused interaction between, on the one hand, rival ideas about the role of women and the family and, on the other, the urgent economic and labour-control imperatives of a late-industrial society. What is clear overall, however, is that motives of economic and industrial control took precedence over pronatalism, anti-poverty strategies or considerations of the position of women, children and the family. To be sure, campaigners such as Eleanor Rathbone, Richard Arthur, A. B. Piddington and Father Leon Lebel may have thought profoundly about the need to challenge gendered inequalities in the labour market and in the home by a redistribution of wages: indeed this issue of wage-redistribution was potentially one of the most radical social questions of the twentieth century. A central concern of Rathbone's *The Disinherited Family* (1924) was that the problem of income distribution within the household needed thorough examination – after centuries of neglect by male economists – and that enforced redistribution from husband to wife via cash family endowment would recognize the importance of motherhood, would give women some modicum of independent income and would encourage further discussion of the issue. But even these reformers' imaginations were constrained by the knowledge that industry either would not or could not pay an adequate three-child minimum-wage to all its workers. Indeed, the radical aspect of their case – that family allowances would open the way to equal pay for women – was balanced by a conservative acceptance of what industry could afford. The earliest initiatives in the European movement came from employers, who were far more concerned with economic questions than they were with preserving inequalities of gender. State intervention on any significant scale only took place in the 1940s, again primarily for reasons of economic management. Hence a highly 'feminized' analysis, stressing the primacy of patriarchal relations, only tells part of the story. Family allowance systems emerged as a consequence of the wider industrial and economic conflicts that capitalist democracies experienced in the turbulent first half of the twentieth century. Though introduced in the name of the child, they served other purposes.

NOTES

1 Eleanor Rathbone, *The Ethics and Economics of Family Endowment* (Beckley Social Service Lecture, 1927), London: Epworth Press, 1927: 74.
2 Joan Higgins, 'Comparative social policy', *Quarterly Journal of Social Affairs*, 1986, 2: 227.
3 The literature on comparative social policy analysis is now quite extensive. Very useful discussions, including attempts at model-building, are contained in: Joan Higgins, *States of Welfare: comparative analysis in social policy*, Oxford: Basil Blackwell and Martin Robertson, 1981; Catherine Jones, *Patterns of Social Policy: an introduction to comparative analysis*, London: Tavistock, 1985; Peter Flora and Arnold J. Heidenheimer (eds) *The Development of Welfare States in Europe and America*, New Brunswick: Transaction Books, 1981; Barbara Rodgers, with John Greve and John S. Morgan, *Comparative Social Administration*, London: Allen & Unwin, 1971 edn.
4 John Macnicol, *The Movement for Family Allowances, 1918–45: a study in social policy development*, London: Heinemann Educational Books, 1980; Hilary Land, 'The introduction of family allowances', in P. Hall, R. Parker, H. Land and A. Webb (eds) *Change, Choice and Conflict in Social Policy*, London: Heinemann Educational Books, 1975: 157–230.
5 See, for example, Paul Douglas, *Wages and the Family*, Chicago: University of Chicago Press, 1925.
6 D. V. Glass, *Population: policies and movements in Europe*, Oxford: Clarendon Press, 1940: 100.
7 Hugh H. R. Vibart, *Family Allowances in Practice*, London: P. S. King, 1925. Vibart's study orginated as a post-graduate thesis, and is supplemented by a typescript bound volume (deposited at the British Library of Political and Economic Science) containing extraordinarily detailed tables giving information on over one hundred European 'equalization funds'.
8 Glass, *Population*: 100–1; Vibart, *Family Allowances*: 27.
9 Vibart, *Family Allowances*: 6.
10 Paul H. Douglas, 'Family allowances and clearing funds in France', *Quarterly Journal of Economics*, 1924, 38: 257–8.
11 United Kingdom Committee on Industry and Trade, *Survey of Industrial Relations*, London: HMSO, 1926: 124.

12 Vibart, *Family Allowances*: 31; J. H. Richardson, 'The family allowance system', *Economic Journal*, 1924, 34: 382–3.

13 International Labour Office, Studies and Reports, Series D, no. 13, *Family Allowances – the Remuneration of Labour According to Need*, Geneva: International Labour Office, 1924: 31; Family Endowment Society pamphlet, *Family Allowances Abroad and in the British Dominions*, London: Family Endowment Society, 1932; Douglas, 'Family allowances and clearing funds': 265.

14 Douglas, *Wages and the Family*: 79–88; Jacques Doublet, 'Family allowances in France', *Population Studies*, 1948, 2: 219. An excellent account of French developments is to be found in Susan Pedersen, 'Social policy and the reconstruction of the family in Britain and France, 1900–1945', Ph.D. thesis, Harvard University, 1989: ch. 5.

15 Eleanor Rathbone, *The Disinherited Family*, London: Edward Arnold, 1924: 193–6.

16 Douglas, *Wages and the Family*: 62; Family Endowment Society, *Monthly Notes*, January 1925.

17 Douglas, 'Family allowances and clearing funds', op. cit: 261.

18 *Family Endowment Chronicle*, 1932, 1: 37.

19 Quoted in James C. Vadakin, *Family Allowances: an analysis of their development and implications*, Miami: University of Miami Press, 1958: 30.

20 International Labour Office, op. cit: 61.

21 Douglas, *Wages and the Family*: 89–90; for a detailed table of how family allowances affected wage levels, see Vibart, *Family Allowances*: 167–71.

22 Vibart, *Family Allowances*: 158–60.

23 Ibid.: 159.

24 Quoted in Douglas, *Wages and the Family*, p. 62.

25 Ibid. 67; R. Picard, 'Family allowances in French industry', *International Labour Review*, 1924, 9: 172.

26 Quoted in Eleanor Rathbone, *Family Allowances in the Mining Industry*, London: Family Endowment Society, 1925: 8.

27 Vadakin, *Family Allowances*: 35–6.

28 Douglas, *Wages and the Family*: 95–109; E. Susswein, 'Family allowances in Belgium', *Population Studies*, 1948, 2: 278.

29 Quoted in Family Endowment Society pamphlet, *Will Family Allowances Mean Lower Wages?*, London: Family Endowment Society, c. 1925.

30 Susswein, 'Family allowances in Belgium': 279; *Family Endowment Chronicle*, 1931, 1: 27.

31 Eduard Heimann, 'The family wages controversy in Germany', *Economic Journal*, 1923, 33: 509–12; Douglas, *Wages and the Family*: 144–8; Family Endowment Society pamphlet, *Family Allowances Abroad*.

32 For an account of such developments, see Mary T. Waggaman, '"Family wage" systems in Germany and certain other European countries', *United States Department of Labour. Monthly Labour Review*, 1924, 18: 25–9. Detailed information on schemes for public servants is

contained in the Family Endowment Society pamphlet, *Memorandum on Family Allowances Presented to the Royal Commission on the Civil Service*, London: Family Endowment Society, 1930: Appendix B.

33 Information in this and subsequent paragraphs is from: A. B. Piddington, *The Next Step: a Basic Family Income*, Melbourne: Macmillan, 1925 edn; H. Heaton, 'The basic wage principle in Australian wages regulation', *Economic Journal*, 1921, 31: 309–19; Rathbone, *The Disinherited Family*: 166–92; D. T. Sawkins, *The Living Wage in Australia*, Melbourne: Melbourne University Press, 1933; P. G. Macarthy, 'Labour and the living wage, 1890–1910', *Australian Journal of Politics and History*, 1967, 13: 67; P. G. Macarthy, 'Justice Higgins and the Harvester Judgement', in Jill Roe (ed.) *Social Policy in Australia: Some Perspectives, 1901–1975*, Melbourne: Cassell, 1976: 41–59; M. A. Jones, *The Australian Welfare State: growth, crisis and change*, Sydney: Allen & Unwin, 2nd edn, 1983: 7–9; Ray Markey, 'The ALP and the emergence of a national social policy, 1880–1910', in Richard Kennedy (ed.) *Australian Welfare History: critical essays*, Melbourne: Macmillan, 1982: 105–15; Diane Kirkby, 'The Australian experiment of compulsory arbitration', in D. C. M. Platt (ed.) *Social Welfare, 1850–1950: Australia, Argentina and Canada compared*, Basingstoke: Macmillan, 1989: 107–24.

34 Sawkins, *Living Wage*: 13–14; Piddington, *Next Step*: 13; Markey, 'ALP and national social policy': 115.

35 Frances G. Castles, *The Working Class and Welfare: reflections on the political development of the welfare state in Australia and New Zealand, 1890–1980*, Wellington: Allen & Unwin, 1985: 14.

36 Peter Beilharz, 'The labourist tradition and the reforming imagination', in Richard Kennedy (ed.) *Australian Welfare: historical sociology*, Melbourne: Macmillan, 1989: 139.

37 Bettina Cass, 'Redistribution to children and mothers: a history of child endowment and family allowances', in Cora V. Baldock and Bettina Cass (eds) *Women, Social Welfare and the State in Australia*, Sydney: Allen & Unwin, 1983: 62.

38 *Report of the Royal Commission on the Basic Wage*, 1920: 7 (contained in *Australian Parliamentary Papers*, IV, 1920–1).

39 Ibid: 12–58, 66–84.

40 Rathbone, *The Disinherited Family*: 176.

41 Piddington, *Next Step*: 21–7.

42 Jones, *Australian Welfare*: 29–30.

43 T. H. Kewley, *Social Security in Australia, 1900–72*, Sydney: Sydney University Press, 1973: 136–40; Family Endowment Society pamphlet, *Family Allowances Abroad*; J. B. Beyrer, 'Family allowances in Australia', *Bulletin of the International Social Security Association*, January/February 1961: 47.

44 Kewley, *Social Security in Australia*: 137. For a brief account of events in Queensland, see University of Tasmania, *Employment Relations and the Basic Wage*, Hobart: University of Tasmania and the Pitt-Cobbett Foundation, 1925: 17–19.

45 Richard Arthur, *State Endowment for Families and the Fallacy of the*

Existing Basic Wage System, Sydney: New South Wales Government, 1919. For an interesting account of this reformer's life, including his commitment to family endowment, see Michael Roe, *Nine Australian Progressives: vitalism in bourgeois social thought, 1890–1960*, Queensland: University of Queensland Press, 1984.

46 *New South Wales Industrial Gazette*, 1919, 16: 448.

47 Eleanor Rathbone, 'The New South Wales scheme for the grading of wages according to family needs', *Economic Journal*, 1920, 30: 551–2; Rathbone, *The Disinherited Family*: 185–7.

48 Piddington, *Next Step*: 3; *Family Endowment Chronicle*, 1932, 2: 4; J. C. Eldridge, 'Motherhood endowment in Australia', *Eugenics Review*, 1922, 14: 54–8; Cass, 'Redistribution to children and mothers': 66–9, 71–5; A. H. Charteris, 'Family endowment in New South Wales', in Jill Roe, *Social Policy in Australia*: 148–64.

49 R. M. Campbell, 'Family allowances in New Zealand', *Economic Journal*, 1927, 37: 369.

50 J. B. Condliffe, *The Welfare State in New Zealand*, London: Allen & Unwin, 1959: 243.

51 Castles, *Working Class and Welfare*: 25.

52 For the debates, see *New Zealand Parliamentary Debates*, 210, 3–28 August 1926: 587–633, 667, 762–74, 833–45.

53 Campbell, 'Family allowances in New Zealand': 370–2; Peter Kaim-Caudle, *Comparative Social Policy and Social Security*, London: Martin Robertson, 1973: 251.

54 Glass, *Population*: 269–75.

55 Ibid: 287–8; D. V. Glass, *The Struggle for Population*, Oxford: Clarendon Press, 1936: 22–31.

56 D. V. Glass, 'The Berlin Population Congress and recent population movements in Germany', *Eugenics Review*, 1935, 27: 210–1.

57 Marie Kopp, 'The nature and operation of the German eugenical programme', *Marriage Hygiene*, 1937, 3: 283.

58 Glass, *Population*: 291, 299–303.

59 Kopp, 'German eugenical programme': 285.

60 Quoted in Glass, *Population*: 220.

61 'Notes of the quarter', *Eugenics Review*, 1935, 27: 5; Glass, *Population*: 248–55; Eva Hubback, 'Family allowances in relation to population problems', *Sociological Review*, 1937, 29: 282.

62 Glass, *Population*: 106–218; Susswein, 'Family allowances in Belgium': 278–80; Doublet, 'Family allowances in France': 219–22.

63 Frank Lorimer, 'Population policies and politics in the communist word', in Philip Hauser (ed.) *Population and World Politics*, Glencoe, Illinois: Free Press, 1958: 219; Bernice Madison, *Social Welfare in the Soviet Union*, Stanford: Stanford University Press, 1968: 42–4; David Heer and Judith Bryden, 'Family allowances and fertility in the Soviet Union', *Soviet Studies*, 1966, 18: 154.

64 Eleanor Rathbone, *The Case for Family Allowances*, Harmondsworth, Penguin Books, 1940, p. 99.

65 John S. Morgan, 'Canada', in Barbara Rodgers et al., *Comparative Social Administration*: 159.

66 Veronica Strong-Boag, '"Wages for housework": mothers' allowances and the beginnings of social security in Canada', *Journal of Canadian Studies*, 1979, 14: 24–34.
67 League for Social Reconstruction, *Social Planning for Canada*, Toronto: University of Toronto Press, 1975 edn: 373–80.
68 J. L. Granatstein, *Canada's War: the politics of the Mackenzie King Government, 1939–1945*, Toronto: Oxford University Press, 1975: 261–3.
69 Leonard Marsh, *Report on Social Security for Canada*, Toronto: University of Toronto Press, 1975 edn: 196–203.
70 Granatstein, *Canada's War*: 279.
71 Brigitte Kitchen, 'Canadian controversy over family income support policies, 1928–1976', Ph.D. thesis, University of London, 1977: ch. 10.
72 Cass, 'Redistribution to children and mothers': 78–9.
73 Condliffe, *Welfare State in New Zealand*: 261–8.
74 Both quoted in Joseph M. Willard, 'Some aspects of family allowances and income redistribution in Canada', *Public Policy*, 1954, 5: 202.
75 *Social Insurance and Allied Services*, Cmd 6404, 1942: 164.
76 Willard, 'Some aspects'; Joseph M. Willard, 'Family allowances in Canada', in Eveline M. Burns (ed.) *Children's Allowances and the Economic Welfare of Children*, New York: Citizens' Committee for Children of New York, 1967: 62–3; Daniel P. Moynihan, 'Foreword', in James C. Vadakin, *Children, Poverty and Family Allowances*, New York: Basic Books, 1968: xvi.
77 Heer and Bryden, 'Family allowances in Soviet Union': 160.

INDEX

Bristol 60, 214; Child Guidance
  Clinic 215
British Association for the
  Advancement of Science 47
British Cameroon 231
British Child Study Association 48
British Institute of Preventive
  Medicine 133, 140
British Journal of Psychology 201
British Medical Association (BMA)
  47, 56, 59, 62
British Medical Journal 67n.12, 193
British Museum 33
British Paediatric Society 17n.43
British Psychoanalytic Association
  215
British Psychoanalytical Society
  201
Broca, Paul 41
Broken Hill Mine agreement,
  Australia (1909) 256
Bromley 68n.29
Brook Hospital, Woolwich 137
Brown Animal Welfare Institute,
  London 133
Brown Dog libel suit 120n.42
Brown, Sybil Clement 189, 207,
  218n.22
Brunton, Sir Lauder 52
Buhler, Charlotte 182, 183
bureaux d'assistance, Paris 130, 135
bureaux de bienfaisance, Paris 130
Burke, Dr Noel 184
Burnett, John 85
Burroughs Wellcome 140
Burt, Cyril 184, 201–2, 206–7, 212,
  216; and *The Young Delinquent*
  201, 202, 203, 204
Butler-Sloss, Lord Justice 147, 167

Cadbury, Geraldine 214
Cadbury, Mr and Mrs Barrow 76
Calmette, Albert 139
Calmette, Gaston 138
calorimetric studies 113
Cambridgeshire Education
  Committee 77
Canada 256–8, 271; 'Beveridge
  Plan' 266; Family Allowances

Bill (1944) 267; labour
  unionization 265; Select
  Committee on Industrial and
  International Relations 265
Cannon, Walter Bradford 108–11
capital and labour polarization 247
Carlson, A.J. 114
Carpenter, Howard C. 104, 106
Carpenter, Mary 63
Carr-Saunders, Alexander 218n.22
Cass, Bettina 257
Central Association for Mental
  Welfare 206, 214
Central Association for the Care
  of the Mentally Defective 206,
  207, 218n.18
Charité state hospital, Berlin 130,
  133, 135
Chadwick, Edwin 128
Chamber of Deputies, France 249
Chapman, Nathaniel 98
character-building, in schools 90
charity organization 160
Charity Organization Society 47,
  132, 171n.59, 198n.79
Charlottenburg 128
Chelsea Hospital for Women 133
Cheltenham Ladies' College 48
Chemical Society, London 140
Cheyne Hospital for Incurable
  Children, London 131–2
Chicago 84, 98, 204
Chicago University 114
Child 79, 80, 86, 203
child (the): 'abnormal/normal' 53,
  64, 86, 225 see also development;
  body 9, 24–5, 31, 54, 64, 175
  see also physiology; as death
  40; different from adult 8, 205;
  'discovery' of 26, 32; 'of nature'
  226, 236; as patient or 'welfare
  object' 2; as potential rescuer
  34; romanticized 20, 31–2, 34–5,
  37; sacralized 22, 23; see also
  parent–child relations
child abuse: of babies and infants
  162; case reporting patterns
  154–6, 165; and child welfare
  texts 148; in Cleveland, *Report*